Management and Organization of Program Evaluation

Robert G. St.Pierre, *Editor*

NEW DIRECTIONS FOR PROGRAM EVALUATION

A Publication of the Evaluation Research Society

RONALD J. WOOLDRIDGE, ERNEST R. HOUSE, *Editors-in-Chief*

Number 18, June 1983

Paperback sourcebooks in
The Jossey-Bass Higher Education and
Social and Behavioral Sciences Series

Jossey-Bass Inc., Publishers
San Francisco • Washington • London

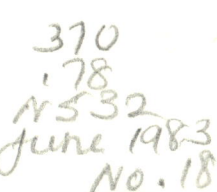

Robert G. St.Pierre (Ed.).
Management and Organization of Program Evaluation.
New Directions for Program Evaluation, no. 18.
San Francisco: Jossey-Bass, 1983.

New Directions for Program Evaluation Series
A Publication of the Evaluation Research Society
Ronald J. Wooldridge, Ernest R. House, *Editors-in-Chief*

New Directions for Program Evaluation (publication number
USPS 449-050) is published quarterly by Jossey-Bass Inc.,
Publishers, and is sponsored by the Evaluation Research Society.
Second-class postage rates paid at San Francisco, California,
and at additional mailing offices.

Correspondence:
Subscriptions, single-issue orders, change of address notices,
undelivered copies, and other correspondence should be sent to
New Directions Subscriptions, Jossey-Bass Inc., Publishers,
433 California Street, San Francisco, California 94104.

Editorial correspondence should be sent to the Editors-in-Chief,
Ronald Wooldridge, Bureau of Forecasting and Modeling,
44 Holland Ave., N.Y. 12229, or Ernest House, CIRCE-270,
Education Building, University of Illinois, Champaign, Ill. 61820.

Library of Congress Catalogue Card Number LC 82-84200
International Standard Serial Number ISSN 0164-7989
International Standard Book Number ISBN 87589-966-8

Cover art by Willi Baum
Manufactured in the United States of America

Ordering Information

The paperback sourcebooks listed below are published quarterly and can be ordered either by subscription or single-copy.

Subscriptions cost $35.00 per year for institutions, agencies, and libraries. Individuals can subscribe at the special rate of $21.00 per year *if payment is by personal check.* (Note that the full rate of $35.00 applies if payment is by institutional check, even if the subscription is designated for an individual.) Standing orders are accepted. Subscriptions normally begin with the first of the four sourcebooks in the current publication year of the series. When ordering, please indicate if you prefer your subscription to begin with the first issue of the *coming* year.

Single copies are available at $7.95 when payment accompanies order, and *all single-copy orders under $25.00 must include payment.* (California, New Jersey, New York, and Washington, D.C. residents please include appropriate sales tax.) For billed orders, cost per copy is $7.95 plus postage and handling. (Prices subject to change without notice.)

Bulk orders (ten or more copies) of any individual sourcebook are available at the following discounted prices: 10–49 copies, $7.15 each; 50–100 copies, $6.35 each; over 100 copies, *inquire.* Sales tax and postage and handling charges apply as for single copy orders.

To ensure correct and prompt delivery, all orders must give either the *name of an individual* or an *official purchase order number.* Please submit your order as follows:

Subscriptions: specify series and year subscription is to begin.
Single Copies: specify sourcebook code (such as, PE8) and first two words of title.

Mail orders for United States and Possessions, Latin America, Canada, Japan, Australia, and New Zealand to:
Jossey-Bass Inc., Publishers
433 California Street
San Francisco, California 94104

Mail orders for all other parts of the world to:
Jossey-Bass Limited
28 Banner Street
London EC1Y 8QE

New Directions for Program Evaluation Series
Ronald J. Wooldridge, Ernest R. House, *Editors-in-Chief*

Contents

Editor's Notes

Program evaluation research typically involves evaluators at the federal, state, and local levels of government who either conduct in-house evaluations or prepare requests for proposals (RFPs) and who monitor the resulting evaluation contracts; evaluators in research firms and universities who compete for and conduct evaluations; administrators and practitioners whose programs are being evaluated; and members of Congress, federal agency officials, state legislators, local officials, and other evaluation audiences. While the technical science or art of conducting field-based evaluations has advanced steadily over the past decades, the management of program evaluation has received little attention.

A review of the literature in this area (St. Pierre, 1982) reveals very few articles. The major evaluation journals and handbooks have ignored the topic. Further, the subject is covered lightly, if at all, in most evaluation texts; it is not a common subject in graduate training; and, according to Anderson and Ball (1978, p. 169), forty-four "people whose opinions we would value and which would seem to carry weight in the field" did not perceive it to be a particularly important topic for graduate training in evaluation research. Of thirty-two evaluation-related skills and content areas, these forty-four experts rated only two—job analysis and case study methodology—as less essential than management skills. It is not incidental that most of these evaluation experts are based in universities or that most could be labeled *evaluation theorists*, not *evaluation practitioners*. As Riecken and Boruch (1974, p. 157) have noted, "the art and practice of managing large-scale field research is not well-developed and is not easy to learn. Furthermore, the education of the majority of university-based social scientists has simply not exposed them to this range of practical problems."

Evaluation management is a skill that evaluation practitioners learn on the job. The experts surveyed by Anderson and Ball (1978) would agree, in that they rate management skills ahead of thirty other skills and content areas as best learned via supervised field experience. This view is supported by Abt (1980, p. 176), who writes, "The kind of social scientist who can cope with all these operational problems...is not directly trained to do so in university graduate schools. Several years of experience actually doing this kind of work are usually essential."

Because evelution management is a largely unstudied domain, this volume is broad in scope; it aims to provide an overview of a substantial amount of territory rather than to focus on one or two specific areas. The first four chapters discuss ways in which evaluation units are organized and managed at the federal, state, and local levels of government. In Chapter One, Michael

Wargo gives an overview of how program evaluation is organized within the federal government. Using examples from three federal agencies, he shows how evaluation units are formed, defines their functions, and discusses the barriers that must be overcome to manage a federal program evaluation office effectively.

In Chapter Two, Jack Radzikowski and Burleigh Seaver describe the role of the federal project officer in evaluation management. They review the life of a federal evaluation and emphasize the management role played by the project officer in understanding the need for information, articulating evaluation requirements, preparing the request for proposals, selecting the research contractor, monitoring the evaluation, and disseminating the findings.

Chapter Three addresses the state level. Recently, Hugh Peck and Suzanne Triplett had the opportunity to establish a unit that is responsible for statewide educational evaluations in Louisiana, and in their chapter, they provide information on its development, structure, mission, rationale, staffing, and operations.

In Chapter Four, Freda Holley relies on her experience in the Austin (Texas) Independent School District to describe the organization and operations of an evaluation unit in a local governmental agency. She concentrates on ways in which local evaluation units manage external relations in order to obtain funding, gain access to data sources, and encourage evaluation use. She also discusses the management of internal operations, including staffing, communication, data collection, and analysis.

The next three chapters focus on evaluation management from the contractor's viewpoint. In Chapter Five, Robert Levine offers his opinions about the ideal organizational configuration for a federal evaluation contractor and the degree to which firms so configured will be able to meet the federal government's informational needs.

In Chapter Six, Paula Nassif and Sherry Rubinstein address the management of research organizations that concentrate on state and local evaluation projects. They deal with such issues as the contractor's mission and philosophy, organizational structure, staffing, and management controls.

In Chapter Seven, Robert St. Pierre considers the ways in which the project director's control over selection of staff for evaluation teams and over technical direction of evaluations first grew and then shrank during the past decade. He examines the ways in which project directors work with project officers in government and with administrative staff in their own research organization, and he draws conclusions about the impact of the present shrinkage in evaluation research on the project director's autonomy.

The last three chapters offer complementary views on evaluation management. In Chapter Eight, Robert Dentler describes and interprets the role of the evaluation research manager. He addresses such issues as what it is like to be an evaluation manager, where evaluation managers come from, how they are selected and trained, and where they go.

In Chapter Nine, Karen Seashore Louis examines the role of the evaluation project director as middle manager, defines five types of evaluation environment, and draws conclusions about the way in which different types of work environment affect the performance of evaluation management tasks.

In Chapter Ten, Eleanor Chelimsky argues that evaluation managers need systems for measuring and interpreting evaluation quality. She describes such a system and shows how it can be used to track changes in evaluation quality over time.

What is to be learned from the chapters in this volume? Some readers may think that they already know much of what it contains. These readers can consider themselves lucky. The knowledge that these chapters convey is held by few people, most of whom possess only individual pieces of the evaluation management puzzle. Further, most of these people have never recorded their thoughts on the topic for the benefit of others. This volume is not meant to be the last word about the organization and management of evaluation research. Rather, it has been conceived as helping to start the dialogue — as containing some of the first words.

Robert G. St.Pierre
Editor

References

Abt, C. C. "Social Science in the Contract Research Firm." In R. K. Kidd and M. J. Saks (Eds.), *Advances in Applied Social Psychology.* Hillsdale, N.J.: Erlbaum, 1980.

Anderson, S. B., and Ball, S. *The Profession and Practice of Program Evaluation.* San Francisco: Jossey-Bass, 1978.

Riecken, H. W., and Boruch, R. F. *Social Experimentation.* New York: Academic Press, 1974.

St.Pierre, R. G. "Management of Federally Funded Evaluation Research: Building Evaluation Teams." *Evaluation Review,* 1982, *6* (1), 94–113.

Robert G. St.Pierre is a social scientist at Abt Associates Inc.,
where for the past eight years he has directed national evaluations
of social programs.

Barriers to efficient and effective management of federal program evaluation are described, and strategies for overcoming them are detailed.

Management of the Evaluation Function Within the Federal Government

Michael J. Wargo

This chapter focuses on the context within which federal program evaluations are conducted and on the barriers that must be overcome to manage a federal program evaluation office efficiently and effectively. Mission options are discussed, evaluation functions are defined, and typical function allocations and operations are described. Organizational and staffing configurations associated with the performance of the evaluation function within the federal government are addressed. Factors that influence the management of evaluation units and the execution of federal program evaluation functions are defined. Next, major barriers to the management of federal evaluation units are summarized, and their effects on evaluation unit organization, staffing, and operation are discussed. Finally, recommendations for overcoming obstacles to the execution and management of federal program evaluations are proposed.

Evaluation Mission and Functions

In establishing an evaluation mission for a federal agency, there are three paramount questions: Whom should evaluation serve, what services

The views and opinions expressed in this chapter are those of the author and should not be construed to be the policy or position of the Food and Nutrition Service, U.S. Department of Agriculture.

R. G. St. Pierre (Ed.). *Management and Organization of Program Evaluation.* New Directions
for Program Evaluation, no. 18. San Francisco: Jossey-Bass, June 1983.

should be provided, and when? Potential audiences for federal program evaluations include federal executive and legislative offices, state and local governments, recipient groups, public interest and advocacy groups, and professional trade organizations. A rational first step in establishing an evaluation mission is to determine which of these audiences must be served and how much priority should be placed on serving each of them. Once audiences have been defined and prioritized, an assessment of audience information needs is necessary. In assessing these needs, priorities must be established, and information content and timing requirements must be determined. Then, on the basis of audience specification, definition of information needs, and timing requirements, an evaluation mission can rationally be specified.

Once the evaluation mission has been established, the issues of function definition and allocation become important. How will various needs be met and by whom? The functions associated with evaluation management are well established: planning, organizing, coordinating, conducting, monitoring, and disseminating. The major options available to an agency involve allocation of these functions to individuals and groups. Functions can be allocated to various offices within an agency at headquarters level, they can be decentralized and allocated to federal regional or local offices, and they can be assigned to state and local authorities; finally, some can be delegated to qualified profit and nonprofit private institutions through the medium of grants, cooperative agreements, and contracts.

Organization of the Evaluation Function

The organization chart of a federal agency suggests how the agency has defined its program evaluation mission and how the evaluation function is allocated throughout the agency. The placement of an evaluation office within an agency and the operations assigned to it are based on a conscious decision about those whom the office serves. If its prime audience is senior agency policy makers, then the office usually reports directly to the agency head. If the primary audience is program management, then the evaluation office most often reports to the program director or to the director of a group of related programs.

The organizational placement of an evaluation office is related to the relative centralization of agency functions. Experts suggest that a centralized organization leads to more coherent activity at the cost of delays in decisions and actions as information and directives move up and down the organizational structure. In a decentralized organization, operations can come closer to satisfying needs of individual operating units, but there is the possibility of duplication and associated resource waste (Raizen and Rossi, 1981).

Federal office functions are centralized and decentralized on a regular basis—most often when a new administration takes over the executive branch or when new positions are taken by incumbent administrations. The most viable organizational model for an agency is partly a function of its size and the scope of its activities. Small agencies and large agencies with a relatively narrow scope of activity tend to have centralized evaluation units, while large agencies and agencies with a wide range of activities tend to have decentralized evaluation units. In the decentralized model, there are several evaluation units, each associated with a cluster of similar programs, and a central coordinating unit.

Whether the evaluation function is centralized or decentralized and whether it reports to the agency head or to lower levels of management, the evaluation office is usually assigned one or more additional agency functions. The functions most often assigned to evaluation offices in agencies of the federal government are policy formulation, planning, budgeting, and research.

The primary evaluation functions of an agency entail planning, coordinating, executing, and monitoring evaluations and disseminating their findings. In some agencies, all these functions are performed by federal employees within the agency. In large agencies and in agencies with large evaluation agendas, at least some of the evaluation execution function tends to be allocated to public and private agencies outside the federal government. The instruments used to allocate the evaluation execution function are contracts, grants, and cooperative agreements.

Evaluation offices in three federal agencies will illustrate the various configurations of evaluation office organization and placement. The paragraphs that follow describe a centralized evaluation office in a department with a relatively narrow mission (U.S. Department of Education), a decentralized evaluation office in a department with a broad mission (U.S. Department of Agriculture), and a centralized evaluation office in a very small independent agency with a mission enormous in scope (ACTION).

Department of Education. The mission of the U.S. Department of Education is to establish policy for the administration and coordination of most federal assistance to education (General Services Administration, 1982). In 1981, most of the department's evaluation activities were centralized in the Office of the Assistant Secretary for Management; that office reported directly to the Secretary of Education. The assistant secretary's evaluation function included both program and management evaluation. In addition to evaluation, the assistant secretary for management was responsible for administrative and financial management and for human resources (see Figure 1).

The Office of Program Evaluation had primary responsibility for program evaluations. The office conducted most of its evaluations by contract with profit and nonprofit organizations and institutions. In-house staff developed preliminary designs for studies, selected contractors through a competitive process, monitored contractor performance, disseminated evaluation results, and acted as primary spokespersons for the studies. Allocation of the evaluation execution function to contractors is typical of centralized evaluation units in departments with extensive evaluation agendas.

Figure 1. Organization of the Evaluation Function in the U.S. Department of Education, 1981

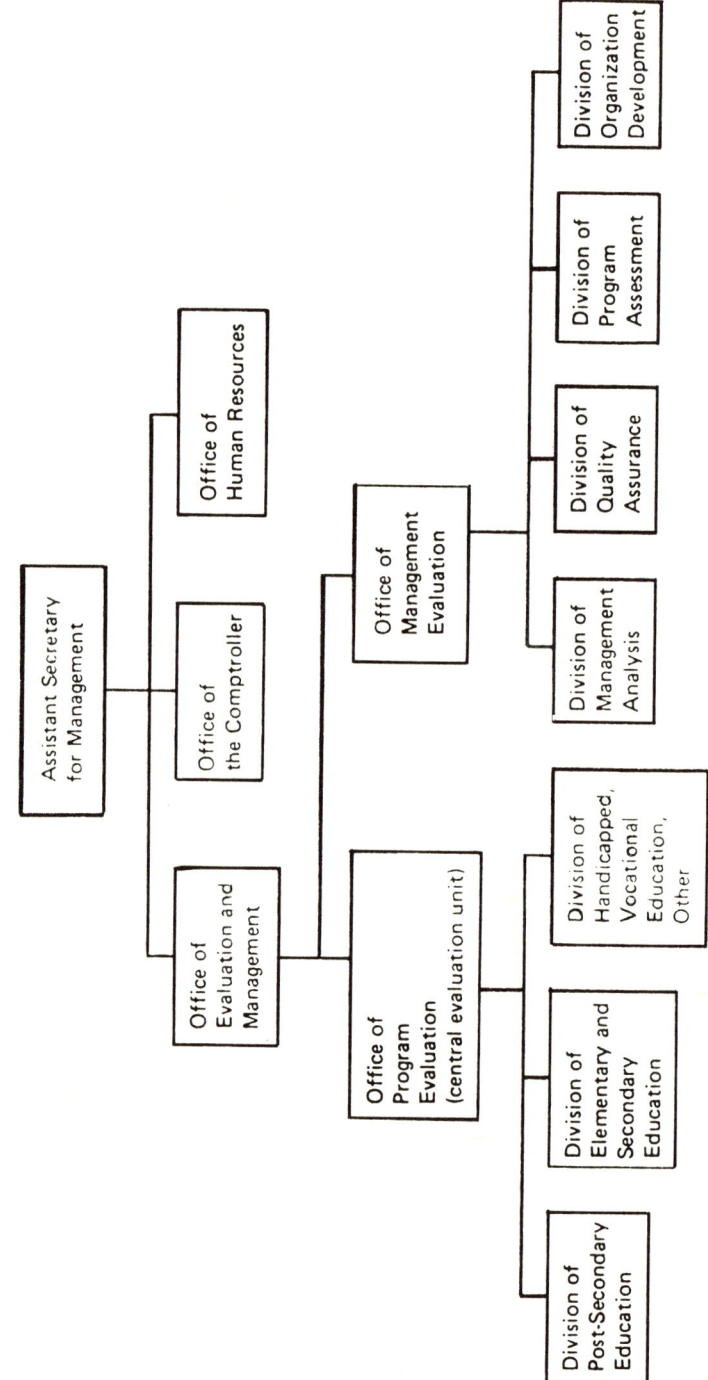

Assistant Secretary for Management

Office of Evaluation and Management

Office of the Comptroller

Office of Human Resources

Office of Program Evaluation (central evaluation unit)

Office of Management Evaluation

Division of Post-Secondary Education

Division of Elementary and Secondary Education

Division of Handicapped, Vocational Education, Other

Division of Management Analysis

Division of Quality Assurance

Division of Program Assessment

Division of Organization Development

The reorganization of the department's evaluation function illustrates several points. First, it typifies an evaluation organization in a relatively large department whose activity is focused in one functional area. Second, it illustrates a centralized organizational structure. Third, the functions that were combined with evaluation—administrative and financial management and human resources—were somewhat unusual for the federal government. Fourth, the two layers of supervision between the central evaluation unit and the Secretary of Education suggest that the evaluation function was considered less important to the department than the functions of other offices that reported directly to the secretary—namely, the offices of public affairs, legislation, civil rights, the inspector general, and planning and budget. Finally, the centralization of evaluation within the office was incomplete, which suggests that several problems remained after reorganiztion was completed.

Even more recently, the Department of Education removed the evaluation function from the Office of the Assistant Secretary for Management and combined it with the functions of planning and budget in the Office of the Assistant Secretary for Planning, Budget, and Evaluation. The second reorganization further centralized the evaluation function and removed one level of supervision between the evaluation office and the Secretary of Education. These changes suggest that the combination of the evaluation function with the management function did not work well and that the stock of the evaluation office had increased with the secretary.

Food and Nutrition Service. The U.S. Department of Agriculture is responsible for the administration of farm income support, conservation, rural development, nutrition, food service, and related programs (General Services Administration, 1982). Its many programs are organized into related clusters and assigned to one or another of the twenty-eight agencies that compose the department. Related programs are managed by one of seven assistant secretaries or the equivalent. The Food and Nutrition Service (FNS) is one of two agencies that report to the Assisant Secretary for Food and Consumer Services. Its mission is to safeguard the health and well being of the nation through the provision of food, food vouchers, and nutrition education programs. FNS administers eleven programs designed to achieve those ends. Its programs include the Food Stamp Program, National School Lunch Program, the Child Care Food Program, and the Special Supplemental Food Program for Women, Infants, and Children (U.S. Department of Agriculture, 1980).

The department's evaluation function is decentralized. Evaluation offices are located in several of its twenty-eight agencies. A staff office to the Secretary of Agriculture, the Office of Budget and Program Analysis, coordinates and monitors the department's evaluation function and prepares periodic status reports to the secretary regarding all evaluation activity. The evaluation function of the FNS is centralized within the Office of Analysis and Evaluation, which reports directly to the agency administrator. As the title of this office indicates, an analysis function is associated with the unit's evaluation function. This analysis function involves policy formulation and legislative, budgetary, and regulatory support. The Office of Analysis and Evaluation is headed by a director, and it is subdivided into two staffs, the analysis staff and the program evaluation staff (see Figure 2).

The mission of the program evaluation staff is periodically to assess the efficiency and effectiveness of ongoing programs as well as of pilot and demonstration programs. The evaluation staff achieves this mission by establishing ad hoc teams for each evaluation. Each team is composed of representatives of the program to be assessed, analysis staff, and other department agencies, if warranted, and it is headed by a project officer. The in-house team is supported by an evaluation contractor, an advisory panel, and various consultants, as required. The evaluation team participates in the design and execution of the evaluation and contributes significantly to dissemination of evaluation results (Wargo, 1981a, 1981b, and 1981c).

The planning, coordination, and monitoring of the evaluation staff's performance is the responsibility of the evaluation staff's director, who is supported by two branch chiefs. This management team is responsible for planning the agency's evaluation agenda, for providing resources to evaluation teams, for monitoring their performance, and for ensuring that the evaluation function contributes to achievement of the agency's mission. The organization of the evaluation function within the FNS illustrates the typical organization of that function in an agency that is one of several in a department with a multifaceted mission and a decentralized evaluation function.

ACTION. Prior to 1981, ACTION was the federal government's umbrella agency for the support and promotion of domestic and international voluntary activities. It administered a major domestic antipoverty volunteer program and several volunteer programs for senior citizens. The scope of ACTION's mission — promotion of world peace, reduction of domestic poverty — was enormous for a small organization with limited resources (General Services Administration, 1979). Between 1976 and 1979, ACTION's evaluation function was centralized within the Office of Policy, Planning, and Evaluation. That office was headed by an assistant director, who reported directly to the agency's director. In addition to policy, planning, and evaluation functions highlighted by the office's name, the agency's budgeting function was also allocated to the office (see Figure 3).

A significant portion of all ACTION's evaluations was conducted in house. This was possible because ACTION made liberal use of various personnel authorities for hiring temporary staff. For most evaluations, former Peace Corps volunteers, hired temporarily to assist them in making the transition back to life in the United States, formed a very large percentage of data collection staff. Attempts were also made to use former volunteers and other temporary staff in technical and managerial positions associated with program evaluation. At times this practice was successful, but most often it resulted in evaluation products of less than acceptable quality.

Figure 2. Organization of the Evaluation Function at the Food and
Nutrition Service, U.S. Department of Agriculture, 1983.

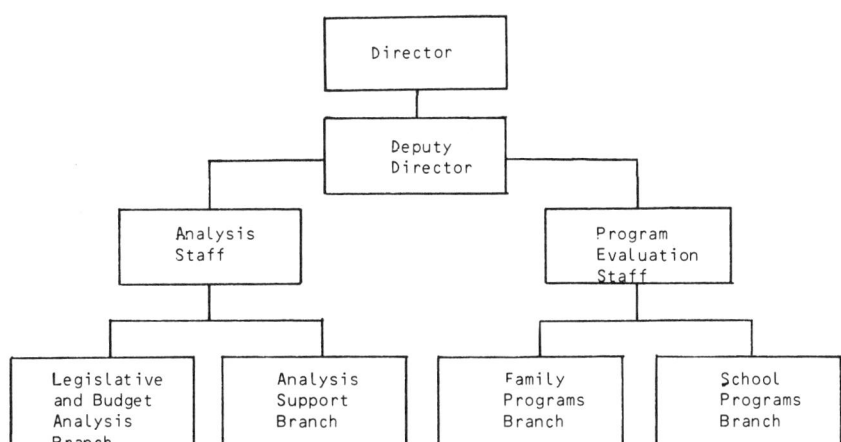

ACTION also supported in-house evaluation efforts with consultants
who were hired for specific tasks (for example, questionnaire development,
data collection) or to support an entire evaluation effort. Finally, for its more
difficult evaluation activities, ACTION obtained significant technical, managerial, and staff support from contractors selected competitively. However,
the total contract activity in any year was usually quite small (less than $2 mil-
lion, as compared to the $10 million to $20 million efforts at the FNS and the
Department of Education).

The preceding discussion illustrates how three different federal agencies have organized the evaluation function. All three evaluation units can be
characterized as centralized. (The FNS unit is located in a department that
decentralizied its evaluation function by allocating evaluation responsibility to
subagencies.) All three units also illustrate the variety of agency functions that
can be combined with evaluation: The Department of Education placed evaluation in an office that also had administrative and financial management functions and human resource responsibilities. The FNS combined evaluation
with an analysis function that consisted of responsibility for policy formulation
and support of the legislative, budgetary, and regulatory processes. In
ACTION, the evaluation function was housed with the agency's policy, planning, and budgeting activities. These three units also illustrate the various
vehicles used by federal agencies to conduct evaluations: At one extreme,
ACTION conducted much of its evaluation in house. At the other extreme,
the department of education conducted almost all its evaluations by contracting with profit and nonprofit research and evaluation organizations. The FNS
takes the third approach, which develops evaluation teams consisting of in-
house staff, consultants, and advisory panels and which also uses contractors
(Wargo, 1981a).

Figure 3. Organization of the Evaluation Function at ACTION Between 1976 and 1979.

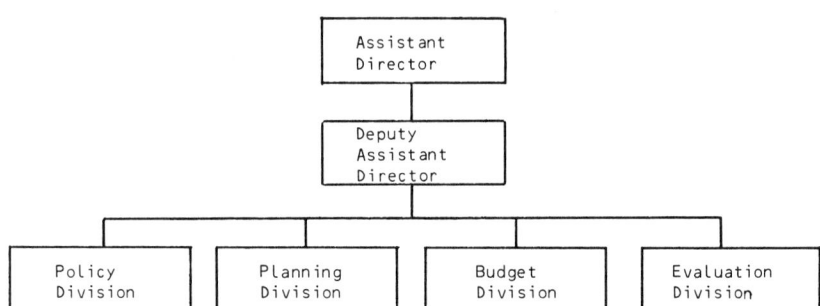

Evaluation Operations

This section describes how the primary management functions associated with the operation of a federal evaluation office are performed. There are four primary management functions: planning and coordination, execution, monitoring, and dissemination of results.

Planning and Coordination. The comprehensiveness and formality of an agency's evaluation planning system is related to the agency's needs. If most of the agency's evaluation activity is mandated by Congress, it has little need for a formal planning system. In contrast, agencies that have discretion as to their evaluation agenda require elaborate, comprehensive, and formal planning systems. As an agency's discretion increases, so does its need to define and prioritize potential audiences for evaluation, to assess and prioritize evaluation needs, and to justify resource allocations.

The budget system is an integral part of the planning system in all federal agencies. It is through the budget process that resources for evaluation are obtained. During most of the fiscal year, an agency and its evaluation offices must deal with three budgets: the current year budget, the proposed budget for the coming fiscal year, and the budget for the fiscal year after that. An agency's evaluation planning system that deals with less than a three-year period is shortsighted, while a system that includes three years or more facilitates intelligent management.

In developing a long-range evaluation plan, consideration must be given to the various sources of funds and to the limitations associated with those sources. Most agencies have several sources for evaluation funds, the most flexible being the salary and expense budget, which can be used both to support in-house evaluations and to obtain evaluation assistance through contracts, grants, and cooperative agreements. The salary and expense budget can also be used to evaluate any program associated with the agency. All other evaluation budgets place restrictions on the programs that can be evaluated with their funds and preclude use of such funds for in-house evaluation activities.

Execution. Federal program evaluations can be designed and executed in house, or those functions can be allocated to external organizations and institutions through grants, contacts, and cooperative agreements. As just indicated, the number and size of evaluations that can be conducted in house are severely restricted by budget. Consequently, in-house evaluation activity is usually small in scale and limited in scope.

In-house activity can focus on the conduct of a few complete evaluations, or it can be directed at parts of evaluations that organizations and institutions outside the federal government will complete. Agencies that take the latter course often focus their in-house activity on developing preliminary designs for evaluations, selecting contractors to execute evaluations, monitoring contractor performance, and disseminating evaluation results. They then obtain outside support (through contracts, grants, and cooperative agreements) to finalize designs, develop data collection and analysis plans, design instruments, collect and analyze data, and write reports. When agencies opt to design and conduct all their evaluations in house, they can still obtain some outside support by hiring consultants through the personnel system or by contracting for consultant services.

Monitoring. The typical federal evaluation office uses contractors to conduct much of its evaluation activity primarily as a result of the severe limitations placed on its salary and expense budget. The major functions performed by nonsupervisory evaluation staff in the typical evaluation office are selecting contractors to conduct evaluations and monitoring contractor conduct of evaluations.

The individual who has responsibility for the selection and monitoring of evaluation contractors is generally known as the *project officer.* He or she is ultimately responsible for the successful completion of an evaluation on schedule and within the resources provided. He or she must ensure that the contractor abides by the statement of work that forms the basis of agreement between the contractor and the government and that the contractor's expenditures are within the resources provided by the contract. To achieve those ends, the project officer monitors the management, technical performance, and expenditures of the evaluation contractor through periodic progress reports, telephone conversations, face-to-face meetings, visits to the contractor's facilities, and review of all evaluation plans and technical reports. The project officer must develop a thorough knowledge of the entire evaluation process, since he or she is expected to be the government's primary spokesperson for the evaluation.

The project officer is supported by staff from the agency's evaluation, program, and contracting offices. Evaluation staff provide technical and procedural support, while program staff provide substantive support relating to program operations and policy. Contract office staff assist in awarding the contract and in ensuring that all contractual terms are met by both the government and the contractor.

Dissemination of Results. When an evaluation is completed, the project officer is responsible for disseminating evaluation results and conclusions. Although the dissemination process varies from agency to agency, most agencies produce at least two documents at the conclusion of an evaluation. The first and primary document is the final report, which describes the evaluation's objectives, methods, results, and conclusions. The second document is an executive summary that provides an overview of the evaluation for program managers and senior policy makers. A few agencies also produce memoranda for agency heads, program heads, or both that detail the policy implications of evaluations and that recommend policy or programmatic action.

The procedures that project officers use to disseminate evaluation results range from informal procedures to elaborate agencywide dissemination plans. In any case, project officers must ensure that evaluation products are reviewed and approved internally before external dissemination begins. Most agencies specify the procedure for such reviews. Whether this procedure is documented or not, most agencies require review and approval by program offices, the major policy office, and senior managers prior to any external dissemination of reports.

Barriers to Federal Program Evaluation Management

Evaluation practitioners are quick to report the many obstacles to design and execution of program evaluations (Cook and Campbell, 1979; Cronbach and others, 1980; Riecken and Boruch, 1974; Wargo, 1977, 1981b). The list of barriers to evaluation increases dramatically when management of an entire evaluation function at a federal agency is the focus of discussion. For the purposes of this chapter, management barriers will be classified as systemic, political, and attitudinal. A systemic barrier is indigenous to our system of government and its bureaucracy. A political barrier is related to the political system or to the politics of government. Attitudinal barriers are associated with individuals and groups that have a stake in the evaluation process and its products and with their manner of feeling, thinking, or acting toward evaluation, government, and government employees. Most of the barriers to the management of federal program evaluation that evaluation practitioners have reported can be assigned to one or another of these categories.

Systemic Barriers. The major systemic barriers to the management of federal program evaluation are related to the principal systems of the federal government; namely, the personnel, budgetary, procurement, legislative, policy, regulatory, and oversight systems. Each of these systems was designed to facilitate government operations and to maintain the system of government defined by the Constitution and expanded by subsequent law and regulation. Nevertheless, many of these systems frustrate the federal evaluation mission in one way or another.

Personnel System. The *Managers Handbook* (U.S. Office of Personnel Management, 1979) defines the rules for job classification, recruitment, hiring, compensation, incentive awards, assignments, promotions, transfers, and other personnel actions within the federal government. The system whose operations it describes was designed to be fair to all job applicants, employees, and retirees. In accomplishing this aim, however, it places restrictions on the program evaluation unit manager. The three aspects of the federal personnel system that cause particular difficulty for managers are the organization establishment, classification, and job selection processes.

The organization establishment subsystem defines the procedure that must be followed to organize or reorganize an agency or subunit (office, division, staff, branch, section) of the federal government. This process requires a description of unit mission, definition and assignment of functions to subunits, and development of an organizational structure that facilitates mission achievement and that justifies the number and grades (rank) of assigned staff. The procedures that must be followed to organize or reorganize an agency's evaluation unit are labor-intensive, cumbersome, and time-consuming. They require the attention of senior agency management and classification specialists as well as an inordinate number of time-consuming reviews and clearances. It is not unusual for the process to take a year or more, during which time most personnel actions associated with affected units are prohibited.

The classification subsystem categorizes positions into a grade structure and specialty series on the basis of job difficulty, assigned responsibility, and knowledge and skills required for job performance. Job classifications and associated position descriptions form the basis for organization justification as well as for recruiting, selecting, placing, promoting, and training actions (U.S. Office of Personnel Management, 1979). A major roadblock that the classification subsystem imposes on the management of federal program evaluation units relates to its impact on grade assignment and salary structure. The classification system rates supervisory responsibility higher than the technical knowledge and skills required for satisfactory job performance. Consequently, it is difficult to maintain productive journeyman evaluators in government or to attract trained and experienced evaluators to government unless they are offered supervisory positions that do not always take advantage of their technical training and experience.

Under the selection or hiring subsystem, it is relatively easy to recruit and hire individuals who are currently part of the career civil service. However, the recruiting and hiring of individuals who are not currently working for the federal government and who have no past experience in federal civil service requires a very formal and long-drawn-out process that can take anywhere from four months to one year to complete. This is particularly burdensome for the evaluation unit manager, since many prime candidates for positions are from outside government.

Another drawback of the federal hiring system is the uncertainty associated with the process. Candidates who have been recruited often have to remain available for a period ranging between four and twelve months before they can be made a firm offer. Further, a manager cannot guarantee that any candidate will be judged highly qualified by the panel assigned to review applications, nor can a manager guarantee that some time during the four to twelve months required by the process he or she will not lose the authority to hire; that there will not be a presidential, departmental, agency, or officewide freeze on hiring; or that there will not be budget reductions or freezes that prevent filling the position.

Budget System. Another major systemic barrier to evaluation operations is the limitations imposed by the budget process on in-house evaluation execution. As indicated earlier, the only funds that can be used to cover in-house evaluation are those provided in an agency's salary and expense budget, which usually is both the smallest of all the agency's evaluation budgets and the one most closely monitored by the Office of Management and Budget (OMB) and by the Congress in their attempts to control the size of government. These salary and expense budget constraints make it nearly impossible to conduct any sizable in-house evaluation activity.

Procurement System. The federal government's procurement system sets the legal and regulatory requirements that must be followed to obtain extragovernmental assistance in the design and execution of program evaluations. The system defines the appropriate vehicles for obtaining assistance, dictates the procedures that must be followed, and defines the standards and criteria that must be met to award contracts, grants, or cooperative agreements. Basically, the procurement system is designed to facilitate the transfer of money for public purposes through grants and cooperative agreements. It is designed so that the acquisition of services by the government for the government's benefit, not for the public's good, is subject to strict control. Unfortunately, support of government evaluation activities is construed to benefit the government, not the public. Consequently, the legislation that regulates the procurement system requires the government to acquire evaluation support services primarily by contractual agreement; such acquisition is more subject to restrictive procedures and regulations than grants and cooperative agreements are.

The use of a contract as the legal instrument for developing a relationship between the federal government and another party imposes a series of requirements on the procurement process that makes awarding of contracts a very complex activity (see the chapter by Radzikowski and Seaver, this volume). The process requires that the government develop a work statement that includes specification of evaluation objectives, an evaluation methodology, a description of contractor tasks, and a schedule for product delivery. The government's contract and grants office adds to the work statement various legal and regulatory requirements that must be adhered to by the parties involved. The statement of work, when combined with these requirements, is known as a request for proposal (RFP).

The availability of RFPs to interested parties is announced in the *Commerce Business Daily.* Interested parties are usually provided thirty to sixty days to submit technical and cost proposals in response to RFPs. A panel of agency officials, at times supplemented by experts from within or outside government, reviews and rates all proposals on the basis of criteria specified in the RFP. The result of the panel's deliberations is usually reviewed by the contracts and grants office for adherence to all required government procedures. Then the panel and the contracts and grants office negotiate with the most technically qualified bidders in an attempt to improve technical quality and reduce the cost of the bids. The most qualified bidders are then requested to submit their "best and final" technical and cost proposals. These revised proposals are again reviewed by the panel, the winning contractor is selected, and a contract is awarded. The length of the procurement process severely restricts the ability of government evaluation offices to respond quickly to evaluation needs. If an office depends on outside support to conduct its evaluation, then it faces a four- to nine-month delay before it can begin a program evaluation. The procurement process is also very costly. At the FNS, for example, approximately 1,000 person-hours of federal employee time and a federal expenditure of nearly $26,000 are required to obtain contractor support for an evaluation, regardless of its size.

Legislative System. The legislative system of the federal government can facilitate evaluation by authorizing the establishment of evaluation functions within agencies and by authorizing specific evaluation studies. However, the legislative process can also become a barrier to effective and efficient management of evaluation activities when specific evaluation mandates are unsound for technical, political, or practical reasons. Some recent mandates for specific studies have placed severe restrictions on the design, conduct, and validity of studies by specifying unattainable objectives, inappropriate sample sizes or site locations, unsound methods for data collection, and unrealistic scheduling.

An integral part of the federal legislative system is the budget process. It facilitates evaluation management by appropriating funds for authorized evaluation activities, for the design and conduct of specific evaluations, or for both. It acts as a barrier to the management of evaluation when insufficient funds are provided, or when general belt-tightening is necessary and discretionary activities or support programs, such as evaluation, incur a disproportionate share of budget cuts.

Policy System. The system used by the federal government to formulate and promulgate policy can also constrain program evaluation units. An agency can have a policy to restrict evaluation to certain types of programs or operations. An agency can specify the preferred methods of evaluation, detail evaluation standards, or specify how often programs should be evaluated (Wargo, 1981b). It is also possible for an agency to be silent on evaluation policy. The restrictive nature of an evaluation policy is directly related to the authoritative nature of its underpinning. If a policy has some basis in statute or executive order, it will be more restrictive than a policy that has no such authority.

Regulatory System. Closely related to the legislative process is the federal regulatory system, which is designed to ensure that laws are properly interpreted and implemented. Currently, four laws and their associated regulations either place or have the potential to place unusual constraints on the management of federal program evaluation: the Federal Reports Act of 1942 (56 Stat. 1078), the Privacy Act (P.L. 93-579), the Freedom of Information Act (P.L. 89-554), and the National Research Act (P.L. 93-348).

As first proposed, the Federal Reports Act of 1942 was intended to reduce and control the data collection burden that federal agencies impose on small businesses. However, as enacted, the legislation covers all reporting or record-keeping requirements that federal agencies impose on state and local governments, businesses, institutions, groups, and individuals. The act affects the evaluation function by requiring agencies to justify completely to the Office of Management and Budget (OMB) any data collection activity that affects more than nine persons or units. The regulations used to implement the clearance process result in inordinate delays and in costs that far exceed the potential benefits associated with the process (see Carter, 1977; St.Pierre, 1982). At the FNS, for example, it requires six months and approximately $65,000 to produce and clear the typical justification package through the OMB.

The Privacy Act of 1974 (P.L. 93-579) was enacted to safeguard against invasions of personal privacy. It permits individuals to determine what records the federal government maintains that pertain to them, it gives individuals access to those records, and it requires the government to safeguard against the misuse of individual records. The Privacy Act is applicable primarily in situations where the federal government collects and maintains personally identifiable data. When data collection ensures anonymity, most provisions of the Privacy Act do not apply. If a federal agency plans to collect personally identifiable data, it must publish an annual notice describing the proposed establishment of the data base, the uses that will be made of the data collected, and the access and security procedures that are planned. Further, the agency must institute safeguards against data misuse and destroy data bases when they have fulfilled their intended purposes. When personally identifiable data are to be collected, the Privacy Act requires that respondents be informed in writing about the authority to collect the information, the purpose for data collection, the intended use of the information, and the effects on the respondent of not cooperating with the requestor, if there are any.

The major negative impacts that the Privacy Act has had on federal evaluations are that it increases the difficulty of obtaining cooperation from respondents when data collection is not specifically required by law and that the requirement to publish a public notice prior to collection of personally identifiable data creates an additional delay in the data collection process.

The National Research Act of 1974 (P.L. 93-348, Title II) places restrictions on biomedical and behavioral research conducted by federal contractors or grantees. Although the act was initially intended to cover only the U.S. Department of Health, Education, and Welfare (DHEW), many departments and agencies have adopted the DHEW's protection of human subjects regulations in whole or in part. The regulations require all proposed research to be reviewed and approved by an institutional review committee located at the principal investigator's affiliation before the research is submitted to the federal government for funding. The institutional review committee must ensure that human subjects give their informed consent before participating in the study, that the benefits of the proposed research far exceed any risks imposed on human subjects, and that the rights and welfare of human subjects will be safeguarded. Agencies covered by the protection of human subjects regulations may not award a grant or a contract for biomedical or behavioral research unless written assurances from the proposer's institutional review committee indicate that the planned research complies with the regulations (U.S. Department of Health, Education, and Welfare, 1971).

Almost all the direct burden of the protection of human subjects regulations is placed on the institutions that conduct federally supported biomedical or behavioral research involving human subjects. Indirectly, the regulations act as a barrier to federal program evaluation by potentially limiting the methods and procedures that can be employed to collect data. When restrictions on methods are based on sound risk–benefit considerations, they are acceptable. However, it is questionable whether local institutional review committees are best qualified to assess the risks and benefits associated with nationwide program evaluations.

The Freedom of Information Act (P.L. 89-554), as amended, was enacted to provide the public with liberal access to government documents. Unless specifically exempted under the act, all documents maintained by an agency must be made available to the public. The major burden that the Freedom of Information Act places on federal program evaluation management relates to the short time allowed for responding to requests for information—ten days—and to the limited resources made available for responding to such requests (U.S. Department of Health, Education, and Welfare, 1974). Most federal evaluation units have a wealth of interesting data, but their capacity to respond to frequent Freedom of Information Act requests without disrupting their principal activities is limited by inadequate resources.

Oversight System. The federal oversight system consists of higher authorities who review and approve the plans and activities of lower authorities. Within federal agencies, senior officials review and approve or disapprove all evaluation plans. Senior officials are also responsible for approving the release of all agency evaluation products. If the agency is located in a department, there is usually another layer of review and approval authority at the assistant secretary level. Across federal agencies, the OMB and the Congress oversee federal evaluation activities.

In addition to the formal federal oversight system, there is an informal evaluation oversight system that consists of state and local government associations, political organizations, national interest groups, lobbying organizations, professional groups, trade organizations, and other evaluation stakeholders. Although the federal government is not required to obtain the approval of these groups in order to conduct evaluations, evaluators and evaluation management must still attend to their concerns.

The major barrier that the oversight process imposes on federal program evaluation management relates to the large number of stakeholders involved and to the inordinate amount of time and money that must be spent in justifying the evaluation function and specific evaluation activities to interested and concerned parties. Responding to both the formal and the informal oversight system can consume between 50 and 70 percent of the federal program evaluation unit manager's time and between 20 and 50 percent of the staff's time. This heavy burden leaves management little time to focus on other matters associated with the operation of federal program evaluation offices.

Political Barriers. Three political barriers to evaluation will be discussed in this section: the political context of the evaluation process, the impact of administration changes on federal operations, and bureaucratic resistance to change.

Political Context. Federal program evaluation is embedded in a context that is extremely political in nature. The systems that keep the bureaucracy operating were developed by elected representatives to Congress, they are implemented and maintained in federal agencies under the guidance of politically appointed senior agency officials, and their operations are monitored by unions, public interest groups, lobbying organizations, and other stakeholders. The programs on which evaluation is focused also contribute to the political context of evaluation. Federal programs are the product of the political system. As such, their maintenance and evaluability is subject to power shifts within the political system. Finally, there is the political nature of evaluation itself. By agreeing to evaluate programs in terms of their intended goals, evaluators help to legitimize both the goals and the programs. Evaluators can also become unwitting advocates of programs as a result of their close association with program managers, participants, and other stakeholders (Lynn, 1977; Weiss, 1975).

Administration Changes. Federal program evaluation offices are often directed by noncareer political appointees. Their tenure in such positions is typically less than the four-year term of the incumbent president. In fact, it is usually about one half as long, due to appointment delays and to the insecurities associated with serving at the pleasure of an agency head or department secretary. During the ten years in which the author has directed evaluations in three federal agencies, he has been supervised by ten different office directors. Such frequent shifts in leadership are very disruptive to an agency's evaluation mission. When a political appointee assumes leadership of an evaluation office, he usually asserts control over the office staff by placing a freeze on hiring and by restricting use of the office's budget. These restrictions are typically imposed for a period of at least a few months; the actual length is a function of the director's assessment of his chances of achieving his desired ends. Such freezes can also be imposed during periods when there is an acting director. These periodic budget and hiring freezes, in combination with freezes imposed by agency and department officials or by the president, can severely restrict evaluation unit expenditures and hiring during much of a president's usual four-year term.

Bureaucratic Response to Change. Another political barrier to the management of federal evaluation units is the bureaucracy's response to change. Federal employees are very sensitive to security. As a group, they develop and perpetuate strategies and tactics to protect their status and turf. Any attempt to change agency operations is perceived by federal employees as either a threat or as an opportunity for advancement. Thus, opportunistic behavior by some employees and heavy foot dragging by others seem the inevitable responses to change.

Attitudinal Barriers. In the political arena, within which federal program evaluation must operate, participants often act on the basis of their perceptions of things, not of the case that actually exists. Two reasons for this are the fast pace of politics and the frequent changes in the political situation. In responding to changes, the politician must often act on the basis of incomplete information. In such an environment, the attitudes and perceptions both of individuals and of constituencies strongly influence decision making.

The attitudes and perceptions of program evaluation stakeholders, whether veridical or not, directly affect the management of federal program evaluation. Negative views of the federal government, federal employees, and the evaluation function have been expressed by congressmen, senior members of the executive branch, special interest and advocacy groups, state and local officials, and the general public. Combating negative attitudes about the subject of evaluations—that is, government operations—the executors of federal program evaluations—that is, government employees—and the conduct of federal program evaluation is a time-consuming activity for agency program evaluation managers. Time and effort taken to correct negative attitudes and perceptions is well spent, but it is time and effort diverted away from achievement of the federal evaluation mission.

Recommendations

The basic premise of this chapter is that efficient and effective management of a federal agency's evaluation unit requires a thorough understanding both of the bureaucratic and political systems in which the agency operates and of the views and attitudes of the agency's key evaluation stakeholders. This section makes some recommendations for overcoming the most common impediments to efficient and effective management of federal program evaluation activities.

Systemic Barriers. The first recommendation is that managers of federal program evaluation offices, their staffs, and their contractors, grantees, and cooperators should possess a thorough understanding of the operation of the primary systems of the federal government. Such understanding confers power to manage program evaluation units effectively. Failure to understand these systems or dependence on others' understanding of these systems will inevitably degrade management performance. Unfortunately, information relative to these systems is not well synthesized, and it is not available in readable form. Most system-relevant information is available in either an oversimplified or an excessively detailed form. The problem is exacerbated by the fact that, in most agencies, the systems experts often have only a superficial understanding of their system; further, they fail to recognize that systems should facilitate, and not impede, efficient management.

A second recommendation for overcoming systemic barriers is that management should document the systemic barriers that it faces, the frequency with which they occur, and the resulting effects of the management and evaluation process. Such documentation is also necessary to promote system modification by informing individuals and groups that have influence over the establishment and maintenance of those systems.

A third recommendation is that system changes should be initiated whenever one finds oneself in a position to do so. It is often possible for a person or group that normally does not influence federal systems to be placed in a position or to assume a position in which he or they can influence system improvements. Armed with a thorough understanding of these systems, with documentation of their negative effects, and with motivation to improve them, program evaluation managers and evaluation stakeholders can have a significant impact on system improvement.

The final recommendation for overcoming systemic barriers is that the federal government should provide all its managerial employees with thorough training in system operations prior to their assignment to a supervisory position. Such basic training is particularly important for noncareer political appointees, who often have little experience with government or with major management responsibilities. The current state of affairs is that few federal senior managers have sufficient understanding of these systems at the time when they assume management responsibilities. Thus, they often learn on the job through trial and error — at best an inefficient and costly method to obtain the knowledge necessary for effective management.

Political Barriers. The political barriers to management of federal program evaluation units are best overcome by a thorough understanding of the political process. One can manage a federal program evaluation office more effectively by operating within the political system than by wittingly or unwittingly attempting to fight it. It is important to recognize the political viability of possible solutions, since the most technically sound evaluation solutions will not always solve problems that are essentially political in nature. In addition, one must also know what means for implementing those solutions are politically acceptable. The political process must be understood and used effectively by managers of federal program evaluation offices if they are successfully to achieve their agency's evaluation goals.

The second recommendation is that evaluation managers should develop and nurture for their unit a broad-based constituency consisting of all major stakeholders in the evaluation process, including agency and department senior management, the OMB, the Congress and its support offices, state and local government, program recipient groups, advocacy organizations, trade groups, and professional societies. These groups need to be recognized as users and critics who have vested interests in the management and operation of evaluation offices as well as in the conduct of specific evaluation studies.

The third recommendation is that evaluation managers should be flexible and adaptable in their interactions with politically significant players. Intransigence is totally unacceptable in the political arena — compromise is the key to achievement. By demonstrating a willingness to consider others' views on matters of mutual interest, the evaluation manager can go a long way toward achieving his agency's evaluation goals.

The final recommendation is that evaluation managers should be as apolitical as possible when performing agency functions. Nonneutrality on political issues can have damaging effects on the credibility of program evaluation offices. It is imperative to the viability of a federal evalution office that all key evaluation stakeholders feel that the unit is unbiased in its assessment of programs and issues that have political overtones.

Attitudinal Barriers. Most attitudinal barriers to the management of federal program evaluation offices can be eliminated by action directed at changing these negative attitudes. Such change can be facilitated by providing information that counters the attitudes and by positive experiences with the subjects of those attitudes. All the recommendations for overcoming attitudinal barriers to efficient and effective program evaluation management made here include one or both of these components.

First, it is incumbent on the managers of federal program evaluation offices, as well as on federal employees in general, to improve the public's negative attitude toward the federal government. Federal employees must demonstrate that they provide efficient and effective services to the public and that they do not hinder the public's conduct of business with the government. The federal civil service must regain the respect of the public by providing courteous service in an efficient and effective manner. Further, the career civil service must monitor its own members, to ensure that only the most qualified individuals are selected for service and that only those who perform satisfactorily remain in the ranks. Federal employees must earn the respect of the public to regain their own pride in government service.

Second, with respect to stakeholder views of federal program evaluation, managers must establish and maintain evaluation offices that provide timely and useful evaluation information to key stakeholders in a cost-efficient manner. Only the best evaluators should be hired, and they should be compensated adequately for outstanding performance. Policies should be promulgated that encourage technical excellence to go hand in hand with concern for evaluation stakeholders (Wargo, 1981a, 1981b, 1981c). In short, steps should be taken to ensure that the public has no foundation upon which to base negative attitudes toward federal program evaluators or their products.

The final recommendation is that federal program evaluation managers should begin to promote their activities with the public in an attempt to change existing negative attitudes toward evaluation and to head off the formation of new negative attitudes. The general public, as well as evaluation stakeholders, need to know that their tax dollars are being used effectively by federal agencies and that evaluation units in those agencies are evaluating programs periodically to ensure that they achieve their goals. The public needs to know the contribution that evaluation and evaluators make to good government. The very survival of federal program evaluation rests on getting this message across to the public. Evaluation managers have a responsibility to their agency, their staff, and themselves to promote their activities and accomplishments and thereby to improve the general public's image of federal program evaluation.

References

Carter, L. F. "Federal Clearance of Educational Evaluation Instruments." *Educational Researcher,* 1977, *6* (6), 7–12.

Cook, T. D., and Campbell, D. T. *Quasi-Experimentation: Design and Analysis Issues for Field Settings.* Chicago: Rand McNally, 1979.

Cronbach, L. J., and others. *Toward Reform of Program Evaluation: Aims, Methods, and Institutional Arrangements.* San Francisco: Jossey-Bass, 1980.

General Services Administration. *The United States Government Manual.* Washington, D.C.: U.S. Government Printing Office, 1979.

General Services Administration. *The United States Government Manual 1982/83.* Washington, D.C.: U.S. Government Printing Office, 1982.

Lynn, L., Jr. "Improving Policy Making." In J. Salasin (Ed.), *The Management of Federal Research and Development.* McLean, Va.: Mitre, 1977.

Raizen, S., and Rossi, P. H. *Program Evaluation in Education: When? How? To What Ends?* Washington, D.C.: National Academy Press, 1981.

Riecken, H. W., and Boruch, R. F. *Social Experimentation.* New York: Academic Press, 1974.

St.Pierre, R. G. "Management of Federally Funded Evaluation Research: Building Evaluation Teams." *Evaluation Review,* 1982, *6* (1), 94–113.

U.S. Department of Agriculture. *Food Programs of the U.S. Department of Agriculture.* Food and Nutrition Service Program Aid No. 1161. Washington, D.C.: U.S. Department of Agriculture, 1980.

U.S. Department of Health, Education, and Welfare. *The Institutional Guide to DHEW Policy on Protection of Human Subjects.* DHEW Publication No. (NIH) 72-102. Washington, D.C.: U.S. Department of Health, Education, and Welfare, 1971.

U.S. Department of Health, Education, and Welfare. *Public Information Regulation.* Washington, D.C.: U.S. Department of Health, Education, and Welfare, 1974.

U.S. Office of Personnel Management. *Managers Handbook.* Washington, D.C.: U.S. Office of Personnel Management, 1979.

Wargo, M. J. "An Evaluator's Interpretation." In M. J. Wargo and D. R. Green (Eds.), *Achievement Testing of Disadvantaged and Minority Students for Educational Program Evaluation.* Monterey, Ca.: McGraw-Hill, 1977.

Wargo, M. J. "Evaluation in the Nutrition Program." In L. E. Datta (Ed.), *Evaluation in Change.* Beverly Hills, Calif.: Sage, 1981a.

Wargo, M. J. "Program Evaluation at Agriculture: The FNS." *Evaluation Research Society Newsletter,* 1981b, *5* (2), 11.

Wargo, M. J. "Research Programs of the Food and Nutrition Service." In C. E. Eshbach (Ed.), *Energy, Government, Research.* Proceedings of the 37th conference of the Society for Advancement of Food Service Research. Fort Wayne, Ind.: Society for the Advancement of Food Service Research, 1981c.

Weiss, C. H. "Evaluation Research in the Political Context." In E. L. Struening and M. Guttentag (Eds.), *Handbook of Evaluation Research.* Vol. 1. Beverly Hills, Calif.: Sage, 1975.

Michael J. Wargo is director of the program evaluation staff at the Food and Nutrition Service, U.S. Department of Agriculture.

The project officer plays a pivotal role in managing the work
of social scientists to serve the needs of federal policy makers.

The Project Officer's Role in Managing Federal Program Evaluations

Jack Radzikowski
W. Burleigh Seaver

This chapter describes the functions of federal project officers in managing program evaluations with support from contract research firms. Four functions have particular interest: articulating evaluation requirements; contracting for assistance from research firms in a manner that provides for fair competition; guiding ongoing studies so they are technically sound, policy-relevant, and compliant with the law; and transmitting evaluation results to decision makers in a timely manner and in a usable form.

The management functions of the project officer are described in terms of the check points and approvals for which the project officer holds major responsibility as a large-scale evaluation study proceeds through its various phases to successful completion. Figure 1 depicts the four management functions just identified and their usual time sequence. It shows the relationship of these functions to management decisions that affect the evaluation and to

The views and opinions expressed in this paper are those of the authors and should not be construed to be the policy or position of the Food and Nutrition Service, U.S. Department of Agriculture.

R. G. St. Pierre (Ed.). *Management and Organization of Program Evaluation.* New Directions for Program Evaluation, no. 18. San Francisco: Jossey-Bass, June 1983.

27

documents and other products of the evaluation; evaluation products appear in boxes. References in the text to functions and products are keyed to Figure 1 by means of parenthetical notes, such as *(1a)*.

Articulating Evaluation Requirements

The project officer's job often begins with vague guidance to conduct an evaluation study. The guidance can come in the form of a mandate from Congress that is part of an appropriation or authorization law. It can also arise from an interest taken by the Office of Management and Budget (OMB) or senior agency officials in particular policy issues, from general agency policy to evaluate all ongoing programs, or from program managers who identify program operations and management issues. Regardless of its origin, the evaluation requirement usually reaches the project officer as a vague set of ill-defined information needs and sketchy ideas about what can be done to meet them. The project officer's first tasks are to translate these vaguely defined needs into an articulate and parsimonious set of evaluation requirements and to obtain the sponsor's endorsement of the study as articulated. The resulting officially sanctioned requirements and the record of discussion surrounding them become critically important to the study's success. Being one of the few aspects of a given evaluation with which most parties concur, the evaluation requirements form a large part of the criteria used to judge the adequacy of the eventual research design, data analyses, and reports.

As an example of congressional guidance available in advance of written evaluation requirements, consider the case of Senate Resolution 90 (Report 98-208, June 20, 1979), which called for a comprehensive assessment of the National School Lunch Program. This assessment was to examine the income and family composition of program participants, the program's impact, and the extent to which program benefits were targeted to participants' needs.

The Senate conference report containing the resolution gave a date for a final report but said nothing about how the evaluation should be conducted or about how much money should be spent on the effort. A review of the rest of the conference report gave few clues about whether there should be one study or several. The only other guidance was that a review of existing data would not itself form an acceptable answer to Senate Resolution 90. After receiving this resolution and confirming the seriousness of the request, senior staff at the Food and Nutrition Service (FNS) took their evaluation director aside and said, "Start making plans." The evaluation director in turn took a project officer aside and said, "Read the conference report, and get started."

At this point, although there seemed to be little to go on, the project officer did have some immediate steps to follow. The first was to review the legislative and regulatory history related to the issues listed in Senate Resolution 90 (1a). In Washington, such documents can be found through a federal agency's congressional liaison office, or they can be located through contact with the Congressional Research Service or the Congressional Budget Office. These sources often turn up other immediately relevant documents, such as recent research findings cited in the public record as influencing program policy. Guidance for the early planning of an evaluation can also be obtained from senior civil servants and political appointees in the sponsoring agency as well as from staff of congressional committees and other agencies, such as the General Accounting Office and the OMB, that have oversight authority for the sponsoring agency's programs.

Conversations with these interested parties inevitably prove more profitable in formulating evaluation objectives than the review of documents alone. In particular, staff from oversight agencies and congressional committees can provide a solid oral history of the intent of decision makers when legislative mandates or requests for studies are forthcoming (1b). Via this process, the intentions behind Senate Resolution 90 were quickly identified, and four conceptually distinct evaluation efforts were conceived.

Next, the project officer wrote two-page concept papers describing the objectives, products, uses, and users for each evaluation (1c). The concept papers were sent up the chain of command to the level of the assistant secretary, and they served as a basis for discussion in seeking the endorsement of senior agency decision makers. At successive levels in the organization, the concept papers were debated, altered, and ultimately endorsed (1d). This process generally bought the needed early support and approval of program managers. The time that elapsed between the formal request for the study—the congressional mandate—and final approval of the concept papers was about one month.

The scope of work for large-scale evaluations usually exceeds the level that can be performed by the internal staff of a federal evaluation unit, and assistance is usually obtained from an outside organization with specialized evaluation capability through a competitive contract procedure. After receiving approval of the concept paper, the project officer begins the process of securing contracted assistance by writing a detailed description of the evaluation requirements and the work to be performed. This statement of work generally has five parts: a synopsis of legislative history and a description of the program's objectives and operations; a statement of the evaluation's objectives and research questions in as much detail as possible, along with uses to be made of evaluation results; a draft research design to give prospective contractors an idea of the sponsor's technical prejudices; a list of the tasks that will form the basis of the contract between the offeror and the federal government; and a schedule and list of deliverables described in sufficient detail to serve as part of the criteria for authorizing payment for the work when it is performed. The period of time necessary to prepare a good statement of work is about six weeks.

The project officer ushers the statement of work through two kinds of review, one for technical acceptability and one for policy relevance, before

Figure 1. The Federal Project Officer's Management Functions for a Large-Scale Program Evaluation

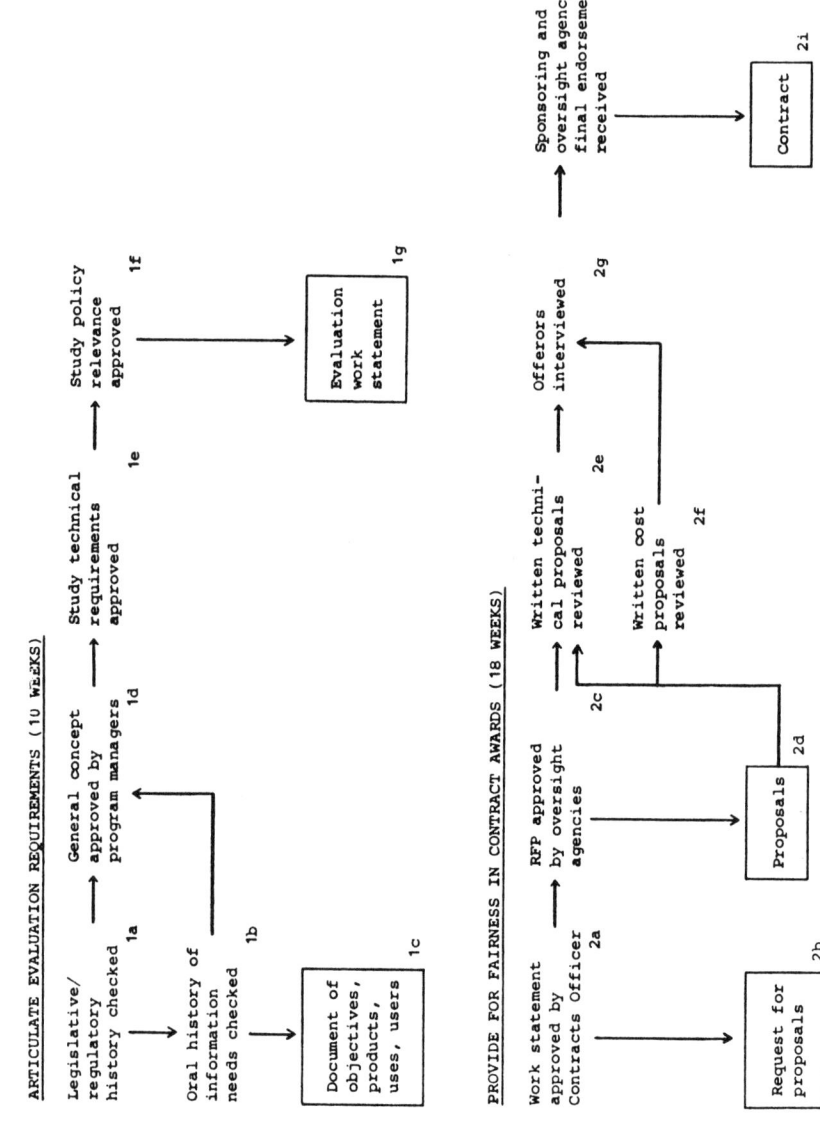

MONITOR ONGOING STUDIES FOR TECHNICAL QUALITY, POLICY RELEVANCE AND COMPLIANCE WITH THE LAW (1 TO 3 YEARS)

Management plans prepared   3a
→ Existing data synthesized   3c
→ Research design/analysis plans debated and approved   3e
→ Instrumentation and data collection plans cleared   3i
→ Analyses/reports reviewed and approved   3m

Contract event schedules   3b

Program operations description/relevant research   3d

External advisors considered   3f

State and local fieldwork problems resolved   3j

Research design and rationale

Analysis Plan   3g   3h

Data collection manual

OMB clearance package   3k   3l

Ad hoc and final reports   3n

Computer tapes   3o

TRANSMIT EVALUATION RESULTS TO DECISION MAKERS (1 YEAR)

Agency and department executives briefed   4a
→ Administration budget proposals supported   4d
→ Congressional legislative alternatives supported   4f
→ Library and information retrieval center dissemination   4h
→ Lobbyists/program constituency groups briefed   4i

Policy memoranda

Executive summaries of results   4c   4b

Memoranda for subcabinet levels and OMB   4e

Q and As to Hill   4g

Journal publications   4j

passing it on to the agency's contracting office, which turns it into a legal instrument. The technical review addresses the scientific quality and logistical feasibility of the proposed evaluation relative to the study objectives and to resource constraints on time and money (1e). The review for policy relevance ensures that the study focuses on concrete issues important to the agency and that the study's products are tied to decisions to be made in the future (1f). The project officer uses the results of both reviews to prepare the statement of work in final form (1g).

Providing for Fairness in Contract Awards

With a sound statement of work in hand, the project officer sets about identifying the organization that will do the best possible job of conducting the evaluation on terms that are the most favorable to the government. The project officer must manage the selection of the contractor in a way that ensures fair and open competition, that prevents conflicts of interest, and that promotes social goals established by Congress, such as assisting small, minority-owned firms and firms located in areas of high unemployment. To ensure fairness in contracting as defined by legislation and by the courts, a complex set of legal and administrative conditions must be fulfilled. While the project officer has a natural interest in doing a proper job as he or she perceives the law, there are others, both within the sponsoring agency and within the so-called over-sight agencies, whose principal function is to see that the project officer does a proper job. This section outlines the steps that proceed from the time when the statement of work leaves the federal evaluation shop to the time four and one-half months later when a research firm signs a contract to begin the tasks specified in the statement of work.

The statement of work goes first to the contracting office, where it is reviewed by contracting specialists (2a) to ensure that the task statements can form the basis of a legal document. Assuming that all the work is described in some detail, the contract specialist must adjust the language so that ambiguous statements concerning what both the contractor and the government will and will not do are made as clear as possible. The contract specialist also checks for adequate cost guidance to see that the task statements and the criteria for acceptable products will allow several hypothetical contractors having similar labor rates, other direct costs, and overhead to provide comparable cost figures. The cycle of contract specialist review and project officer rewrite can take several iterations before the statement of work becomes the request for proposals (RFP). Once sanctioned by the contract specialist, the statement of work grows in stature and weight by gaining the boiler plate—a set of stock legal clauses that apply to the substance of the work at hand and that include everything from the grounds by which either party can abrogate the agreement to the types of contractor-purchased equipment that must be manufactured in the United States. The boiler plate often adds fifty or more pages to the statement of work, which can range from thirty to fifty pages in length.

Approval of the work statement by a contract specialist and the production of an RFP (2b) usually take between two and six weeks. The time needed for the next step, oversight agency approval (2c), is difficult to estimate, because oversight approval for a study costing more than $500,000 means that the RFP must be passed to the sponsoring agency's general counsel, assistant secretary for administration, inspector general, Office of Small and Disadvantaged Businesses, and sometimes the Office of Management and Budget. Depending on the workload of oversight agency reviewers and on their familiarity with the study topic, an RFP can be held as little as three weeks or as long as four months or more, in which case several major rewrites of the work statement can be required from the project officer. Oversight agency reviews bog down less from obvious legal or regulatory violations associated with the proposed work than from simple misunderstandings about the nature of the work on the part of reviewers. This is not surprising when one considers that an oversight agency reviewer has to be quick, intelligent, and thorough and must at least have some knowledge of the program, the objectives of the evaluation, and the proposed evaluation methods. This is a rare mix of skills to find in one person, who often has oversight responsibilities for thirty programs across four or five agencies.

With the RFP in hand, the project officer helps the contracts specialist to publish notices in the *Commerce Business Daily* and the *Federal Register* and to distribute the RFP to known qualified sources and to interested persons and organizations that request it. Offerors have between thirty and sixty days in which to respond with proposals (2d). The typical agency receives between five and ten proposals, each consisting of separate technical and cost parts. If the RFP was well prepared and the topic is at least somewhat interesting to prospective offerors, two thirds of the proposals will be serious contenders for the final award.

The project officer has the lead responsibility for review of technical proposals (2e). The review process typically involves five persons, three of whom have some skills as program evaluators and two of whom contribute detailed substantive knowledge of program policy and operations. All proposals are read by all reviewers at least twice during a two-week period and rated according to the criteria listed in the RFP. During the same two-week period, the cost proposals are reviewed (2f), and offerors' references are checked by contract specialists and the project officer. Offerors who remain in the competitive range after the technical review are invited to Washington for orals (2g). These face-to-face interviews allow the project officer, the contracting officer, and the offeror to address ambiguities in the written technical and cost proposals. At the conclusion of the orals, the contract specialists and evaluation staff decide which proposals provide the most favorable combination of technical and cost terms to the government. The top two or three offerors — the finalists — are requested to go back over their proposals and make their best and final offer.

A recommended winner is selected from these best and final offers.

The project officer and the contracting specialists present the recommended decision and the supporting evidence to the contract board of awards, a formally constituted committee of top agency officers who decide whether to award a contract and to whom to award it. Assuming that the board endorses the recommended winning offer, the offer is forwarded to the final gatekeeper, the agency general counsel, for one more review (2h). Only then is a contract prepared and signed (2i).

Monitoring Ongoing Studies

If one thinks of the contract research firm's project director as the chief executive officer of the evaluation team, then the federal project officer is the chairman of the board. To continue the metaphor, the successful evaluation should have a board that meets frequently and a well-qualified chairman who is very inquisitive. During the active life of the contract, after the procurement process is over and before the final results are presented to decision makers, the project officer is responsible for maintaining the technical quality of evaluation projects, for keeping those products tailored to their evaluation uses, and for ensuring that all project activities comply with the law. As chairman of the board, the project officer must interpret agency policy, frequently reinterpret the evaluation requirements, review all interim and final products, and suggest appropriate revisions in products to the project director.

Despite this seeming obtrusiveness, the project officer must allow the project director sufficient leeway as chief executive officer to manage the immediate tasks of the evaluation efficiently. While there is no simple, universally applicable prescription for success in this monitoring role, several points of intervention occur in most evaluations. These interventions, which for the most part are really checks and approvals, are of two sorts: those that the project officer makes during the life of the project, and, if primary data collection is required, those that officials within oversight agencies make of instrumentation used to collect data. The discussion that follows describes both the key events in a study that the project officer monitors and the typical cycle for clearing instrumentation. Again, while no single model fits all large-scale program evaluations, the discussion in this section roughly describes the experiences encountered by the nutrition evaluation studies conducted in response to Senate Resolution 90. Those studies were national in scope, they involved large amounts of primary data collection, and they enjoyed sufficient lead time to allow detailed planning.

Immediately after award of the contract, the project officer, the project director, and other contract research firm staff meet for an orientation and operational planning session. This session serves the purpose of introducing both agency decision makers and inexpensive, accessible sources of written information to the contractor's evaluation staff. Out of this meeting comes a revised schedule for major project events (3a, 3b). The evaluation team now retraces in detail the trail blazed by the project officer in preparing the statement of work. The research literature is reviewed, and the operational dynamics of the program are fully described (3c, 3d). The literature review and the program descriptions serve the purpose of refining the research questions and of uncovering clues about how program outcomes and factors affecting those outcomes can be measured. During the course of these events, the project officer acts in the capacity of chief referral authority and program contact for the evaluation team.

After the understanding of research questions and the phenomena to be studied has been refined, a detailed research design is prepared. The research design identifies the options for dependent variables of interest, baselines for comparisons, schedules of observation, data sources, sampling procedures, and reasons for the choice of each (3e, 3g). Next comes a plan for analyzing the data generated by the research design (3h). Preparing research design and analysis plans in painstaking detail permits painstaking critiques prior to the expenditure of hundreds of thousands of evaluation dollars. During this methodological planning period, a board of external advisers composed of expert methodological and substantive consultants is usually formed to review and criticize the evaluation methodology (3f). In support of these activities, the project officer must facilitate communication among the many members of the team, who report to different organizations—federal, state, and local agencies, prime contractors, subcontractors, university consultants, program advocates, and lobbyists. In the difficult start-up period, when advisers can agree on very little, the project officer has to give frequent and reasonably consistent guidance to the contract research firm or pay a dear price in false starts prompted by poor or nonexistent directives. Fortunately, the project officer has the luxury of reconciling or rejecting a great deal of conflicting opinion before the methodological plans are firmly cast. The period of time involved in methodological planning can often consume between six months and a year or more, depending on the extent to which the research questions posed are novel.

To this point, much of the planning is conceptual in nature, since it involves the research design and the preferred analytic procedures. With the subsequent need for operations plans—that is, for instrumentation and data collection plans—approvals by persons not in the project officer's immediate span of control are required. The most formidable, and in some cases the most time-consuming, clearance to obtain in the conduct of a large-scale evaluation is that from the OMB. Under the Federal Paperwork Reduction Act of 1980, OMB clearance is required for any data collection instrument to be used with more than nine members of the public (3i). This clearance is intended to minimize the burden placed on the public by federal data collection efforts, whether those efforts recur, as in the case of Internal Revenue Service Form 1040, or whether they happen once in a lifetime. To prove that a given study has practical utility and that it imposes a minimal burden, the project officer must justify its merits both in writing and orally to an OMB examiner. The justification includes authority for the study, such as a congressional mandate; the instrumentation necessary to meet the study objectives; an outline of an analysis plan; and a list of reports. Both because it is long and because it must be developed in a short time, the written justification for clearance is usually prepared by the evaluation contractor (3k, 3l).

Although there is a standard form for obtaining OMB clearance, each justification is very much tailored to the individual needs of the clearance examiner as the project officer interprets them. Experience suggests that obtaining clearance in a reasonable amount of time depends both on the style and specific requirements of the clearance examiner and on the speed with which the project officer can discover and adapt to the examiner's needs. Clearance can take anywhere from one to many months.

Depending on the nature of the study, the project officer may have other data collection clearances to manage as well. At the federal level, approvals are needed to ensure the privacy of respondents and the safety of human subjects. With proper planning and luck, these can be obtained concurrently with OMB approval. Once these clearances have been secured at the federal level, the project officer must obtain approvals to enter the necessary state and local jurisdictions (3j). Geographical jurisdiction approvals most often can be obtained by forwarding all or parts of the OMB clearance justification to relevant state and local authorities. Once clearance has been granted, state and local authorities require a strict entry and exit protocol, which the project officer must handle directly or oversee carefully. If data collectors enter a locale without being preceded by the proper telephone calls or letters of introduction, the project officer can end up spending days or weeks apologizing to a wide range of disgruntled officials.

Assuming that data collection has been completed, the project officer's next to last contract monitoring function, albeit usually a long and enjoyable one, is to review analyses and reports (3m). For large data sets, the analytic and reporting activities are exceedingly difficult to complete in less than a year. This time estimate does not include the effort that both the contractor and, to a much lesser extent, the project officer devote to the reduction of data from hard copy to computer tape. It complicates the job that analytic budgets are invariably insufficient for large studies, in which multimillion dollar or billion dollar decisions hang on the accuracy of analytic estimates. Although analysis plans have already been thoroughly reviewed and revised, the project officer must choose the highest priorities from a list of possible analyses much longer than can be completed. The project officer must also reconvene the study's advisory group to ensure that the final results can withstand rigid scrutiny and maintain a high level of integrity (3n). Here, too, advanced planning (for example, table shells, introductions) helps enormously in the reporting process. Each large-scale evaluation is unique, and a useful final report always takes a lot of careful review and rewriting under the direction of the project officer, no matter how gifted the principal authors are as writers. In part, this occurs because the policy decisions that a study can influence often continue to change up to the last minutes of a contract's life. Finally, in closing out the contract, the project officer must ensure that a door remains open to the data, should the need arise. The project officer's final duty under the contract is to accept computer tapes (3o) that are sufficiently well documented that they can be used readily by staff of the federal government.

Transmitting Evaluation Results to Decision Makers

In an important sense, the project officer's most critical function begins after the final report has been delivered. That function involves dissemination of results to decision makers. If one judges the ultimate success of an evaluation by the extent to which policy makers use the results, then much of that ultimate success depends on the skill of the project officer in selling the product of the evaluation. At the end of a contract, it proves well worthwhile to take stock once again of the decision maker's current needs and to redetermine how and when results should be transmitted. Experience suggests that the utility of a final report soars when a thick, technically oriented document is translated into a variety of smaller reports and oral presentations, each of which focuses on some special issue at a level of technical detail tailored to the interest and sophistication of the particular user.

Before study findings are transmitted to the Congress, oversight agencies, or the public at large, extensive briefings occur within the sponsoring agency (4a). Several versions of an executive summary of results are prepared to explain what the evaluators found (4b). Under separate cover, policy memoranda are prepared suggesting actions that could be based on the results (4c). Within the sponsoring agency, these summaries address the three main issues of interest to federal program managers: budget issues, legislative issues, and issues addressing program regulations. The project officer proceeds up the chain of command within the agency and the department, briefing division directors, office directors, administrators, and assistant secretaries. Staff who manage regional program offices are also briefed. These briefings ensure that all key people receive the official version of the results before they read the unofficial and often misinterpreted version that appears in the newspapers. These briefings also allow the project officer to gauge how well the results play to different audiences; that is, to judge what questions remain unanswered and what clarifications of results may be required.

Results are first given to the public by way of a press release drafted by the project officer. Then, as the evaluation findings are formally released by the sponsoring agency, the OMB and the Congress, particularly the House and Senate committees that have an immediate interest in the program, receive principal attention from the project officer. The OMB receives summaries and explanations that emphasize budget issues (4d, 4e). Senate and House staff receive information sensitive to legislative issues (4f). If a program is up for reauthorization, Congress will typically follow up receipt of an evaluation report with questions to the agency asking for further clarification or an official agency position on a particular evaluation issue (4g). The project officer will usually draft the agency's response to such questions.

The second tier of public constituents to receive evaluation results can be grouped into two broad categories: one made up of the academic community surrounding the program's substantive area (for example, for the FNS, the nutrition community) and one consisting of state and local program operators' professional associations, program advocates (for example, antihunger coalitions), and business interests (for example, commodity producers and processors). The project officer makes full volumes of final reports available to these broad audiences through lending libraries and information storage and retrieval exchanges (4h). Concurrent with release of the report and for a short time thereafter, the project officer is available for briefings at professional meetings (4i). Professional journals and trade association publications are the final forum, in which extended explanations of special issues can be offered and the inevitable critics can be answered (4j).

The four functions described in this chapter are the principal management activities of the project officer through the life cycle of a major program evaluation. These activities demand a major commitment of time, attention, energy, and enthusiasm, and they require substantial skill in working simultaneously in the technical realm of evaluation methodology and in the political realm of public policy. Through managing large-scale evaluations, the project officer provides a point of contact between the information-gathering and information-interpreting capability of modern social science and the decision-making functions of government.

Jack Radzikowski is a member of the program evaluation staff at the Food and Nutrition Service, U.S. Department of Agriculture. He heads a branch that evaluates the commodity donation, national school lunch, and school breakfast programs.

W. Burleigh Seaver is a member of the program evaluation staff at the Food and Nutrition Service, U.S. Department of Agriculture. He heads a branch that evaluates the food stamp program; the supplemental feeding program for women, infants, and children; and other programs that provide food assistance to families.

*The Bureau of Evaluation, created three years ago by the Louisiana
Department of Education, has established policies and procedures
that ensure use of evaluation findings by both policy makers and
program administrators.*

Management and Organization of an Evaluation Unit in a State Education Agency

Hugh I. Peck
Suzanne E. Triplett

Growth of staff, diversity of responsibilities, and development of policies and
procedures have been the hallmark of the Bureau of Evaluation in the Louisiana Department of Education since the bureau was established in 1980. The
bureau has developed policies and established relationships that have mini-
mized conflict with program staff and resulted in substantial use of evaluation
results. This chapter provides information on the development and structure
of the bureau that managers of similar evaluation units can use. The rationale
for the Bureau of Evaluation is discussed in the first section. Next, its organizational structure is described. Finally, some unique operational features that
have contributed to its success are highlighted.

Rationale and Mission

Much of Louisiana's recent educational accountability legislation
requires the State Department of Education directly or indirectly to evaluate
programs and projects in order to determine their impact on the basic skills
achievement of children in public schools. For example, Louisiana's authoriz-

R. G. St. Pierre (Ed.). *Management and Organization of Program Evaluation.* New Directions
for Program Evaluation, no. 18. San Francisco: Jossey-Bass, June 1983.

ing legislation for compensatory education (Louisiana, *Revised Statutes*, 1980, Act 433) stipulates that there must be "evaluation of the program's effectiveness." By 1992, compensatory education will be provided to students at all grade levels who do not pass the annual basic skills test. Even more recent legislation (Louisiana, *Revised Statutes*, 1982, Act 160) provides for review and evaluation of department programs to determine "(a) whether the program is meeting goals and objectives established by the legislature, or in lieu thereof by the department; (b) whether the program is conducted as effectively and efficiently as possible in terms of services rendered, benefits achieved, and purposes accomplished and in terms of economic costs; (c) whether the program should be modified or eliminated; and (d) what specific changes, if any, should be made in the program. Any such review shall develop and employ relevant and valid criteria and techniques of study which will measure real program effects, which will demonstrate in factual terms results or effects of the program which are related to its goals and objectives, and/or which will measure the effectiveness and efficiency of the operations and administration of the program against objective standards."

In addition, the Joint Legislative Committee on Executive Branch Reorganization (1981) recommended that the department "set out the programs and goals of the Department, provide for the evaluation of these on a regular basis, and provide a procedure for recommendations of modifications to improve the programs based on such evaluation." In some instances in which the authorizing legislation did not impose evaluation requirements for funded programs, the State Board of Elementary and Secondary Education directed the department to provide formal evaluation information. Underscoring the importance of evaluation, the state board, in its role as the policy-making body for education in Louisiana, established specific requirements for both the evaluation process and the persons who conduct evaluations of educational programs in Louisiana. Information about these requirements appears later in this chapter.

As a result of the growing demand for evaluation, the Bureau of Evaluation was established on April 1, 1980. It is placed administratively within the Office of Research and Development. The Bureau of Evaluation is responsible for examining the success with which educational policies and programs meet the goals that they are designed to achieve for their targets (for example, individuals, schools, school systems). Through the use of objective and systematic methods, the bureau assesses the extent to which policy and program goals are realized, it analyzes cost effectiveness, and it examines factors associated with successful and unsuccessful outcomes.

The bureau responds to the informational needs of the state legislature and the state board in making policy decisions about education in Louisiana and of the state superintendent of education in executing and implementing the department's educational policies and programs. The Bureau of Evaluation is designed to operate as a service-oriented arm of the Office of Reserach and Development. Although the bureau is an integral part of the department, it provides services independent of program administration within the department. It assumes a posture of objectivity, and it does not advocate any program, project, or activity that does not contribute to improved evaluation.

The bureau implements policies and establishes procedures for improving the quality of evaluations supported by the state board and by local boards of education. The focus of these actions is to broaden the concept of evaluation from one of the simple acquisition of numbers for compliance purposes to one of comprehensive formative and summative reviews of educational elements and programs. Thus, the Bureau of Evaluation was conceived as an integral component of the office of which it is part. It responds to policy makers' needs for information about educational program effectiveness independently of program administration, while it serves a leadership role for the process of evaluation.

Organizational Structure

The Bureau of Evaluation has developed an organizational structure that is conducive to the ordered growth of program evaluation as its responsibility in this area increases, that provides the necessary data and research bases and the necessary analytical and dissemination capabilities, and that ensures direct access to decision makers. This structure was developed for two reasons. First, prior to establishment of the bureau, the department had no unit with overall evaluation functions. Thus, there was neither an existing structure to reorganize nor were there attitudes to change. Second, the first person to be employed after the bureau was established was the director, who immediately assumed all planning and managerial responsibilities, including design of the organizational structure, development of a staffing plan, hiring of personnel, and development and administration of a fiscal plan to support the new organization.

Functions. The bureau performs three major functions: program evaluation, evaluation studies, and quality assurance. Program evaluations are undertaken to gain an understanding of a program or process so that judgments can be made about its relative worth. A second purpose of program evaluations is to identify factors related to program objectives that are important for program improvement. Information is provided to program managers so they can adjust activities so as more nearly to achieve project goals and to department and state board policy makers so they can make judgments concerning funding, expansion, and so forth.

The purpose of evaluation studies is to gain understanding of certain phenomena in order to provide information to decision makers. Evaluation studies provide background information about the consequences that can be expected from alternative policy or program decisions. For example, the bureau conducts evaluation studies on the phenomena associated with basic skills testing of special education children. These studies enable department decision makers to select courses of action that both ensure protection of the rights of handicapped children and maintain the integrity of Louisiana's accountability legislation.

The quality assurance function stems from the bureau's charge to provide technical assistance to local school systems and to assure quality in the evaluation processes and products developed at the local level. This function has been included because there are few trained educational program evaluators or researchers in the state. Consequently, many evaluations are designed and implemented by persons who are not knowledgeable about technical advances in this rapidly expanding field. Moreover, Louisiana educators have not been exposed to comprehensive, responsive, and timely evaluations. For this reason, they are unaware of the potential usefulness of evaluation results in making program and policy decisions. The users of evaluation results do not know what to request or expect from an evaluation of a program or project; hence, they do not demand technical and procedural rigor.

In January 1981, the state board adopted a rule establishing certification criteria for educational program evaluators. This rule made Louisiana the first state to establish a certification procedure for evaluators. The *Standards for Evaluations of Educational Programs, Projects, and Materials* developed by the Joint Committee on Standards for Educational Evaluation (1981) were adopted by the state board in January 1981. The *Standards* provide a common approach to the evaluation of programs, projects, and materials in Louisiana as well as a measure for judging the quality of educational program evaluations in Louisiana. The Bureau of Evaluation provides training for all persons who seek certification as a program evaluator. More than 350 persons achieved certification status in the initial grandfather phase, which lasted from July 1981 to January 1982. It is expected that approximately fifty new evaluators will be certified this year. In the future, basic training in the *Standards* will be supplemented with specific training in evaluation skills.

Fiscal Policy. A two-part policy adopted by the Louisiana Department of Education establishes the fiscal relationship between the Bureau of Evaluation and other department bureaus and programs (Thompson, 1980): "The Bureau of Evaluation will, through regular budgeting procedures and legislative appropriation, have a core budget which provides for (1) the overall administration of the Bureau, (2) the administration and implementation of the quality control functions of the Bureau, and (3) the ongoing evaluation of projects, programs, and materials administered by the Department of Education. The Bureau of Evaluation will negotiate with individual divisions, bureaus, and programs within the Department of Education for appropriate evaluations of specific projects, programs, and materials. These individual evaluation activities will be supported within the budget of the respective project or program in a subcontract arrangement with the Bureau of Evaluation. The evaluation of a project, program, or material will be negotiated at the beginning of the planning process. Upon initiation of the project or program, evaluation funds will be transferred to the Bureau of Evaluation cost center." Further, it is official policy that, to the degree possible, all program evaluations will be conducted by the bureau.

Perhaps this combination of a core budget with subcontracts makes Louisiana's Bureau of Evaluation unique among state education agency evaluation units. In any case, combining funding from a variety of sources has several benefits. The core budget allows the bureau to maintain a small but highly qualified staff, and it demonstrates a permanent commitment to program evaluation. The use of subcontracting gives the bureau maximal flexibility in responding to new legislative, state board, and department initiatives without building a large permanent staff. Under this arrangement, new federally funded programs are evaluated by adding project staff on a one-, two-, or three-year basis. Professional personnel employed for specific projects enhance the capabilities of bureau staff. One more benefit of subcontracting is that it improves cooperation among program managers and staff in the implementation of evaluation. When funding for the evaluation is a part of their budget, program staff are more likely to provide requested data and to use information produced by evaluation.

Staffing. The bureau employs three types of evaluation professionals: managers, associates, and assistants. Education program evaluation managers have administrative responsibilities from the design phase through day-to-day operations of the evaluation to preparation of written technical reports and presentation of results to users. All managers have the doctor's degree and at least three years of experience in program evaluation. Education program evaluation associates work under the supervision of managers. They can be administratively responsible for small evaluations. Associates must have the doctor's degree or the master's degree and experience. Education program evaluation assistants provide support at all stages of evaluations conducted by the bureau. Usually, assistants have special skills in one or more areas, such as data management, statistics, or computers.

The bureau's staff is relatively small. In addition to the director, there is a chief of program evaluations and four managers, two associates, three assistants, three word processor operators, and a word processor operator supervisor. Staff members are either permanent core staff or project staff on limited assignment of one to three years. During the 1981–82 school year, bureau staff completed five major studies (that is, studies that required more than one person-year) and thirteen smaller studies and implemented a statewide training and technical assistance program in evaluation. In addition, staff members served on numerous department program and study committees and provided technical assistance in evaluation-related efforts by the department.

Evaluation managers are assigned to direct evaluations. Frequently, they must direct more than one evaluation at a time. Depending on the level of effort, other managers, associates, and assistants provide help with areas in which they have particular expertise. Staff work together in evaluation teams to enhance and expand both group and individual capabilities. A matrix staffing pattern is employed, which matches staff expertise with evaluation functions. This pattern allows a minimal number of staff members to conduct evaluations of a wide range of educational programs and projects.

The bureau's matrix staffing pattern requires identification of needed competencies. The director of the bureau used a compendium of competencies developed by the Dallas Independent School District (1980) in preparing job descriptions and in employing staff. Each new staff member brings new skills and experiences to the team. Competencies in the areas of evaluation, research, psychometrics, statistics, evaluation design, and data processing are particularly sought. Each staff member must have demonstrated experience in working with people and writing skills.

As part of their job, all staff members, including clerical and support staff, are expected to upgrade their technical skills and to demonstrate professional growth and development during the year. Activities can include, but they are not limited to, improving proficiencies in computer language, expanding capabilities in statistical procedures, and preparing research papers for juried journals or national research groups.

The Bureau of Evaluation is highly production-oriented. Quarterly personnel evaluations are conducted to assist all staff in assessing their performance against specific, written standards. Bureau policy is that, to the degree possible, promotions are made from within.

Interrelationships. The emphasis in Louisiana on improving accountability within education, the increased sophistication of state and local policy makers regarding the use of empirical data in decision making, and continuing demands by local, state, and federal fiscal agents for technically adequate evaluations of educational programs and projects all demand that local education agencies improve their evaluation capabilities. However, only a few of the larger school systems in the state can afford to maintain staff to conduct program evaluations. Smaller, less affluent systems must often depend on program personnel who have little or no training or experience in program evaluation. Thus, one of the bureau's major responsibilities is to assist local education agencies and personnel in the area of program evaluation. The bureau meets this responsibility by providing training and technical assistance in evaluation, not by conducting actual program evaluations. Such services as workshops on evaluation methodologies and on use of evaluation results are provided on request to local school systems. Certified evaluators and users of evaluation results are involved in determining the topics for ongoing evaluation training and skills upgrading offered by the Bureau of Evaluation.

It is incumbent on the Bureau of Evaluation to demonstrate educational program evaluation excellence and to provide models that can be used throughout the state. Two mechanisms have been identified to assist in the accomplishment of the goals. First, the bureau provided the leadership to establish an education program evaluators' round table for persons employed by local school systems to conduct evaluations. The round table provides a forum in which approximately twenty professional evaluators can learn about bureau activities and question and critique the bureau's methodologies and findings. The round table provides the bureau with the perspective of local school systems on projects, and it provides participants and bureau staff with opportunities to interact and grow professionally. Second, the bureau is establishing an advisory council to provide it with overall guidance.

Unique Operational Features

Evaluation Design Document. For every evaluation that the bureau conducts, it develops a design document that specifies the research and policy questions to be examined and the instrumentation, data collection, analysis, and reporting procedures to be followed. The document is negotiated with program administrators to ensure the appropriateness and efficiency of the design, and subsequently it serves as a formal agreement between the Bureau of Evaluation and the program being evaluated. It is, in fact, an accountability mechanism for both the Bureau of Evaluation and program management.

Evaluation Reports. The ultimate measure of the effectiveness of any evaluation is the degree to which its findings are used by program and policy decision makers. To enhance evaluation use, bureau staff devote considerable attention during the design phase to identification of the needs and interests of all potential audiences. These needs help to determine the format of the reports written and disseminated by the bureau, which range from lengthy technical volumes to brief summaries of single aspects of a given study.

Dissemination of evaluation results is not left to chance; the bureau takes a proactive stance on disseminating its findings. Bureau staff make oral presentations on evaluation findings to the state superintendent, his cabinet, the state board, and the legislature as a matter of course. Other audiences for such reports include program administrators, program participants, teachers, local and state educational administrators, and department personnel with an interest in developing or improving the program.

Since evaluation is conducted to inform decision makers, results must be presented in time for effective decision making. For example, programs that run during the school year often require that interim reports be made to the legislature or the board before school ends. The bureau provides such interim reports. In addition, educational decision makers sometimes need information about emergency situations. Typically, the bureau can respond to such requests within a few days, developing formal reports for the superintendent, the state board, and the legislature. Such requests can include literature reviews, development of survey instruments, data collection, and brief policy analyses.

Credit to Program Evaluators. The bureau gives credit for the work done by its staff in two ways. First, the bureau evaluation managers are responsible for presenting their findings to various audiences. Second, although evaluation reports are publications of the Louisiana Department of Education, all reports identify their individual authors. These factors, simple as they may seem, have been mentioned by state board members and department administrators as improving the credibility both of evaluation findings and of the bureau. In addition, credit to the authors serves as a means of providing visibility for staff members and of documenting professional developmental activities.

Conclusion

The Bureau of Evaluation of the Louisiana Department of Education has the responsibility for providing valid, relevant, and timely information to assist in making choices — such choices as whether to start, modify, expand, contract, or terminate major educational programs and projects. It is the bureau's charge to provide evaluations that are high not only in technical quality and policy utility but also in credibility. Three major factors affect the credibility of bureau efforts: First, evaluations must be unbiased and administered independently of the program's administration. Second, evaluations must be valid and reliable representations of the programs or projects that they purport to evaluate. Third, evaluations must be managed by highly competent professional staff.

The organizational structure and the processes described in this chapter grew out of the author's beliefs that evaluation is a service to program managers and department administrators and that evaluations should be conducted only if it is probable that their findings will be used. These structures and processes are themselves being evaluated to determine their validity within the state education agency. Early indications suggest that they are successful.

References

Dallas Independent School District. *Senior Evaluator Competencies.* Dallas, Tex.: Department of Research, Evaluation, and Information Services, Dallas Independent School District, 1980.

Joint Committee on Standards for Educational Evaluation. *Standards for Evaluations of Educational Programs, Projects, and Materials.* New York: McGraw-Hill, 1981.

Louisiana, *Revised Statutes* (1980), 17:394–400.

Louisiana, *Revised Statutes* (1982), 36:8, 36:51.1, and 36:629b.

Louisiana Legislature. *Report of the Joint Legislative Committee on Executive Branch Reorganization.* Baton Rouge: Louisiana Legislature, May 1981.

Thompson, C. E., deputy superintendent of the Louisiana Department of Education, Baton Rouge. Memorandum. September 1980.

High I. Peck is associate superintendent for research and development in the Louisiana Department of Education. Prior to joining the department, he directed evaluation units in local school districts and for private and nonprivate research firms.

Suzanne E. Triplett is director of the Bureau of Evaluation in the Office of Research and Development, Louisiana Department of Education. She has thirteen years of experience in conducting local, state, and national evaluation studies.

*Management issues relevant to the internal operations and external
relations of local-level evaluation units are identified, and
solutions are offered.*

Of Tugboats and
Local Education Agency
Evaluation Units

Freda M. Holley

There are few descriptions of what the ideal local-level research and evaluation
unit looks like. Since 1965, when these units first began to emerge, noteworthy
departments have developed in Dallas, Cincinnati, Louisville, Philadelphia,
Portland, and other cities. One interesting thing about these units is that,
despite some similarities, most are unique to their time and situation.

Differences among local research and evaluation units are due to two
factors. First, outstanding units have had strong, charismatic leadership. As
the personalities and interests of the directors have differed, so have the units
themselves. Second, the school system in which each unit operates has shaped
it. A successful unit must be responsive to its environment. As the school systems vary, so do the units. To illustrate why this is so, I like to use the analogy
of the harbor tugboat.

The tugboat's purpose is to guide, nudge, and pull the ship that it
guides to safe harbor. The tugboat corresponds with the mission of the good
research and evaluation unit. The ship which has its own driving mechanisms,
must allow the small tug to direct it, just as the local education agency with its
day-to-day operating forces must accept guidance to achieve better educational
practice. It, too, must be nudged and pulled. The form that the tugboat's effort

R. G. St. Pierre (Ed.). *Management and Organization of Program Evaluation.* New Directions
for Program Evaluation, no. 18. San Francisco: Jossey-Bass, June 1983.

takes depends on the condition of the waters, the velocity of the wind shoals, the ship's load, the ship's crew, and other externals which change from ship to ship. At the same time, the tugboat captain must command both the tug and its crew. So, the local research and evaluation unit must both understand and respond to its external environment and have good internal management. This chapter examines some management aspects of local research and evaluation units from both perspectives.

Managing the Externals

Research and evaluation units have three basic needs that must be met from external sources: resources, data, and constructive uses of the information that they produce. Assuring that these needs are met is the major management task, of the research and evaluation unit's director. Indeed, this can consume most of the director's time and energy. Each need presents its own particular management issues, but the issue of organization power is common to all. High organizational placement and personal persuasiveness are the director's keys to meeting the unit's needs. Although information is in itself powerful, it is rarely powerful enough to bring about major change or to permit the unit to meet its external needs.

Securing Resources. The work of the research and evaluation unit is expensive, and school systems are reluctant to allocate funds to anything other than direct classroom services. Therefore, securing funding adequate for high-quality work is a continuing struggle. Research funds for local education agencies typically come from state, federal, or local sources. Occasionally, research and evaluation units also receive grants from private foundations.

State resources are likely to flow to local research and evaluation units in two ways: as general personnel funding and as special program funding. For example, in Texas, general personnel funding is provided by the minimum foundation program. Personnel slots are granted on the basis of a school system's average daily attendance. Slots are defined in terms of teachers, administrators, and clerical staff, and if research and evaluation unit personnel are certified teachers, they can be funded under this formula. This can be a benefit, but it is more likely to be a handicap, since many school systems are unwilling to hire staff who are not certified teachers, and most persons with strong research and evaluation competencies do not have certification. As a result, research and evaluation units are often staffed by persons who are not equipped to do complex research and evaluation work. State funds also come through special grants allocated to compensatory education, gifted and talented, special education, community schools, and other programs. Again, practice varies from state to state, but in most cases state funds are allocated to research and evaluation if evaluation is mandated for the special grant.

Federal evaluation funding is usually limited to categorical grant programs. The level of evaluation funding trades off against the provision of services, and it is largely a local decision. One evidential test of management skill involves securing adequate levels of funding from these sources. Persuading the school district to adopt a policy whereby a set percentage of grant funds is allocated to evaluation is a good management device.

In general, most of a unit's funds come from local sources, and they are secured through a formal budget process, which is the most highly political event in school district administration; and perhaps for that reason, it is also one that varies from year to year. Budget games are played at every organizational level. Knowing the games and using the rules to advantage are where real management skill becomes evident. Although most school systems have taken a fling with such notions as zero-based, programmatic, and priority-centered budgeting, in most cases the actual procedure relies on a base budget equal to the budget of the previous year, plus or minus some increment. In good years, debate centers on additions; in bad years, it centers on deletions. In most districts, final budget decisions are made either by the board or by the superintendent. These are the unit's paying clients. If their needs have not been served by evaluation, the resource decisions are likely to be unfavorable. However, good services to school principals and teachers are not necessarily rewarded by increased funding.

Data Access. The work done by research and evaluation units requires data to be collected with tests, questionnaires, rating scales, interviews, and other instruments. Here, the situation is likely to counter that which prevails in the matter of securing resources. That is, good service to the board and the superintendent is likely to decrease the willingness of school staff to respond to data requests, while good service to schools is likely to have a positive effect. Few soldiers, after all, relate well to the inspector general.

Data collection must be managed to minimize respondent burden. Although this responsibility belongs to the research and evaluation unit, the manager must coordinate the unit's data needs with school district procedures. For example, a few years ago, my district instituted a procedure that required all correspondence with school campuses to receive approval signatures from department directors plus the signature of the director responsible for supervision of school administrators. Initially, I had strong objection to a procedure that added one or two days to the process of getting most correspondence to the schools. In time, however, it became clear that these signatures were a tremendous aid in gaining responses from school personnel. Our return rates on most data requests are very high. As one addressee asked, Who, after all, can reject a request that looks like a declaration of war. Therefore, although the district as a whole has abandoned the procedure, we continue to use it to our advantage.

Here are some other tricks that foster good response to data collection efforts: A year-long data collection schedule should be prepared, reviewed, and published in advance. Data collection instruments should be attractive, eye-catching, and short. In our district, we try to use one annual teacher and administrator survey to obtain all data from these two groups. Computer-generated questionnaires with matrix sampling for respondents cover many questions and permit us to keep the forms short. Occasionally, we collect data outside this main survey, relying on interviews wherever feasible. People prefer interviews to questionnaires.

Feedback to respondents is also essential. One way of providing feedback is to send a news sheet to all staff, students, and parents involved in a survey. Test results should also be reported as quickly as possible. When tests are turned in by Friday, we strive to return scores on Monday.

Use of Research and Evaluation Information. Unless its evaluation products are being used, the research and evaluation unit is not likely to enjoy resources or data responsiveness. The literature on this topic is increasing (Alkin, Daillak, and White, 1979; Boruch and Cordray, 1980; Kennedy, Apling, and Neumann, 1980), but it provides little practical direction for the research and evaluation unit manager on how use can be facilitated.

Various school districts have developed formal procedures for responding to evaluation reports. In most cases, the procedure involves some type of directive and response form from the superintendent to officials responsible for the given program. However, such formal mechanisms are not very successful, and they do not substitute for bright administrators and teachers. In districts with strong staff, information use is seldom a problem.

In districts that do not have strong staff, the best alternative is persistent, persuasive repetition of important information by research staff until findings become part of the local memory. This alternative dictates low reliance on formal, written reports and high reliance on memos, brochures, newsletters, lunch or coffee break exchanges, and verbal presentations at meetings or workshops. It is helpful to repeat the same information in a variety of formats.

Managing the Internals

In order to guide a ship successfully, the tugboat must control its own movements. Similarly, if a research and evaluation unit has major internal management problems, it is unlikely that it will achieve external success. While use and impact of research and evaluation information is the chief goal of the unit's external management, the production of high-quality information relevant to important issues is the end goal of internal management. In seeking to achieve the latter goal, management issues arise in connection with staffing, communication, targeting, data collection and management, data analysis, data processing, and information retrieval.

Staffing. Competent staff are the key to high-quality evaluations. Knowing the areas of competence that a unit needs is, of course, prerequisite to finding competent personnel. Webster and Mendro (1974) developed a list of required research and evaluation competencies and job descriptions keyed to those competencies. Most of us would agree with their competency categories, which include planning and management, instrument development, measurement, computer use, statistical analysis, and other analytic skills.

Research and evaluation units differ in how they gain these skills. Some units hire evaluators who are expected to have all the necessary skills themselves; they receive only secretarial support. Other units have differentiated staff, including evaluators, programmers, data collection specialists, graphics specialists, and clerical staff. As stated earlier, state and local certification requirements can have considerable impact on staffing decisions. For example, in one district that I know of, no professional research and evaluation staff can be hired who have not worked in district schools for two years. Thus, research and evaluation unit staff members in this district tend to have minimal statistical skills but excellent knowledge of school curriculum and operation.

Recruitment efforts also differ. Since school districts rarely pay for interview visits or moving expenses, it is necessary to look to local sources. Cities with major research and evaluation units can usually draw staff from nearby universities. This often results in a staff whose members all have the same background, which can be a major problem. However, it can also help to build a unity of approach and concern that can be helpful, considering the stresses under which most units work.

Retaining good staff can also be difficult. School district tenure policies that offer security can be one good holding mechanism, but good salaries are even better. There is strong pressure for an office to build hierarchical positions as a way of providing promotion opportunities for staff. For example, my office has three levels for evaluators, three levels for evaluation assistants, and two levels for programmers. The levels recognize experience and training more than they do exact job assignments, although those at the higher level are generally assigned to the tougher jobs. Career paths involve important morale issues, and some of our best staff have grown from one position type to another. We have provided some internal training opportunities, flexible time schedules to permit class attendance, and internship positions to aid graduate study. Several of our evaluators and one programmer began as evaluation assistants, and one top-level evaluation assistant began as a secretary.

Another important staff motivator is membership in professional organizations. Participation in national and regional research groups helps evaluation staff members to view their work with more respect and care. This is important in local research and evaluation units, which lack career rewards for publication and research that exist in higher education. In my office, we have worked hard to obtain funds to enable staff to attend annual meetings of research groups. There is a congruent requirement that staff members submit papers for consideration as a prerequisite to attendance.

Communication. Internal and external communication pose constant problems in the research and evaluation unit, just as they do in any other organization. The unit manager needs to have good lines of communication, but the manager rarely has time to develop them. A few techniques that the author has found helpful are illustrative.

One external communication technique that our unit uses is to assign each unit staff member a school for liaison purposes. The staff member tries to be available to that school for service consultation and for faculty meeting presentations on testing and evaluation. The staff member also tries to cultivate some personal communication lines with that school. Recently, we tried the same approach with central office departments.

One of the more difficult aspects of internal communication is to assure that staff keep the manager informed of problems as well as of successes. It is important for employees to know that the unit manager wants to be the first to know when something goes wrong. This is easier when the problem deals with external situations, since employees usually know that the manager will hear about the problem from others if not from them. Equally important, however, are internal errors of data analysis or interpretation.

Another productive idea is the quality circle concept. In our office, secretaries, programmers, and evaluation assistants have regular sessions, as do evaluators. Secretaries solve problems, such as where to get the best prices on supplies, telephone answering procedures, and work sharing. Programmers have developed data documentation procedures and forms. Minutes are kept and circulated on all meetings.

A procedures manual, in which most of the routine activities of the office are described, has been very helpful. Procedure descriptions cover everything from how to get a purchase order through the business office to personnel evaluation procedures. We also use standardized design and report formats, which reduce the time spent on routines. Typing guides for these formats lay out requirements, and many standard pages are prelettered with titles and headings.

An advisory committee can assist with communication within the unit as well as with outreach to various groups. The committee can be composed entirely of community members, or it can combine school and community representatives. The committee can be a sounding board, a review body for designs and data collection instruments, and even an advocate. It can be useful in establishing priorities. It is helpful if members' actual appointments are made by the superintendent, the board, or some other administrator to whom the evaluation unit is assigned.

Targeting. Determining how and on what an evaluation unit spends its time is not always an internal issue. For example, funding can be so intimately tied to the tasks required that there is not much choice about requirements for specific objectives and congruent measurement. Or, the evaluation model in use can constrain the focus and topics of evaluation. If the district views evaluation only as program evaluation, limited types of studies will be assigned. Nevertheless, an evaluation unit usually has considerable control over at least the questions addressed in various evaluations.

Fortunate units may even be able to assist in identifying the evaluation targets. Such assistance can be provided by drawing attention in reports to important issues that should be investigated, by enlisting the advisory committee, and by making presentations to groups concerned with a particular issue. Where this kind of influence is possible, the evaluation unit should identify targets that are likely to involve issues with high payoff. That is, researchers who stay in contact with the research on teacher effectiveness recognize that time-on-task studies are potentially rewarding. Those who follow the rising cost of lunchroom services have to recognize that a study of alternatives to traditional patterns of service provision can produce a high-interest and perhaps a high-reward study. To increase its ability to identify targets with high potential, the unit should stay in touch both with national research and evaluation and with the local school and community environment. Thus, it is important for the research and evaluation research manager to attend meetings of the school board and of advisory and professional groups of all types and to make frequent visits to school sites of all types.

Data Collection and Management. Years ago, our unit tried to coordinate data collection across a number of major evaluations, including a bilingual program, the district's ESEA Title I program, an instructional aide program, an individualized instruction program, and a class size reduction effort. The result was very frustrating. Although coordination problems were exaggerated by such a major collaborative effort, the effect was to create a keen awareness of the need for coordination. The communication required by this effort revealed the multitude of discrete data collection activities that had been imposed on the schools.

Now, every project in our unit develops schedules of all data collection requirements as a part of the design phase. A data collection calendar is developed, and one staff member is assigned the task of reviewing all data collection instruments and plans prior to their approval. One multi-purpose questionnaire for staff is used annually. A central roster of staff members can be used to identify special data-collecting efforts and prevent staff members from being sampled twice. Districtwide tests serve outcome evaluation purposes for all programs.

Contracted services are useful in taking care of huge data-handling tasks. If regular staff members have to code tests for scoring, the task becomes impossible or much delayed; temporary, hourly workers can make coding a task that takes only a day or two. When the number of such tasks reaches fair proportions over a year, it is possible to develop a corps of well-qualified persons who like temporary work. Keypunching or data entry for tapes can be contracted to local university computer centers or commercial firms. A few districts even contract major evaluation efforts. If so, the request for proposals approach is generally used.

It helps to describe standard data collection procedures in writing. Such standard procedures can include a list of advance planning activities, such as makeup date, sequencing of schools, and scoring procedures. Procedures for contracting with and paying temporary workers, training, and scheduling can all be put in written form. It is also wise to have a written reminder list on required behavior and protocol to be followed by staff when in schools. A similar write-up on typical problems and ways to avoid or to solve them can also help. Development of data collection instruments and scanning forms can involve special considerations for the particular type of equipment or the unit's preferred procedures. Written directions save training time. Data management will probably include a set of required procedures for accuracy checks, confidentiality controls, documentation, and special codes. Committing these to writing and developing monitoring procedures will help to see that these required procedures are followed.

Data Analysis. Typically, data analysis is the domain of the individual evaluator. While much external input is sought when deciding on the questions to be asked, deciding on the most appropriate kind of analysis is usually an internal unit decision. Of course, there are constraints. For example, the inability of most school systems to support strict experimental research conditions limits analysis in a major way.

Within the unit, data analysis is a continuing source of concern and communication. Usually, some staff members have special skills in this area, and it is wise to try to budget extra time so they can consult with other staff members. Our unit draws on the expertise of colleagues in nearby universities when particularly troublesome issues arise.

Data Processing. Data processing is a problem area for many school districts. Typically, research and evaluation offices emerge as a separate unit. Data processing handles only payroll and related functions. As a consequence, the research and evaluation unit often has little control over one of its key resources. Evaluation has broadened its focus from programs to larger educational questions and as larger data bases have become necessary, the absence of such control has had serious consequences. In recent years, a number of school systems, including those of Dallas and Houston, have merged the research and evaluation and the data-processing functions in one unit. Other school systems have added programmers to the evaluation unit. This approach has only been partially satisfactory, since research and evaluation tasks have low priority for data processing staff.

Regardless of the overall school system organization, important questions about the best management of programming resources will remain. Should the capability operate on a service basis across evaluations, or should programmers be assigned to specific evaluation? Again, various school systems use different approaches. The need to make interface among data files possible and to document programs sufficiently well to prevent total loss of files when a programmer leaves requires specific rules for data processing to be developed and followed. Security of data, proper backup of data, and data maintenance all become issues of crucial importance in research and evaluation unit management.

Changes in the computer world, including both distributed processing and microcomputers, are having substantial impact on research and evaluation units, and the effects are likely to be even more substantial in the future. They could, in fact, completely change many aspects of local research and evaluation work.

References

Alkin, M. D., Daillak, R., and White, P. *Using Evaluations: Does Evaluation Make a Difference?* Beverly Hills, Calif.: Sage, 1979.

Boruch, R. F., and Cordray, D. S. *An Appraisal of Educational Program Evaluations: Federal, State, and Local Agencies.* Evanston, Ill.: Northwestern University, 1980.

Kennedy, M. M., Apling, R., and Neumann, W. F. *The Role of Evaluation and Test Information in Public Schools.* Cambridge: Huron Institute, 1980.

Webster, W. J., and Mendro, R. L. "A Pragmatic Model for a Comprehensive Public School Research and Evaluation System." Paper presented at the annual meeting of the American Educational Research Association, Chicago, 1974.

Freda M. Holley has directed the Austin (Texas) Independent School District's Office of Research and Evaluation since 1973.

What kind of contract evaluation firm is most likely to survive and profit in Washington today? How can such firms fill the government's needs for valid and objective evaluation information at minimum cost?

Contractor Evaluation for the Federal Government

Robert A. Levine

The author of this chapter has a rather eclectic background within the broad area of public policy research and analysis. He has been a data-using policy analyst as well as a data-producing evaluator. He has carried out these activities for local and federal government. He has been employed by not-for-profit organizations and by for-profit firms. Finally, he has worked within the government, sponsoring and using the products of external research, and he has worked outside the government, where he produced such products.

The variety of his experience enables him to examine contractor evaluation for the federal government from several viewpoints. It facilitates the evaluation of evaluation organizations against two different sets of criteria. From the viewpoint of the evaluation organization itself, the key criteria are those associated with any business endeavor: survival, growth, and profit. (The first two, of course, are key criteria for most not-for-profit organizations as well.) From the viewpoint of the federal customer, the key criterion is the provision of valid and objective evaluation information at minimal cost. Clearly, the two sets of criteria are not identical. The extent to which they reinforce or countervail each other is the major consideration here.

Evaluation is only one of a number of possible topics within the broad area of public policy research and analysis. In this chapter, discussion focuses on evaluation, not on policy analysis. Evaluation and policy analysis overlap;

R. G. St. Pierre (Ed.). *Management and Organization of Program Evaluation.* New Directions for Program Evaluation, no. 18. San Francisco: Jossey-Bass, June 1983.

there is no clear boundary between them. Nonetheless, evaluation involves the gathering and analysis of data that enable the value of the object being measured to be compared with some other object or standard. Policy analysis involves the use of primary or secondary data to examine the policy alternatives available to decision makers.

One major implication of the evaluation focus is that it calls for staff whose members have training in statistics and psychology and skills in statistical analysis and survey techniques, including fieldwork and instrumentation. It also calls for people who have subject matter expertise in the fields being evaluated. Only to the extent that the analysis verges into policy analysis (as noted later in this chapter, it must to some degree in order to be meaningful) will staffing begin to extend into economics, systems analysis, operations analysis, and the like.

The discussion covers the federal government, not state and local governments. The focus on the federal government implies that marketing is concentrated. It is not for state or local government, although for an organization that targets a single large state like California might find that it was. However, even within the federal government, choices must still be made—an organization that tried to perform across the board from agriculture to unemployment compensation would go nowhere—but these choices must be made from a relatively small set, and ordinarily they allow marketing to be concentrated in the Washington area. The federal focus also means dependence on the federal budget, with all that that implies.

This chapter discusses private, for-profit firms, not universities or other not-for-profit organizations. This implies the kind of financing that makes between-project staff continuity far more difficult than it is for universities, where core personnel are on the academic payroll, or for not-for-profits, many of which typically have some nonproject money available, if only because they collect nonprofit fees.

One final dichotomy, both sides of which will be covered, is whether the evaluation organization is standalone or part of a firm involved in several kinds of activities. Standalone status has the advantage of concentrating overhead and other activities on the evaluation business. Coupling has the advantages of increasing access to a wide variety of skills and of covering nonevaluation staff between evaluation contracts.

The first section of this chapter discusses contractor evaluation from the contractor viewpoint, the next section looks at the government interest, and the last section addresses some issues of government evaluation policy that can affect the ways in which these things are done. The fact that government now has little interest in using evaluation information will structure evaluation and evaluation contracting for the foreseeable future, and the resulting structure will be small indeed. However, before I discuss the implications of the government's current lack of interest in evaluation, I will examine the contract evaluation industry as it was until recently and as it might be again, if government seeks to revive it.

The Contractor Viewpoint

Notwithstanding the occasional newspaper story about the dangers of close federal agency relationships with consultants, in whose number evaluation contractors are ordinarily included, the world of the federal evaluation contractor is highly competitive. Typically, between three and ten or even more contractors bid for any one effort, but only one wins. From the firm's point of view, what kind of configuration allows it to exist and prosper in this world?

While no pattern can hold for all conditions and times, the best configuration for a contract evaluation firm at the present moment—with one major caveat—is that the firm is small, which means that it has between fifteen and seventy-five professional employees; it performs policy analysis as well as evaluation; and it stands alone, in that its evaluation and analysis activities are not coupled with anything substantially different, such as production of computer software or the sale of real estate. (Neither example is hypothetical.)

Size. The fifteen-person lower limit placed on size is based on two considerations. First, below this level, the firm can risk demise from accidental fluctuation. Of course, this is not true of all policy consulting firms. Several do quality work with very few principals and academic backup brought in as needed. The second reason for the lower limit applies specifically to organizations specializing in evaluation. The gathering of evaluation data is a massive activity, and a work cadre cannot be brought together on an ad hoc basis as easily as it can for policy analysis. Indeed, the fifteen-person lower limit may be too low. It assumes that such a small cadre can organize interviewing, data processing, and so forth by calling in other temporary resources. This can be done, but the results are not always satisfactory. The upper limit—seventy-five, more or less—is a very rough estimate of the number of professionals that, if exceeded, will cause the organization to be dominated more by bureaucracy than by either substantive evaluation or business incentives. Of course, bureaucratic organization is not always fatal to evaluation endeavors, but neither is it ideal.

Evaluation Coupled with Policy Analysis. The need for evaluation to be coupled with some policy analysis is a relatively recent phenomenon and an important one. Federal social programming expanded rapidly in the mid 1960s, and after about a five-year lag, a need to evaluate these programs was felt. Thus, the 1970s saw a rapid expansion in federal evaluation. When budget and other considerations slowed social programming in the mid 1970s, the desire for evaluation also slowed; the lag was about the same, with the visible decline beginning around 1980.

During the 1970s, the peak period for evaluation of social programs that began in the 1960s, most evaluation was based on the biological model: Set up an experimental group receiving program treatment, set up a control or comparison group resembling the treatment group as closely as possible, and compare the two. This was by no means simple. It took sophistication in statistics and survey techniques, including such skills as psychometrics, and it took at least some knowledge of the substantive areas of the evaluation. But, it did not require much policy analysis of the kind carried out by economists, systems analysts, and the like — designing systems to aid in public decision making, modeling systems, and fitting the evaluation information to be gathered to systems. On both sides — the government agencies that contracted for evaluation projects in the mid 1970s and the evaluation contractors that carried the projects out — it was felt that evaluation was the contractor's responsibility and that policy implications belonged to the agency.

As the need for large-scale program evaluations wound down in the late 1970s, most new evaluations were coupled with policy analyses, and evaluation organizations came under substantial pressure to adapt. Whether this is a cyclical phenomenon which indicates that a renewed need for big biological evaluations lies just over the horizon or a longer-run change is not certain. It does seem certain that, for a future long and foreseeable enough to determine organizational structure, the ideal evaluation firm should also have a capability for policy analysis. Perhaps any evaluation firm should have such a capability in order to survive.

Status. Finally, embedding the evaluation capability within a diversified organization raises different issues. Currently, evaluation groups are either standalone or they exist within firms devoted largely to policy analysis, a structure which, as the preceding paragraph suggests, appears to be strong. Other evaluation units, however, are contained in military systems analysis companies, software houses, testing groups, hardware manufacturers, and even real estate firms. Conjunctions like these have one major advantage: When the demand for evaluations drops sharply, as it has in the 1980s, the capabilities can be maintained — and at least some of the evaluators can be assured of continued employment — by turning those capabilities to other things. The disadvantage is that, if the major thrust of the overall organization is not evaluation, then the evaluation unit can come to the table as a poor relation. A standalone evaluation and policy analysis company can direct its overhead expenditures — for publications, library, public relations, fringe benefits, and government-funded independent research — toward winning and performing evaluation and analysis contracts. An organization in which other functions dominate is likely to allocate these overhead expenditures and functions in ways that are less than optimal for evaluation business.

On balance, then, the ideal evaluation firm is the relatively small evaluation and policy analysis organization that focuses its efforts on those two activities. But, a major caveat must be entered here. Small size, particularly at the low end of the scale, together with the standalone status of the ideal firm, can mean that, when evaluation contracts are scarce, the firm may have a hard time finding enough business to remain alive. Yet, for firms strong enough to survive, business life is likely to be most satisfactory with the configuration just outlined.

The Government Viewpoint

How well will an evaluation industry made up of such firms satisfy the government's requirements for valid and objective evaluation information at minimum cost? First, it is important to specify what this industry cannot do. It cannot carry out long-run policy analysis — analysis that has little relevance for the immediate concerns of government agencies or that questions fundamental assumptions. The reason does not lie in the particular configuration suggested here; it lies in the basic assumption of an industry made up of private for-profit firms. These firms live by satisfying the needs of funding organizations, as the funders see these needs. Private for-profit firms cannot afford to market something to the government that the government does not want. Nor, except within some rather narrow limits, can they build and continue staff other than by winning government contracts. Long-run analysis, questioning assumptions, and building staff to perform these functions are far better suited to universities and other not-for-profit groups. By the same token, however, evaluation is not a natural realm for most not-for-profit organizations. Evaluation activities must be highly responsive to agency definitions, which often are made under congressional mandate, of what needs to be evaluated. Further, many necessary evaluation activities, such as organization of field data collection, are not comfortable for universities and other not-for-profits. Thus, the industry made up of for-profit firms is appropriate, for evaluation as such. But, how do the government's needs affect the other firm-oriented parameters — size, scope, and status?

Size. From the government's viewpoint, the size defined earlier in this chapter as best for the firm itself may be too small, particularly at the lower end of the range but perhaps even at the upper end. There are two reasons for this. First, an evaluation effort carried out within a single organization is likely to be both more effective, since it is apt to be better coordinated, and less costly, since there is less pyramiding of overhead and profit, than an evaluation performed by a contractor-subcontractor team. But, an industry made up of small firms necessitates teaming for most evaluations, so that evaluation and subject matter expertise can be combined. The one exception to this rule may be the contractor that specializes in a single area, such as health. However, if the specialist firm has a high level of evaluation expertise, then the government loses by not having that expertise used more widely. In addition, the firm runs extra risks of demise if there is slack in its area of specialization. Second, as already noted, the large firm can risk substituting bureaucratic motivations for substantive or business motivations. But, from the point of view of government bureaucrats in such functions as contracting, it is useful to deal with business bureaucrats. Whether it is useful to the public as well will be considered later in this chapter.

Evaluation Coupled with Policy Analysis. The ideal evaluation organization couples evaluation with policy analysis. Such coupling serves the gov-

ernment (and the public) well. The tendency in the mid 1970s to conduct
public program evaluation on the biological model and to set policy aside in a
separate compartment guarded from the evaluation contractor can be viewed
as a historical aberration — for two reasons. First, it is fraudulent to apply the
biological model to social programs. Social program data can never be as clean
and accurate as biological data, true control groups are politically and morally
difficult to create, and so forth. To display the results of such compromised
evaluations as if they were the outcomes of true experimentation is mislead-
ing. Second, it is impossible to decouple evaluation from policy. Policy sets the
criteria — the values against which a program is to be measured. These are
never clear-cut, particularly when the criteria are established by Congress;
indeed, they never can be. They must be adjusted continually as evaluation
data confront criteria and as evaluators confront public officials. In practice,
therefore, evaluators must help to define the policy space into which the evaluation fits, and this brings policy analysis intoevaluation. The error of the biological evaluators who guarded policy against contractor involvement in the
mid 1970s was that they failed to draw the line between policy implications
appropriate for examination by technical evaluation expertise ("Current targeting of this program misses 54 percent of those whom the law said should be
reached") and policy recommendations, which are best left to the democratic
process ("Therefore, we should shift money from rural areas to cities"). The
line is difficult but not impossible to draw. The congressional Budget Office,
for example, managed to draw it successfully during the same time period.

Status. Does standalone status for the evaluation contractor serve the
government's interest? Here, the argument becomes more conjectural. For the
firm, the pluses of standalone status are relatively clear. The chief advantage is
that overhead expenditures, research, and so forth can all be focused on building evaluation business. Of course, this has advantages for the government,
too: It maximizes both the quantity and the quality of the effort that goes into
evaluation. But, the way in which this tight focus on evaluation works out in
practice raises some broad questions. What has happened, particularly in recent years, is that some social scientists have gone into standalone evaluation
organizations; others, particularly information analysts, computer scientists,
and the like, have gone to work for firms that may have had evaluation components in the past. The former evaluate social programs. The latter, insofar
as they do government work, are in the defense business. As a result, the
nation, social programs, defense efforts, even the companies themselves have
all suffered, since this trend tends to prevent the cross-fertilization between the
soft and the hard sciences that took place in the past.

Government Evaluation Policies

At least some dissonance exists between the ideal evaluation organization as seen by the firm and as seen by the government. The viewpoints

coincide only in the need for coupling of evaluation with policy analysis. From the government viewpoint, the public interest might be better served if the firm was larger than seems best for the firm. From the public viewpoint, the separation of evaluation and policy analysis from other activities that current private incentives encourage may be a dangerous trend indeed. If these suggestions are well based, certain changes in public policy could still improve the effectiveness with which the evaluation industry fills public needs.

Size. It seems simple enough for government evaluation authorities to increase the emphasis on integration of evaluation activities; that is, on having all tasks carried out by a single organization. The list of weighted criteria for award that accompanies almost every government request for proposals could stress such integration. It seems simple enough to do this, but it is not, because there is no central evaluation authority that has the power to decree that integration should be stressed. Indeed, there probably should not be such an authority. Nonetheless, individual government agencies dismayed by the lack of coordination in contractor-subcontractor projects could make individual moves in this direction.

Recoupling Hard and Soft Science. If anything is to be done here, it must be done by the Department of Defense. Although this chapter is written from the standpoint of the soft program evaluator, the soft scientist is, as usual, the rabbit in the Defense Department's rabbit-and-elephant stew. Current Defense Department policy discourages such coupling. To be sure, it does not discourage social science as such. But, by encouraging defense firms to concentrate only on defense, it decouples most of the available policy-oriented social scientists, who are doing other things. Here is an example: Federal contracts typically allow companies specific costs for independent research and development not directly related to the contract itself. This is true of Defense Department contracts. It is also true of contracts let by the Education Department. In firms where the split between Defense Department contracts and Education Department contracts is perhaps 90 percent–10 percent, all the funds go into a single reserach and development pool, the allocation of which is reviewed periodically by the elephant. Since the Defense Department gives credit only for militarily relevant research and development activities, it ensures that all the funds, including those that came from the Education Department, go for military research.

Other Issues. Some other, more general, issues and trends are also important in shaping the evaluation capabilities available to the government. Three will be mentioned here: stability, government contracting procedures, and information needs.

Stability. From the industry viewpoint, stability is crucial. From the public viewpoint, it may have less importance. One implicit theme in the above discussion of the evaluation firm's incentives is that the firm needs stability. Evaluation has been a volatile industry, and in recent years, a number of firms have been wounded, some mortally. This may affect some of the variables discussed here. One certain effect is that it will discourage risk taking and innovation. Thus, there are occasional cries from within the industry for a source of greater stability — perhaps some more or less well-disguised form of institutional funding. It is unrealistic to expect such funding. The evaluation industry stands somewhere near the end of the queue of claimants for such stabilizing funding — and some claimants, like arts organizations, are better at public relations. Further, the industry as it has been defined here should not be looked to for innovation. The for-profit incentives simply do not move that way. As already suggested, innovation is the social role of the not-for-profits — and a major reason for the advantages accorded to them by public policy.

Government Contracting Procedures. Real improvement and reversal of prevailing trends in government contracting procedures are needed. Fifteen years ago, evaluation and policy analysis were initiated when the analytical personnel of a federal agency figured out what they wanted done, decided who could do it best, and telephoned him to come in and negotiate a contract. This produced first-class evaluation and analysis, but clearly it was liable to the same abuse as the spoils system was after the Civil War. The remedy of strictly competitive contracting has brought with it the same degree of efficiency that we have learned to appreciate in the federal civil service. To be fair, the informal method probably could not have worked when evaluation hit its full stride in the mid 1970s, and it might have been subject to real abuse. Nonetheless, competitive bidding has gone overboard in recent years. Indeed, the process has become a ritual that frequently comes into conflict with the government's need for valid and objective evaluation information. Two examples are offered.

The major criteria for award of a competitive evaluation contract typically include, besides cost, the quality of the competing firms' written proposals describing how the project is to be carried out and the capabilities of the firms and individuals who will do the work, as demonstrated by their past record on similar work. The difficulty is that the proposal is concrete, while the reputations are not. The government technical experts involved in the award process know that they can be held accountable to the strict rules of the ritual, so they tend to place more weight on the concrete and therefore defensible proposal than on the record of past performance, which, by all the rules of common sense, should be the best guide to future performance. The author of this chapter has been told by a federal official: "We didn't want to give it to them, because they have performed so abysmally for us in the past, but we had to, because they wrote a considerably better proposal than their competitors." As one result, of course, sophisticated evaluation firms know enough to put their resources into proposal writing. Then, they slight on contract performance so they can still make a satisfactory profit. Further, because most evaluation contracts are written on a cost-plus basis (if the contractor's actual costs exceed the estimate in the contractor's proposal, the government reimburses the contractor for the extra costs), sophisticated bidders estimate less than their expected costs in order to win with the low bid; later, they reclaim the actual costs. Thus, under current procedures, neither the reality of the contractor selection process nor the incentives that it sets up tend to produce good, or acceptable, or even cheap evaluations.

In the preceding example, at least the substantive experts controlled the award process. Recently, however, the government's contract officers have taken control on several occasions to override the preferences of substantive experts who were trying to meet the government's evaluation needs. Legally, the contract officers have always had the final authority. For most of the past, however, they have used this authority only to impose a proper appreciation for low costs and acceptable rituals on the substantive people; in short, they worked with the substantive technicians to obtain the best product, subject to reasonable constraints. In one recent and notorious case, however, the contract officers began the competitive process by requiring that the work be done in one of a number of areas around the nation where unemployment was high. This requirement had been designed for a completely different kind of contract. Worse, the contract officers had neglected to inform their substantive counterparts, who protested vigorously but too late. Then, in making the award, the contract officers dealt only with the low bidder, in spite of ordinary procedures that encourage negotiations with a range of bidders so that the high bidders can lower their prices and the technically less acceptable bidders can improve their substance, both to the benefit of the government. In this case, which involved an evaluation mandated by Congress concerning a major and controversial national issue, the government's substantive experts had severe doubts about the quality of the low bidder and wanted the negotiations opened to others. The contract officers refused. At this writing, the issue remains unresolved.

Information Needs. The preceding material suggests that, no matter how successfully the evaluation industry responds to the incentives created by government evaluation policies, the government will not get a very good product until some rather fundamental changes are made. In fact, it is not clear that the government, as managed by the Reagan administration, feels much need for any evaluation product — good, bad, or indifferent. Evaluation is by no means the province of the Democratic Party. The evaluation boom began the the 1970s under the Nixon administration, in large measure as a result of prodding from the now senior senator from New York, Daniel Patrick Moynihan, who as a Nixon staffer wanted to pinpoint what worked — and, even more, what did not work — in the programs of President Johnson's Great Society. Given this beginning, department officials in the Nixon, Ford, and Carter administrations made major attempts to obtain evaluation data, to learn from it, and to use it. The Reagan administration came into office with no felt need for information about its predecessors' programs. Combining strong ideology with the impressive intellectual efforts of a few conservative foundations, it based its programs on a different sort of evaluation, which asked not, How well does it work? but If it works, will it move America in the direction in which we were elected to move it? This absence of felt need for evaluation information, combined with the strong budget reductions imposed by the administration on all government activities, has meant a sharp downturn — which sometimes resembles a death knell — for the evaluation industry. It can be predicted that either this administration or one of its successors will ultimately feel a need for valid and objective information about what works and what does not work in government programs. It can be predicted, but it is by no means certain. The United States almost made it through its second century without evaluation as we know it.

At present, the federal contract evaluation industry exists mainly as the shadow of a shambles. It it revives, its shape will depend, first, on what has survived — with all the strictures noted here, what survives may well be the evaluation remnants of nonevaluation organizations, plus what can be regenerated from universities and other not-for-profits — and, second, on the structural incentives set up by government programmers who interpret the new needs as evaluation requirements. This chapter is intended to help in that process, if and when it occurs.

Robert A. Levine has been vice-president and general manager of the Human Systems Division of System Development Coporation since 1979. Previously, he was deputy director of the Congressional Budget Office, president of the New York City Rand Institute, and assistant director of the Office of Economic Opportunity.

*The special challenges of procuring business from and doing
business with state and local clients present the evaluation
manager with distinct choices.*

Management of Contract
Organizations Specializing
in State and Local
Evaluation Projects

Paula M. Nassif
Sherry A. Rubinstein

Management of evaluation research for state- and local-level programs has
much in common with the management of anything else. To be accomplished
competently, it requires strong planning, excellent project knowledge, effective team building and delegation, vigilant monitoring and quality control,
and fiscal responsibility. What distinguishes this management enterprise from
any other is the context in which these functions are performed — a context
whose parameters are the nature of the client and the nature of the work itself.
Firms engaged in evaluation research constitute a service industry, because
they deliver a professional service, and managing a professional service carries
with it special challenges in the areas of marketing, recruitment, staff development, and ongoing corporate maintenance. An organization comprised largely
of professionals will, by virtue of that fact alone, be managed and organized
differently than an organization whose work force is largely involved in
machine or other production functions. The purpose of this chapter is to illu-
minate the features unique to the management of evaluation organizations
that work primarily with state and local education agencies.

R. G. St. Pierre (Ed.). *Management and Organization of Program Evaluation.* New Directions
for Program Evaluation, no. 18. San Francisco: Jossey-Bass, June 1983.

Evaluation contractors can be entire organizations devoted to the pursuit of evaluation activities, or they can be components of larger, more diverse organizations. The distinction is virtually irrelevant to the management issues addressed, and both types of agencies have been successful in the state and local markets.

The Context

Nature of the Work. The work of a contractor is represented by a portfolio of projects, each of which represents a single contract specifying evaluation services to be delivered to a particular client. Evaluation services broadly defined include research design, instrument development (tests, questionnaires, interview schedules), sampling techniques, data collection methodologies (including extensive field contact), data reduction and analysis, and dissemination activities. All these services are typically called for in state- and local-level evaluation work—often in full service contracts, but sometimes one at a time in projects that are pieces of a larger undertaking managed principally by the client agency itself.

State-level evaluation projects can vary considerably in size and scope. They tend to be smaller and shorter than federal contracts and, perhaps as a result, more intense in the scheduling of activities. The typical contract is in the $30,000 to $200,000 range, with the relatively small proportion over $200,000 limited to states that conduct large-scale testing and assessment programs. At the local level, the range in project size is equally wide. The biggest municipalities and school districts in the country run programs as large as those of some states, while smaller agencies typically need evaluations requiring no more than a few professional person-months of service. Both state and local projects are generally shorter than federal projects. Almost without exception, they last between nine and eighteen months from start to finish.

Nature of the Client. State agencies form a well-defined market with relatively stable areas of interest. Clients direct bureaus of higher education, vocational and occupational education bureaus, Title I offices, research coordinating units, and state offices of licensing and certification, to name a few. Also noteworthy are ad hoc task forces constituted to address specific policy issues; their lack of permanent staff and the speed with which their work must be done often require them to contract for evaluation work.

At the local level, clients are primarily housed in district offices of education; only in rare cases are clients single schools. Their substantive needs typically reflect state or federal priorities for evaluation. Thus, local education agencies focus heavily on the collection of data to document program effects and, therefore, need or eligibility for funding. While state-level clients also conduct evaluations in response to federal requirements, they use contractors for a far greater variety of work than local districts do.

The Management Choices

The special challenges of procuring business from and doing business with state and local clients present the evaluation manager with distinct choices. Managing a contract evaluation firm involves an ongoing process of balancing priorities, weighing advantages and disadvantages, and compromising to resolve conflicting interests—in short, of making professional judgments that can preserve the integrity of evaluation research projects, the confidence of clients, and the stability and viability of the contract firm itself. The remainder of this chapter describes eight of these choices: two bearing on the contractor's mission and philosophy, two bearing on organizational structure, three related to staffing, and one in the area of management control.

Corporate Mission and Philosophy. The corporate mission and philosophy is a set of broad goals and guiding principles for the contract firm as it grows and develops. To the extent that management makes these goals and ideals clear and explicit, it provides direction and leadership for all units of the firm, and staff can merge personal and corporate goals. The unity of purpose benefits all. This section reviews two of the many possible dimensions that can be addressed in statements of corporate mission and philosophy.

Specialization Versus Diversification. As a function of its focus on process skills and research tools, evaluation is a particularly transportable enterprise, and it is applicable in a wide array of settings and content areas. Every decision to bid on or to ignore a particular job is, in part, a matter of deciding on the extent to which the contractor wishes to diversity or specialize. Diversification is a vehicle for ensuring the stability of the contractor, since the ability to provide a wide array of services minimizes vulnerability to sudden shifts or skrinkage in any one market. In contrast, specialization is an effective vehicle for developing a clear and proven track record in a given area, and it creates technical and substantive depth as a major selling point for the organization.

The tension between specialization and diversification has two aspects. The first aspect relates to definition of the service portfolio. The contractor can elect to define its services in the consulting mode and focus narrowly on labor-intensive activities. The consulting mode heavily emphasizes services in the form of person-days either on site (for interviews, observations, shirtsleeve work sessions, workshops) or in the office (performing data analyses, writing reports). By contrast, the broadly defined full service contractor is likely to focus on building up in-house capabilities for large-scale production tasks (test item writing, graphics production, printing, data processing services).

The second aspect of the tension between diversification and specialization involves defining the client base. At a bare minimum, the manager must decide whether to market in the local market, the state market, or both. In some respects, this decision amounts to one on the minimum contract size that the contractor is willing to handle. Further, the state-level contractor must decide either to target specific bureaus or units as potential clients or to pursue them all. This is a matter of content focus, since projects conducted for particular client offices — Title I evaluations, vocational education studies, and statewide assessments, for example — are considered specialties in themselves.

The contractor who develops a track record in a particular service area, such as survey research, can market that service successfully to other client groups. At the same time, the understanding of policy perspectives that a contractor gains in the process of serving a client in one service area can give the contractor the competitive edge needed to win another contract with the same client in a tangential service area, such as developing curriculum materials. In weighting the relative merits of specialization and diversification, the contractor must remain flexible and versatile to ensure that the organization survives, but it must also not be so flexible and versatile that it gains the reputation of being a jack of all trades but a master of none.

Proactive Versus Reactive Marketing. Businesses are typically driven by one of two forces, marketing or finance. That is, the corporate goals and corresponding business plan are based either on such matters as cash flow and return on investment or on matters of market share and life cycle strategies for various services. The evaluation contractor that has public sector clients is more likely to be driven by marketing factors, principally because the method of securing business is so prescribed. The request for proposal (RFP) is the bread and butter of state contracting. The jobs that are contracted without an RFP are typically very small (under $10,000 in some states, under $20,000 in others). It is in this area that state-level contracting is most like federal work and least like local-level work. By definition, the marketing effort for state-level clients is principally reactive: It responds to activities in the market, and it has little or no avenue for stimulating the market or for creating a need for evaluation services. Even if the contract were to identify a need, the likelihood of sole-source business is low. The clear limits imposed by the market therefore serve as the starting point for business planning.

Within this context, there exists an array of choices and decisions in setting goals for the contract organization. These include size of market share, optimal distribution of work, and configuration of the project portfolio. The size of market share desired can be specified in terms of dollar volume of business or in number of contracts to be secured in a specified service area or with a specified client group. The optimal distribution of work over the calendar or fiscal year not only affects the financial health and growth of the organization but also dictates staffing needs and to some extent the corporate structure. A company whose business cycle suffers severe peaks and valleys needs a corporate structure that can accommodate growth and shrinkage in staff size and fluidity in staff assignments. Clearly, it is desirable to distribute the work more evenly over the year. To accomplish this in an environment in which business opportunities cannot be made but, instead, must be captured when they appear, some attractive business opportunities may have to be ignored in the interest of planned corporate development. Of course, management can always choose the opposite course, abandoning corporate development plans in favor of a very attractive business opportunity, but the organization may suffer tremendous growing pains as a result. As for the configuration of the project portfolio at any given point in time, the nature of each contract can be defined in terms of content area, type (labor-intensive or production), and size. Each of these variables has implications for the number of staff needed and for the training and expertise that they must possess. Sophisticated business planning requires projections of the changing portfolio of contracts to assure the necessary internal flexibility and capability to accommodate the combined impact of project demands.

To capitalize on the well-defined nature of the state market, managers typically conduct annual or semiannual surveys of specific bureaus across all state agencies both to obtain advance notice of RFPs to be released and to gain information about new legislation or agency regulations that are likely to result in contract work. General intelligence on new and emerging research interests and policy directions and information on budget constraints are valuable for business planning. In short, if one's marketing effort must be reactive, it is worth finding out exactly when and to what one should be ready to react.

Organizational Structure. Developing an organizational structure is as much a matter of managerial expertise as operating effectively within one is. This section addresses two organizational design issues that have particular relevance for the evaluation manager. It is important for the organizational structure to be examined on a regular basis. A shifting emphasis of the project portfolio can require temporary departures from the structure (for example, as a function of corporate downsizing) or permanent structural changes that serve to accommodate the work more efficiently.

Isolating Versus Integrating the Marketing Function. There are two distinct choices in organizing to accomplish the marketing function. Each has its advantages and disadvantages. Some contractors separate marketing from operations organizationally but establish the necessary professional relationship by ensuring strong liaison between the two areas. In this structure, marketing is responsible for identifying and securing business, and operations is responsible for completing it. The liaison functions include cooperative review of RFPs, proposals, and bids, but the responsibility for initiating and managing the marketing effort, including the major proposal writing, rests clearly with the marketing staff. This model takes advantage of specialized marketing talent and creates a team of professionals to spearhead corporate development. At the same time, it permits the hiring of project directors who are technically strong and capable but not necessarily entrepreneurial in orientation.

In the alternative structure, the marketing and operations functions are performed by the same group of professionals, who in essence are responsible for bringing in business to maintain their jobs. This model has an obvious drawback in the inherent conflict of priorities, since RFPs seem to have a way of arriving in the middle of major data collection activities or major report writing efforts for existing projects. The major advantage is that this model maximizes use of technical expertise, inasmuch as project work plans are conceived and drafted by those who later perform the work.

While both models are workable, the state market probably lends itself more readily than the federal to the separate marketing function. There are two main reasons: First, the RFPs issued by different states tend to display commonalities that allow proposal content to be standardized. Second, state-level projects are not as large or complex as federal projects. This allows the proposal writer to function with the project staff in a cooperative but distinct role in the design phases. These factors notwithstanding, no separate marketing function can succeed without a strong liaison function that ensures input and review by technical professionals whose product knowledge is honed by ongoing work in the substantive area.

Pure Team Management Versus Functional Division of Labor. It is often maintained that teamwork is the foundation of evaluation research, because teamwork is the mechanism that brings together the knowledge and skills required to conduct an evaluation in a particular substantive context. In the pure team model, staff are generally identified in terms of project assignment, and the corporation is composed almost entirely of satellite project teams. Each team is an independent, self-contained unit, and each unit possesses all the expertise needed to complete the job. These satellites may be supported by limited line management functions, such as vice-presidents or area directors in charge of specific subsets of teams, and by limited staff management functions, such as offices of personnel or budget. Nonetheless, this structure is clearly distinguishable from one that assigns staff to functional departments and that reflects an organization plan based on specialization and division of labor.

The team approach has the obvious advantages of close coordination, good cooperation, and ease of quality control, and for these reasons it has tremendous appeal at the individual project level. It has distinct disadvantages, however, at the corporate level. Each team, for example, is subject to peaks and valleys in the workload of individual members at various times in the life of the project. Multiplied across teams, the valleys mean a significant loss in productivity and efficiency. The alternative, functional specialization, has the disadvantage of fragmenting services, dividing their control among a variety of functional area managers. Coordination is cumbersome, and the absence of unifying leadership makes it difficult to ensure the integrity of the study as a whole.

The optimal solution is matrix management, an organizational structure in which each project is controlled by a management team that advocates for its success and each of several production functions (word processing, data processing, graphics) has a management team responsible for performing the function in the best possible manner. Individual projects use departmental services as needed and perform all other professional tasks themselves. Matrix management guarantees coherent teamwork at the same time that it maximizes efficiency. It is a workable solution if the corporation has developed sufficient stability and size to support the functional areas. The only serious threat to its success is posed by retreat from the practice of selecting as project directors professional evaluators who can play substantive roles as research and product designers, act as technical advisers to clients, and control final quality. If project team leaders become content-free managers, the model degenerates into pure line management, in which a public relations–oriented account executive acts as client interface. For organizations that contract with state or local agencies, the account executive model is neither desirable nor acceptable, since state clients expect their contractors to provide technical and program guidance as a primary service on any contract.

Staffing. There is no more critical management challenge than that represented by the array of staffing decisions that confront the evaluation manager. The quality of the contractor's staff is virtually equivalent to the quality of the service delivered to the client. As in any environment, staffing is the backbone of general corporate capability, overall productivity in work performed, and accurate, precise, technically strong products. Beyond these essentials, staffing in a professional service environment means corporate credibility in the eyes of prospective and existing clients. Most staffing efforts focus on locating and affording appropriate staff and on matching staff background and expertise to specific projects. Three related issues are discussed in this section.

Core Staff Versus Consultants. Some contractors are managerially loose associations of professionals whose connection with the corporation is limited to the project on which they were bid and hired to work. These operations are characterized by a small core of management staff, a cadre of staff hired for the duration of their respective contracts, and numerous consultants and stringers. By contrast, a contractor that primarily hires core staff does so with an eye both on the needs of the immediate project and on likely future contract assignments. Each new professional staff member is selected not only to handle a specific project but also to round out or otherwise to expand the expertise of the corporation as a whole. Because even temporary consultants often find ways of extending their associations with the firm from one contract to the next, it can seem trivial to distinguish them from core staff. But the distinction implies a very real difference in the nature of the organization's commitment to the professional. The state market seems more suited to the core staff model than the federal market does, primarily because it has opportunities to repeat the same type of business for numerous clients.

Backup Versus Bare-Bones Staffing. A contractor that elects to pursue the core staff model immediately faces another issue, which is a matter of timing more than anything else. The question is whether to hire a new staff person on award of the contract or in anticipation of winning the contract. The problem lies in the lag time needed for hiring and staff orientation processes; such time is scarcely available once a project has been awarded. While this issue is rarely applicable to the project director or project manager positions, since these staff are typically bid with supporting resumes in the proposal, the issue does apply to the variety of professional, technical, and administrative staff required to support major contracts.

In projecting or anticipating new business, the contractor walks a fine line between optimism (based, we hope, on past experience, track record, and intelligence) and conservatism (regarding allocation of resources and commitments to new staff). Within the core staff model, it is clear that backup hiring allows the contractor to begin work immediately upon receipt of the contract. By contrast, the bare-bones approach protects the unit from overextending itself or from having to find alternate assignments for new staff for whom the proposed contract does not materialize. Experience indicates that the tendency to take the backup staffing approach increases with size. It must be observed that larger agencies are relatively more capable of sustaining staff until other contracts arrive. Even where backup staffing is not financially viable, focused recruitment efforts, if not actual hiring, must begin well in advance of anticipated contracts. Two to three months of time can easily be consumed in the process of locating appropriate professional staff.

Managers Versus Technical Specialists. Once the questions of when to hire and for how long have been answered, the question of whom to hire still remains. As in every hiring effort, the challenge is to identify those who possess the skills needed to perform the job capably. The job of professional evaluator, however, has a dual nature: There are substantive and technical responsibilities, and there are managerial responsibilities. Ascertaining whether a candidate has the skills needed for the former is less difficult, since advanced degrees and academic excellence speak plainly. However, managerial competence is far more difficult to assess. Without strong managerial skills, all the technical excellence that a professional has cannot effectively be brought to bear on contract services. It remains a problem that evaluators rarely receive formal training in management skills and that they must come to the job with management intuitions and be amenable to developing management skills on an inservice basis.

Management Control. A primary goal of management is maximizing the quality of products and services. Quality control, however, must be reconciled with cost containment, since efforts to maximize the former can affect the latter adversely. Cost-effectiveness and quality control are relevant in two distinct phases of the evaluation activity: pricing tasks to bid on the project and managing the job. Competition at the state and local levels for medium-sized evaluation jobs is fierce, because a large number of contractors can manage contracts of reasonable size and have respectable track records. It is significant that the majority of state and local contracts are awarded to the lowest qualified bidder. Technical expertise may qualify the bidder, but the right price wins the job. This criterion for successful bids challenges the prospective contractor to find ways of minimizing costs without backing away from state-of-the-art service. This emphasis on cost-effectiveness heightens the importance of sophisticated pricing strategies.

Given that many state and local contracts are let out for bid on an annual or cyclical basis, one strategy is to take advantage of incumbency. The incumbent contractor who seeks contract renewal under competitive circumstances can capitalize on knowing the nature of the client and how the client defined the services on the previous job. The incumbent has realistic cost information, can use it to explore ways of doing the job more cost-effectively, and can pass on savings realized by eliminating the entire orientation and learning phase of the project. While the incumbent can use these factors to distinct advantage, the experience gained can backfire in favor of challengers. A challenger's lack of detailed knowledge of the job can cause him to underbid the incumbent. The successful incumbent does not set a final bid price without considering how the project looks from the perspective of the naive challenger.

In the project implementation phase, the demand for cost-effectiveness places a premium on sophisticated management strategies. The framework for these strategies is provided by thorough specification and documentation of all deliverables at the outset of the project. Unambiguous definition of products and services is particularly important, since most state contracting is fixed price, not cost reimbursable. Increases in the scope of work once the contract is signed either result in financial loss to the contractor or require a service trade-off to balance the net effect on cost. Where negotiated changes prove necessary, clear and mutual understanding of what the client bought serves to protect the working relationship from conflict.

Management strategies must be in place to ensure that products and services meet technical specifications and client expectations for quality and appropriateness and that they are delivered on time. The manager's two goals, quality control and efficiency, can both be served by an accountability system. A management-by-objectives (MBO) system, for example, is one way of tracking key project milestones and critical delivery dates. Such a system, tailored to the contractor's needs, can be used to exert management control over a given project and, at the corporate level, to monitor overall effectiveness of planning and service delivery. The complete MBO system includes procedures to maintain standards of quality, including scheduled internal reviews against prespecified criteria by quality-assurance staff as well as scheduled external reviews by content experts, ad hoc committees, and client agency staff.

Summary

Effective management of evaluation projects produces the same results as effective management of any other enterprise: efficient and timely completion of activities; satisfied, well-informed clients; and products and services of high quality. The manager makes choices in advance of contract awards and throughout contract life cycles. All these choices are critical determinants of individual project successes and overall corporate health.

Paula M. Nassif is vice-president for research and operations at National Evaluation Systems, Inc., where she has responsibility for operational control of three corporate divisions. Her functions include long-range planning and overall quality and cost control of products and services.

Sherry A. Rubinstein is director of the Division of Project Services at National Evaluation Systems, Inc., which houses the firm's project management teams. She has directed statewide assessments and evaluations in more than twenty state and local educational agencies over the past eight years.

The degree of control that project directors exert over the technical direction
of evaluations and the selection of evaluation staff is examined,
and the way in which it has grown and shrunk over the past decade
is considered.

Managing Evaluation Projects in a Contract Research Organization: Constraints on the Project Director

Robert G. St. Pierre

This chapter examines selected parts of the project director's role in managing research and evaluation projects for organizations that conduct social program evaluations, policy analyses, and other technical research projects primarily for the federal government. It focuses on the degree of control that project directors exert over the selection of staff for evaluation teams over the technical direction of evaluations and on the way in which this control first grew and then shrank during the past decade.

Organizational Structure of Federal Evaluation

Many demands placed on project directors who manage evaluations for research organizations grow from the organizational structure within which federal evaluations are conducted. This structure defines the network of relationships that must be formed and maintained by the evaluation project director. Congress is the source of much evaluation activity, as are policy makers in federal administrative agencies. Regardless of source, management

R. G. St. Pierre (Ed.). *Management and Organization of Program Evaluation.* New Directions for Program Evaluation, no. 18. San Francisco: Jossey-Bass, June 1983.

of any federal evaluation is influenced by three key groups in the federal agency: a contracts unit, which has legal authority to commit government funds by entering into contracts with research organizations; an evaluation unit, which has formal responsibility for technical oversight of the evaluations; and a program unit, which funds and monitors the social programs being evaluated.

When Congress, federal policy makers, or the program unit need evaluation information, the federal agency's contracts unit works with its evaluation unit to award an evaluation contract to a research organization. The research organization is the legal entity that enters into contracts with the federal government. It is responsible to the federal contracts unit for the proper expenditure of evaluation funds and to the federal evaluation unit in technical areas.

Large research organizations engage in several research and evaluation projects at the same time. Each requires an in-house evaluation team, headed by a project director. Each in-house team is a subset of a larger evaluation team that includes other key evaluation actors (St. Pierre, 1982). The client—the federal evaluation unit's project officer—is part of the evaluation team. Although the contractual relationship for any given evaluation is between the federal agency's contracts unit and the research organization, the technical and substantive work on the evaluation is carried out by the federal evaluation unit's project officer and the research organization's in-house evaluation team. Finally, the evaluation team also involves staff from the social program being evaluated. Cooperation must be obtained from the federal program unit responsible for national program direction and oversight as well as from program implementers at the local level.

The Project Director. Traditionally, the research organization's project director has had the responsibility for building the evaluation team just described. Thus, the project director sits at the center of several forces, which can pull in opposite directions. In terms of evaluation management, the most important conflict involves the project director's training and standards for conducting an evaluation, the training and standards held by the client's project officer, the working relationship formed between the project director and project officer, and the degree of autonomy that the project director has within the research organization.

The role of the project director as manager and evaluator was influenced greatly by the increased need for evaluation information felt by the federal government during the late 1960s and the 1970s. It was not that the 1960s lacked excellent researchers but that few had specialized in evaluation and that even fewer understood the complexities of managing large field studies. The demand for technically trained persons who could conduct evaluations led to new graduate programs, new journals, and new professional societies. Many evaluators trained during this period of growth opted for employment in private research organizations, not in academia, in part because many if not most large and interesting evaluations are conducted in nonacademic settings. Their choice was due also to the relatively higher salaries offered by research organizations and to the growing recognition that conducting evaluations is as honorable as teaching about them (Rossi and Wright, 1977).

Finding project directors who can provide technical and intellectual leadership as well as managerial leadership is one of the most difficult problems faced by research organizations. Since most program evaluators are trained as social scientists, their academic backgrounds are technical and substantive. They often join research organizations right out of graduate school and do technical work, such as preparing questionnaires, analyzing data, or writing reports. As they acquire experience, they become project directors. Yet, there is no guarantee that good evaluators will become good evaluation managers. In addition to qualities necessary to be a good technical evaluator, a good evaluation manager must be able to plan well, deal with details, interact well with groups interested in the evaluation, hire and fire staff, prepare budgets, be concerned with timeliness, and so on. Persons with these skills are not trained in graduate school. Rather, they are trained on the job.

Thus, a cadre of evaluators now has experience at managing evaluations. However, the expertise of these project directors still does not entitle them to complete control over the way in which their evaluations are conducted. In part, this is due to the fact the evaluation research operates in a policy context, which means that an evaluation cannot be conducted in a vacuum. It requires input from several groups, including clients, Congress, program administrators, and program recipients. In the evaluation research arena, no single person has the level of control over a study that the academic grant holder expects and receives. Thus, the autonomy of the research organization project director is limited by the nature of the evaluation research enterprise. In addition, I argue that the growth of evaluation research in the 1970s and the subsequent retrenchment in the 1980s have limited the project director's span of control. This has both positive and negative consequences.

The Project Officer. From the point of view of the project director in charge of an in-house evaluation team, the federal evaluation unit's project officer is the client. Although federal evaluations are typically designed to be of use to Congress or to federal agency program staff or policy makers, the federal evaluation unit's project officer has immediate responsibility for monitoring the evaluation contractor and for approving evaluation plans, methods, analyses, and reports.

The role of the project officer is not well defined, and the expectations for what a project officer does vary from one federal evaluation office to another (Raizen and Rossi, 1981). When the number of large-scale evaluations started to grow in the late 1960s, federal evaluation offices tended to be staffed by civil servants who had little or no background in conducting such studies. At that time, many project officers preferred to play a minor role in the technical conduct of evaluation contracts and delegated most of the responsibility for evaluation to the presumably greater expertise of specialists in research firms. In these cases, the role that the project officer played was largely occupied by such activities as participating in meetings, reviewing reports, and approving expenditures. In these early evaluations, the research organization's project director had as much autonomy in setting technical directions as one can have under a contract-based system, although the project director in many early studies, while a good researcher, had little experience in managing large-scale evaluations.

The same rapid growth in the evaluation profession that led project directors to be upgraded in research firms had an impact on federal project officers. At the same time that newly trained evaluators were entering research organizations, the federal government became an attractive place of employment for evaluators. The result was professionalization of many federal evaluation offices and upgrading of staff in these offices. Naturally, well-trained project officers want to play an important part in the projects conducted by their contractors, and so over the past decade there has been a clear move toward more active involvement by federal project officers in the conduct of evaluations. The center of decision-making authority in large-scale evaluations thus has moved from the research organization to a point somewhere between the research organization and the federal evaluation office. In cases where the federal evaluation office has capable staff, this arrangement works well. Evaluations benefit from the combined efforts of a strong project officer–project director team. Still, a wide range remains in the capabilities and interests of federal project officers, and the contractor's project director must be flexible and adaptive, since much of an evaluation's success depends greatly on the ability of project officer and project director to work together.

Working Within a Research Organization

Research organizations are not simply places where several in-house evaluation teams work on different problems until the job is done. Rather, they are fluid organizations faced with the continuous problem of matching the skills of in-house staff with the work available. This problem exists for the management of many organizations. What distinguishes contract research firms is that they must match staff with work in an environment where it is difficult to predict the amount of work available and where the flow of work is not uniform. In this setting, project directors must interact with administrators of the parent organization in three key areas: staff management, quality control, and fiscal management.

Staff Management. The best way to ensure that an in-house evaluation team does high-quality work is to make sure that it is appropriately staffed (Kelling, 1979). The most important areas of interaction between in-house evaluation teams and their parent research organizations involve staff use. Each in-house evaluation team needs staff with three types of skills: managerial, substantive, and technical. Responsibility for staffing and managing the in-house team is split along ill-defined lines between the evaluation project director and the research organization's administrative staff.

A project director can obtain the substantive and technical expertise needed for an evaluation in several ways: by using in-house staff who already possess the appropriate knowledge, by hiring new staff, or by using consultants or subcontractors to augment in-house staff. The best option is to have staff in house who already understand the program being evaluated and who have the requisite analytical talents. This means that the evaluation team can be formed of staff with proven capabilities, that it can proceed with a minimum of read-in time, and that many false starts in preparing the design and instrumentation for the evaluation can be avoided.

If an organization's current staff does not have the necessary substantive or technical background, hiring new staff members is an option. During the period of growth that many organizations experienced during the 1970s, hiring new staff was the preferred course. This raises the issue of whether substantive specialists or technically skilled persons who also have the appropriate substantive backgrounds should be hired. The second category is much more difficult to find, but it is also much more valuable, because technical skills can be transferred from one evaluation to another, while a person whose background is mainly substantive has limited utility to a research organization. During periods of growth, this problem was less critical, since there were reasonable chances that the substantive staff member would be needed for other studies.

During the period of retrenchment now being experienced, research firms are much more cautious about bringing on new staff, especially those who are limited technically. Of course, there are other options available, but they also have drawbacks. Subcontracting part of an evaluation to another research firm is not desirable, but sometimes it is necessary. Arguments in favor of subcontracting generally follow the line that the capabilities of two or more firms are better than the capabilities of one. In other cases, the contractor does not want to build the in-house capacity to do a particular kind of work and subcontracts to buy the needed skills. University-based consultants can be used on evaluation teams to augment the skills of in-house staff by supplying expertise in particular areas. Finally, many federal evaluations require an advisory panel of technical and substantive experts to be assembled to provide guidance and to review the study's progress.

Times of resource shortages can produce tension between project directors and research organizations over use of external sources of assistance. Not having the appropriate in-house skills available, a project director may want outside assistance from a consultant or subcontractor. Wanting to conserve in-house staff, the research organization would rather see the project director use a suboptimal in-house staff member than give support to persons outside the organization. Such conflicts can be negotiated. Success in such efforts depends on the degree of mismatch between the needs of the evaluation and the available in-house skills.

Changing Staff Needs. Five technical functions are necessary for most evaluations: design and sampling, instrument development, data collection, analysis, and reporting. These five functions necessitate staff with diverse skills. Some functions require highly paid, technically trained professionals. Others can be performed by inexpensive, relatively untrained staff. Moreover, the fact that the five functions are relevant at different times in the life of an evaluation has consequences for staffing. Evaluation design and instrument development take place early in the evaluation, data collection in the middle, and data analysis and reporting run from the middle (as soon as data become available) to the end. First, a team of senior professionals reads in, designs the evaluation and the instruments, and prepares written plans to guide the study. Next, staff organize, monitor, and conduct the data collection effort. Finally, the senior professionals analyze the data and prepare reports. While this pattern makes perfect sense to the project director, the changing staffing needs place a tremendous strain on the research organization. What happens to senior evaluators during data collection? It is both a misuse of skills and prohibitively expensive to have them spend a lot of time monitoring the data collection or collecting the data themselves, although some data collection is essential, so that senior staff can gain an understanding of the program being evaluated.

Ensuring both a smooth flow of work for staff and that staff are available for specific evaluation when needed is one of the major problems that any research organization must solve. Thus, it is one of the major management areas faced by the project director of an in-house evaluation team. The general rule is that the research organization wants to preserve staff, to keep the organization's capabilities as strong and broad as possible. In a time of growth, the research organization will have other evaluations for these persons to work on that can use their skills in a productive manner. This can create another problem, because senior evaluators must be free to return to the original evaluation when data collection is complete in order to analyze the data and prepare reports. Just as it is sometimes difficult to find work for professionals when they have a slack period, it is sometimes difficult to get them back once they have found work on another evaluation.

In the current time of retrenchment, finding work to occupy staff when they are not needed on a given evaluation is becoming increasingly problematic. Pressure is placed on project directors to use staff who may be marginally useful, technically inappropriate, overpriced, or otherwise not exactly right. This causes serious management problems for the project director, who can be faced with the choice of supporting key staff during slack periods or having them leave the organization. Both choices are detrimental to the evaluation, since, to be as efficient as possible, the evaluation project director wants to use the best appropriate staff only when they are needed, and the project director does not want to have to support these staff members when they are not needed. If the project director chooses to support a staff member, evaluation funds will be expended faster than planned. But, if the staff member leaves, the evaluation will incur the costs and the disruptive effect of adding a new member to the evaluation team and having that person read in.

Related problems occur when an evaluation requires skills that are not readily available in house. In research organizations preoccupied with finding work for in-house staff, the pressure on project directors to use in-house staff who are not exactly right for the job, and to cover valuable staff who are lacking work, increases. Although these demands can lower the quality of an evaluation, they cannot always be resisted. Suppose, for example, that a project director needs a highly trained data analyst half-time for the next year and that such a person is not available in house. The project director's ability to fill this need by hiring outside the organization is severely constrained by the fact that the position is only half-time, and the research organization may not have other work. Thus, the project director's only recourse may be to use an in-house staff member whose skills are passable but not top-notch.

Quality Control. Research organizations are concerned about the quality of the work done by in-house evaluation teams. Most research organizations want to grow or at least to maintain themselves, and one of the best methods of ensuring a steady flow of work is to build a reputation for high-quality work. Thus, research organizations perform quality-control functions, such as monitoring the progress of each evaluation; reviewing plans, data collection instruments, and reports before they are delivered to clients; visiting clients to discuss progress and satisfaction from the client's point of view; and obtaining formal written assessments from clients of the performance of each in-house evaluation team.

Yet, quality-control operations are quite difficult to maintain, and they work better in theory than in practice. This is not to say that research organizations doubt that quality control is important but that it tends to rank low on the ladder of functions that need to be accomplished and that it can create conflict between the project director and the research organization. Given the minimal involvement that a research organization can have in any single evaluation, the project director usually feels that quality control functions are hopelessly out of touch with the day-to-day technical operations of an evaluation. Further, quality control often manifests itself when reports are being written and can take the form of criticism offered too late to affect an evaluation's design or instrumentation. Such criticism after the fact can help to polish a report, but it is of limited assistance in other areas. The in-house evaluation team sometimes profits from corporate quality control, but a research organization's contribution to the quality of an evaluation is more likely to come from wise staffing decisions or from fiscal control than from ongoing quality control.

Fiscal Management. Research organizations are concerned with expenditures on individual evaluation projects and are much better equipped to help project directors with fiscal management than with quality control. The organization is legally responsible for spending evaluation funds according to contract specifications and for ensuring that funds are used only for activities allowed by the contract. Therefore, research organizations keep close track of such evaluation expenditures as labor, travel, computer time, and reproduction costs. Management information systems are used to bill clients and to provide project directors with spending summaries. This type of information is of great assistance in the conduct of any evaluation, and the conflicts that occur between the project director and the research organization in this area are typically related to mistakes in the information provided, not to the need for such information.

In addition to monitoring the appropriateness of expenditures, research organizations monitor the timing of expenditures. The overhead dollars used to support corporate personnel, pay the rent, provide fringe benefits, and so on are all tied to actual expenditures on evaluation contracts. If work on an evaluation proceeds slower than planned, the costs being incurred are lessened, and the corresponding overhead dollars that flow into the company are reduced. Because research organizations make plans based on assumptions about the amount of overhead funds available during a given time period, they have a strong stake in ensuring that each evaluation project spends according to its schedule. Often, this causes conflict between the research organization and the project director, since the spending patterns of evaluations can easily alter if a data collection effort must be postponed or a report date has been changed. Such changes may or may not benefit the evaluation, but they always cause headaches for research organizations because of their impact on spending patterns.

Conclusions

The past decade has seen a substantial increase in the number of technically trained evaluators who are capable of managing large-scale evaluations. In the late 1960s and for much of the 1970s, these project directors were often granted a great deal of autonomy (although clearly less than the academic grant holder) both in setting technical directions for the evaluation and in staffing the evaluation team. However, the autonomy of the project director has diminished in recent years as a result of the increased role of the federal project officer in designing, conducting, and seeing to the use of evaluations as well as of shrinkage in federal evaluation activity during the late 1970s and early 1980s and the effect that this shrinkage has had on research organizations and their ability to staff evaluation projects.

What can the project director do about this situation? How can encroachment on responsibility and power be accommodated? It is essential to realize that heavy involvement by the project officer is not essentially negative. In fact, the most productive evaluation teams are formed when the project director and project officer see each other as colleagues and work as partners throughout the evaluation, sharing ideas, drafts of design documents and reports, and solving problems. This type of relationship is productive and stimulating for both the client and the contractor.

Thus, rather than regarding substantive and technical involvement by a project officer in an evaluation as a threat to the contractor's independence or to the objectivity of the study, the project director profits from having a close working relationship with a competent and informed project officer. First, the project officer is often a good researcher and evaluator who has devoted a great deal of thinking to the problems at hand. Participation by this project officer in planning the evaluation, in conferences, and in solving day-to-day problems can be a great help. Second, the project officer often has a good grasp of the policy issues involved in the study and can direct the evaluation team's attention to key areas and help to interpret analyses and to draft and revise reports. Although incorporation of the project officer into the evaluation team will not directly increase the project director's span of control, it can improve the quality of the evaluation, and it will assure the client that any surprises are functions of the phenomena under study, not of a failure of communication. Despite the advantages of working with an informed client, however, the skill level of individual federal project officers is still quite variable. Thus, project directors must be able to deal with well-trained and not so well-trained project officers. Moreover, some will defer to the contractor in almost all areas, while others will play a much more direct role in the evaluation.

From the perspective of the research organization, project directors must be able to balance several competing needs in order to manage high-quality evaluations. They must be able to conduct evaluations within a specified budget, so the client can see that the research organization is cost-conscious. Next, they must be able to prepare spending plans for their evaluation activities, and those plans must be accurate enough that the research organization can count on a certain level of overhead funds. Project directors must also be able to balance their staffing needs with the reality which dictates that they may sometimes have to use inexperienced or overpriced staff. In addition, the complex structure that surrounds the practice of federal evaluation research requires project directors to be able to work successfully with the groups that compose the evaluation team, including the client, the research organization from which the evaluation is conducted, the in-house evaluation team, subcontractors, consultants, and advisory panels.

Each of these management demands is simplified in times of prosperity. If a research organization has sufficient work, individual project directors can exert substantial control over the staffing and conduct of individual evaluations. This scenario changes in times of shrinkage, when organizational survival often takes precedence over the needs of specific evaluations.

References

Kelling, G. "Development of Staff for Evaluation (A Retrospective View)." In L. Secrest and others (Eds.), *Evaluation Studies Review Annual.* Vol. 4. Beverly Hills, Calif.: Sage, 1979.

Raizen, S. A., and Rossi, P. H. *Program Evaluation in Education: When? How? To What Ends?* Washington, D.C.: National Academy Press, 1981.

Rossi, P. H., and Wright, S. R. "Evaluation Research: An Assessment of Theory, Practice, and Politics." *Evaluation Review*, 1977, *1* (1), 5-52.

St.Pierre, R. G. "Management of Federally Funded Evaluation Research: Building Evaluation Teams." *Evaluation Review*, 1982, *6* (1), 94-113.

Robert G. St.Pierre is a social scientist at Abt Associates Inc., where for the past eight years he has directed national evaluations of social programs.

The functions and career paths of evaluation research managers,
their duties and generic styles, and some indicators of performance
quality are outlined, and a better way to assess and select
them in the future is proposed.

The Occupational Role of the
Evaluation Research Manager

Robert A. Dentler

The literature on evaluation research—its history, conduct, and effects—is extremely dense with ideas, opinions, and facts pertinent to the technology of inquiry. A newcomer to the field who spends a week ingesting a hundred representative books and articles on the subject can conclude that the work life of the American program evaluator is filled with questions and dialogue about matters of design, instrumentation, data collection and management, and statistical analysis. The much smaller literature on evaluation research management follows the same tradition, so the newcomer could be tempted to imagine that the manager's hours on the job were filled with the challenges of technical planning, costing, technical supervision of staff, and dissemination of technical findings.

    Neither literature is invalid in its emphases. The issues inherent in the technology of inquiry and how they are treated does indeed affect the quality and utility of evaluation research products. Both sets of literature are incomplete, however, as descriptions and interpretations of the evaluation research role and of the role performance of evaluation research managers. This chapter tries to correct one shortcoming of reports on evaluation research management—they overlook the occupational psychosociology of the position—not because the correction will contradict the literature, but because it will augment and perhaps even humanize the newcomer's sense of the situation.

R. G. St. Pierre (Ed.). *Management and Organization of Program Evaluation.* New Directions
for Program Evaluation, no. 18. San Francisco: Jossey-Bass, June 1983.

For the purposes of this chapter, an evaluation research manager is a person who occupies a position above the level of project director and below the level of chief executive officer. Both roles are indeed managerial, but the former is primarily supervisory, and the person who fills it is a collegial member of the study team, while the latter has general executive authority over all aspects of the firm or agency. As understood here, the role excludes such specialized staff leaders as legal counsel, controller, and personnel director. It includes middle managers who preside over clusters of projects, vice-presidents, assistant commissioners or superintendents, and the like.

The Managerial Niche

By definition and social history, evaluation research is a technical activity subsystem. It can be carried out as a solo performance, to be sure, but it rarely ever is. Instead, its players span a series of other activity subsystems— program policy and fiscal sources, program implementors, question askers, beneficiaries, users, and the like—and they are organized within or through a field of complex formal organizations. No other feature of the evaluation research managerial niche has greater primacy.

Because the evaluation research manager is expected to devise, maintain, and reach closure on a complex series of technical activities, whose ingredients are partly arcane, partly undisclosed to others, and partly intended to be executed without interrupting activities unrelated to evaluation research that evaluation research depends on for its existence, nearly everyone in the evaluation research community develops certain expectations about evaluation research managers. As a class, they are expected to exhibit some or most of these attributes: They are self-reliant, technically inventive or adaptive (but not original), calm, organizationally earnest, conflict-avoidant, cool or matter-of-fact, and prudent. This cluster of attributes derives from the legend of expectations surrounding the applied scientist. The basic research scientist seems to have a radically different legend, while engineers are expected to be aggressive on demand, in order to build things or to make things happen.

In addition, the evaluation research manager occupies a niche that is only partially defined by its place in the hierarchy. Even in local, state, and federal agencies where status hierarchies are explicit and prescriptive for most staff, evaluation research managers can enjoy or suffer considerable status ambiguity. They exercise some authority, but it does not ramify outward or downward in any predictable pattern. Their niche is always located on a tangent off other line and staff positions. Moreover, their prestige and influence seldom stem from their position within the organization; instead, they come from the importance that other influentials ascribe to their performance.

The evaluation research manager's niche is somewhat peculiar in another respect. Sales managers do not have to keep on selling in order to preserve their position. Financial managers move along a career path that increasingly separates them from accounting operations. In contrast, evaluation research managers try to keep a hand in evaluation research work or risk losing their credibility both with colleagues and with clients. Substantive changes in field are feasible for them, but separation from the technical practice of design, analysis, and interpretive reporting is usually a dangerous career step. A deep emphasis on managerial role performance can induce evaluation research managers to neglect research skills and thus erode their long-term career prospects.

The Manager's Role Obligations

If environmental conditions within evaluation research organizations were stable and regular, we could say that evaluation research managers are expected to organize the work setting; to allocate marginal resources; to supervise, evaluate, and help to develop staff; to mediate disputes and arbitrate claims or grievances; and to represent or speak for the firm. However, conditions have been unstable for many years, veering from situations in which projects and resources are abundant to situations in which there is a shortage of both.

As a result, evaluation research managers are looked to for help in meeting frequent and pervasive challenges. They are called on to protect the quality and integrity of evaluation research itself; to find new ways of maintaining financial viability; to keep staff encouraged and oriented as prospects for doing good research become uncertain; to enhance productivity and counter staff burnout; and to develop administrative procedures that are flexible and facilitative, not rigid and obstructive. Thus, what began as a set of agency maintenance roles shared by middle managers everywhere has become an extremely challenging, creatively demanding set of obligations.

Occupying the Manager's Role

Evaluation research managers come from evaluation research teams. There are many pathways of preparation, yet the door to the project directorship — the one room that one must inhabit in order to begin to become an evaluation research manager — is opened only to those who have had some research team experience. In emergencies, persons from other specialities can be brought in, to be sure, but almost no one in the business takes such recruits seriously, and managers who begin in this way must often make a career out of apologies for the next fifteen years.

The extreme credence given to job experience in selecting evaluation research managers stems in part from the fact that evaluation research is a very young and underdeveloped profession. It also stems from the fact that the activity subsystem is too unstable to be learned in any other way. An apprentice manager is therefore someone who gathers and stores the lore of ways of handling project contingencies that most evaluation research veterans accumulate in an agency, firm, or department. Such lore conveys norms that govern how evaluation research challenges should be met. The norms are not written down, so the apprentice has to memorize them. Unfortunately, the norms seldom fit issues that emerge in an unstable environment, since they are based on precedents that no longer characterize the situation.

Researchers can aspire to become evaluation research managers for extrinsic motives. Autonomy, mobility, and increased income are the obvious motivations. The career path is too uncertain to be planned in advance, however, and little guidance on how to become a manager is passed through the ranks. To become a project director is both tangible and, for many workers, desirable. The project director position signifies an opportunity to shape the technical portent of the effort and to get credit for the results. The first rung on the evaluation research managerial ladder, project directorship, is thus fairly well marked and within reasonable reach, and it seems to be worth standing on.

Project directors become curious about the next rungs, of course. They consider the roles of evaluation research managers and even imitate the moves of their favorites. They watch the unit middle managers, the vice-presidents, or assistant commissioners closely, yet both the pathways to these positions and their merits can remain obscure. Project directors who are explicitly ambitious for wealth or power often conclude that movement to a line or central staff management position in a different activity system is a surer route to their objectives than movement to an evaluation research middle managership. Other, more technically centered project directors prefer to remain in that position indefinitely.

Thus, senior evaluation research managers tend to be recruited from a very small and shallow pool of candidates. This pool contains project directors and former project directors with strong maintenance skills but weak technical and intellectual qualifications. It also contains research technique-centered candidates who often have few observable qualifications as managers of people or of interorganizational relations. Staff and clients alike keep yearning for candidates in the middle place, of course, where the two kinds of essential leadership skills are merged.

The paradox is that evaluation research, as a craft-type technology, remains a kind of cottage industry nested in larger and more formal bureaucratic settings. Evaluation research tends to simulate the forms of business and public administration, just as it often behaves like a first cousin of academic scholarship. Locating, recruiting, and conserving senior leadership for evaluation research agencies therefore remains an extremely chancy undertaking. Mooveover, the task remains forever in the hands of those in charge. Among privately owned firms, firms owned by employees probably have the best chance of choosing good leadership, but there are very few such firms.

In spite of their expanding obligations, evaluation research managers discover that they are in authoritative charge of very little. Long immersion in evaluation research agencies prior to appointment as an evaluation research manager blunts and eases this discovery. The veteran arrives in middle management with low expectations based on lore of the house built up during stable periods. The role carries with it many responsibilities for adaptive patching, compromising, rescheduling, and other maintenance work. The hours are long, and the communications obligations are heavy. Except in the domain of new project entrepreneurship, most aspects of evaluation research manager behavior are predetermined by the contractual complex, agency norms, and the internalized blueprints carried by agency staff.

For this reason perhaps, evaluation research managers often recognize and reward one another by the standard of entrepreneurial success, even where profitability is not part of the agency's mission. A larger share of current markets, new market inroads, and futures speculation with the anticipated products of a project become the stuff from which many managerial reputations are made. Where this tendency becomes excessive, the manager's ability to improve workmanship and delivery can be threatened. Both in periods of resource abundance (1966–1975) and in periods of severe relative scarcity (like the present) the same tendency can be invoked for different reasons.

Most evaluation research managers work with a matrix type of staff deployment scheme. As a result, very few managers have full-time assistance. Therefore, few staff build up social sentiments, including loyalty, toward such people. This contrasts with life within the evaluation research team, where the project director can enjoy close and warm interdependence as a result of continuous, shared interaction. Managerial roles are often described as lonely, and senior evaluation research manager roles can become even lonelier. Moreover, the sentiments that can evolve from within the senior management group are often stifled by the intense interunit competition around targets of entrepreneurial opportunity. Such competition is exacerbated by the facts that content boundaries are seldom kept firm and that cases can be made by peers for transferring initiatives from one unit to another.

An undergraduate summer intern once told me when I was directing a large research and development agency, "Before this summer, I wondered how people got into jobs like yours. Now, I know the answer, but I wonder who would ever want to." I was amazed, because I regarded it as a wonderful job, and I told him so, but he held to his point of view. He thought the evaluation research manager's work was insufficiently rewarding, filled as it was with pressured, rueful clients and ideologically mulish policy makers on the outside and overworked, brutishly scheduled, and intensely individualistic staff on the inside. As a youthful beginner, he could not appreciate the psychic gratifications that come from guiding a fact-finding process and from building the team that can get the best possible intellectual results. These gratifications combine the pleasures of prospecting for gold and administering a college, while they lack the almost total uncertainty of the former and the ceremonial pomp of the latter. As in airline management work, you probably have to have flown a lot yourself in order to enjoy it.

Performing the Manager's Role

So much for the peculiarities of landing in the job and occupying it. What about the nongeneric features of performing the role? Neither the quantity nor the quality of evaluation research production provides an adequate or valid measure of an evaluation research manager's performance. The role is too contingent on market forces to enable quantity to signify. There is a lot of talk about diversifying markets and services, of course, and the manager of a nonprofit unit can be expected to cultivate usership and hence demand. But, the whole truth probably includes the fact that needs and interests rise and fall among clients and other users quite independently of the behavior of even the ablest managers. The enterprise will never enjoy what some economists call the casino condition, in which people gamble when they are rich because they can afford to and when they are poor because they yearn for a windfall. So too, quality is too complex to be appraised accurately over the short term. Moreover, in an agency that conducts ten or more evaluations a year, the terms and conditions governing excellence are not controllable. Of course, the evaluation research manager can always strive to earn the firm a reputation for distinction, but that is a mere proxy, and over time the reputation itself can hamper opportunities to innovate.

In circumstances as freighted with indeterminacy as these are, what do evaluation research managers do to appraise their own worth and that of their peers? In scholarship and in scientific research, merit appraisals tend to be grounded in the respect accorded the published work of the research manager, and this grounding tends to hold fast, at least within disciplines, across many years. Roughly equivalent grounding has built up from a decade and a half of large-scale cross-disciplinary evaluation research, but so many researchers move out of evaluation research after a three- to five-year stint that the demand for research managers far outstrips the supply of candidates with established publication records, and in any event such records do not always have much standing with evaluation research staff.

Cultivating clients and building a wide-ranging network of prospective coparticipants probably carries more weight and enables managers to base their leadership on comparative insights. This sociometric form of achievement has obvious pertinence to individual worth, yet it is attained through personal charisma or social desirability, and it is not in itself a clear indicator of leadership competencies. Alternatively, a concentration on the tasks of technical review, like the approach of devising mechanisms for upgrading research productivity, can indicate leadership quality, but it can also fall wide of the mark, since the details of design, data collection, and analysis tend to govern project team operations, and these details are seldom amenable to quick or superficial scrutiny. Only the wisest and most delicate intrusions by evaluation research managers are likely to have positive consequences.

Only the very ablest evaluation research managers ground their performance in what seem to be two empirically accessible tests of evaluation research leadership performance. The first is conservation of manifest talents in both researchers and support staff. Conservation is accomplished by keenly appraising the talents of research staff at the very start and by maintaining a cool yet hospitable work milieu that sustains these talents. Both these efforts can be evaluated reliably through a good system of upward evaluation, and research managers who consistently earn a poor rating should be counseled out within two or three years. The second test is whether the evaluation research manager can preserve a reasonably even keel while sailing the turbulent waters of clients. Does the manager hold a fairly steady and even course yet come about without jibing if the winds shift? Does the manager mediate sensibly between client demands and staff convictions? Risking too much and risking too little in the process of negotiating between the two are observable hallmarks of evaluation research leadership failure.

Neither of these indicators suffices to determine whether individual research managers are capable of meeting the many challenges created by rapid political and economic change. Here, the importance of leadership rises as our ability to test it empirically falls. Nonetheless, it is worthwhile to try to imagine some tests. Does the evaluation research manager locate alternative ways of organizing or conducting evaluation research that are reported in the literature, both fugitive and published? Does the manager share these alternatives with staff? Does the research manager identify possible shortcuts and other cost-saving procedures that seem to staff to preserve quality while reducing sweat equity? Does the research manager's leadership become more, rather than less, inclusive of advice from staff as working conditions become harsh? Is a changing vision of the possible uses of evaluation research products—a deep interest in knowledge exchange—apparent in the manager's day-to-day work? If retrenchment is necessary, does the research manager offer to step down and merge his unit with others? Above all, does the research manager uphold the worth of the enduring purposes of evaluation research in ways that staff can see?

There is some congruence between all three types of indicators and the activity patterns characteristic of good evaluation research design, data collection, analysis, and reporting. Those who do really well leading evaluation research projects should become leading candidates for evaluation research management positions. The major source of discrepancy springs from the weak association between cognitive critical skills basic to the technology of inquiry and the interpersonal skills basic to leadership.

Conclusion

Organized evaluation research is still too young to let us know whether the evaluation research manager's occupational role is a career episode or a life calling. How many evaluation research managers become managers at age thirty-five and then age gracefully into a thirty-year career of service? Within agencies where units have been ongoing since the 1930s, one catches an occasional encouraging glimpse. There one sometimes finds the wise and still vitally engaged unit director in the sixty- to sixty-five-year-old range. The federal agency record is becoming less encouraging, however, as the last decade has degraded the federal civic service unmercifully. Ten years ago, however, there were evaluation research managers who entered the government between 1935 and 1945 and who laid the permanent foundation for large-scale evaluation research as an adjunct of policy and program planning. The last few years have largely passed in personal planning for early retirement.

The Evaluation Research Society (ERS) has performed an important service in recent years by awarding recognition to exemplary researchers in the field. These awards have been hard to make, although there are adequate technical standards for making choices. If the evaluation research manager's role is to become something more vital than a kind of symbol, then ERS officers might want to consider the more difficult task of awarding recognition for senior leadership. This task should not be conceived of as a search for the women and men who symbolize evaluation research at its best but for outstanding exemplars of evaluation research management as a special role.

Whether funds for evaluation research continue to dwindle as the 1980s continue or they begin to increase, the need for effective evaluation research management will be intensified by changing conditions in the political economy. The challenges mentioned in this chapter will multiply, not decrease. As similar circumstances have emerged in public school systems, an increasing number have begun to make impressive improvements in their procedure for selecting school administrators (Baltzell and Dentler, 1982). These improvements range from greatly strengthened training and internship activities to adaptation of sophisticated versions of leadership assessment clusters developed for business and industry. Some school systems are now selecting principals on the basis of both merit and equity criteria, and their efficacy is astonishing, given the long history of selection by cronyism and seniority. The evaluation research community might do well to imitate these innovating systems, since many are clients or part of the evaluation research tradition.

Reference

Baltzell, D. C., and Dentler, R. A. *Selecting American School Principals.* Cambridge, Mass.: Abt Associates, 1982.

*Robert A. Dentler is senior sociologist and former education area
manager at Abt Associates, Inc. He managed his first program
evaluation in 1958 at NORC, the National Opinion Research
Center and he was director of the Center for Urban Education,
a regional educational laboratory, from 1965 to 1972.*

*The organizational setting of an evaluation has a significant impact
on the resources available for managing individual evaluation projects.*

Organizational Contexts
for Evaluation

Karen Seashore Louis

Social scientests prefer to compare themselves with autonomous professionals, such as lawyers or doctors, not with administrators. Yet, much of what the project director or principal investigator of a moderate- to large-size applied social research project does on a day-to-day basis involves tasks similar to those performed by middle managers in other contexts. Middle managers are typically in close contact both with subordinates, whose work they supervise, and with administrative superiors, who set policy and control organizational resources that the middle manager needs in order to complete the job effectively. Research on this role suggests that the job of middle manager differs from that of top manager across many different types of settings. First, middle managers have less well-differentiated roles. They perform almost all tasks in the organization to some degree, but they often spend less time on each one (Campbell and others, 1970). The work of the middle manager entails less overall responsibility in such areas as finance and personnel, but in some ways there is also more pressure, because decisions must be made much faster (Campbell and others, 1970). In other words, the middle manager deals with crises, while the top manager deals with long-range planning (Pfiffner and Sherwood, 1960). The pressure associated with the middle manager's role is affirmed by Kahn and others (1964), who find that role conflict is higher among middle managers. In sum, the middle manager position can be viewed as inherently stressful.

R. G. St. Pierre (Ed.). *Management and Organization of Program Evaluation.* New Directions
for Program Evaluation, no. 18. San Francisco: Jossey-Bass, June 1983.

This chapter speculates about the ways in which common organized settings for applied social science research affect the middle management components of the principal investigator's job. How this context can increase and reduce job-related tensions is emphasized.

Data and Methods

My interest in this topic derives largely from my own experience, which has included employment in a major private research center, a small non-profit center, two university-based centers, and a small academic department. With each change of organization, I was struck by differences in the structures, norms, and processes of these settings that both supported and inhibited research management. This chapter started out to be about the differences and similarities between these contexts. However, before beginning to write, I tested my hypotheses by systematically seeking out and interviewing a number of colleagues whose primary professional commitments were to research, not teaching, and who had acted as project director in two or more very different research centers. I wanted to find out how the work environment had affected their performance on key middle management tasks (St. Pierre, 1982). These tasks included gathering resources (otherwise known as writing proposals); recruiting and retaining staff; managing resources; maintaining technical quality, particularly of reports and publications; and maintaining good relationships with the funding agency. The research management experiences of seven individuals in fourteen different research organizations are reflected in this chapter. The respondents reported on a total of sixteen different management experiences. Five were in independent for-profit firms, five were in independent nonprofit agencies, and six were in university-based institutes.

Universities and Independent Agencies

Universities are often regarded as a poor context for policy research, because they do not provide management support or leadership for the effective and timely completion of large-scale research. Instead, universities are viewed as places where courses and teaching obligations, coupled with respect for the notion that the researcher alone should decide what the important research topics are, prevent evaluation and policy research from taking place. In contrast, independent agencies are viewed as supportive and concerned about these issues, able to develop flexible staffing policies that can match a project's needs with a national talent pool, more conscious of time and money, and more accountable (Coleman, 1972; Rossi, Wright, and Wright, 1978; Bernstein and Freeman, 1975).

My interviews suggest, however, that organizational auspices were not always a key factor in determining management experiences. The same issues and problems were reported by people who had worked in prestigious university-based centers and in small profit-making independents. The common distinctions between these settings have validity where the comparisons are between university departments and independent corporations. However, where the comparison is between organized research settings, the distinctions can blur in both contexts. Thus, the interviews revealed that there is no ideal setting for the conduct of policy and evaluation research. Rather, each setting has some weaknesses and some strengths, both from the perspective of a government agency that needs timely, high-quality answers to pressing questions at relatively low cost and from the perspective of the project director as middle manager.

Technical Focus and Administrative Support

In a research setting, the leadership provided by the director or other top management is often channelled into two independent areas. The first area involves the degree to which the director or other core administrators provide a clear technical focus or research mission governing the organization's activities. Many research institutes spring from the vision of a single individual, who is committed to a given area of inquiry. Often, such institutes have an accompanying social mission, such as improving early childhood education or reforming the penal system. People are attracted to the center by the vision and because the successful intellectual leader can build a constituency in funding agencies and among research colleagues that enhances visibility. Sieber and Lazarsfeld (1964) and Sieber (1972) have called these founding fathers "entrepreneurial scholars." Although the zealous commitment to the organizational mission can dim as the years pass, organizations that are still led by the founder tend to retain a strong attachment to the particular problems that stimuated their creation. With appropriate selection of successors, a mission can even be transmitted over time.

Not all research settings have their origins in a research vision. Some successful institutes arise primarily for administrative reasons: Faculty wish to have better research facilities than they can obtain from their department, some researchers feel that they have skills that would allow a new firm to be both distinctive and fiscally viable, or the government wants to fund a center that can respond directly to its research needs. While there may be some constraints on the type of research done under the center's auspices, in general the organization supports whatever research is funded.

The second area involves the degree of administrative support committed to research management and allocation of organizational resources to back up that commitment. The research settings described by respondents varied. In some, the only form of identifiable support was an inaccurate monthly printout of expenditures. In others, support was provided for all managerial functions. In some cases, corporate support is a function of available money.

Some independent centers choose to keep their overhead low in order to improve their competitive position for research grants. This decision limits the funds available to support administrative services. In other university settings, the larger organization retains all or most of the overhead on grants and contracts and returns few services that are tailored to the needs of a research setting. However, in the preponderance of reported cases, the availability of administrative support systems was in large measure the result of organizational choice. For example, in one university center, several full-time administrative staff were supported with university funds, but their efforts were devoted primarily to external and internal liaison, not to providing assistance to faculty whose grants were funded through the center. In another independent agency, the assumption was that the director and associate director could provide all the necessary administrative support, despite the fact that the agency's size and complexity had increased enormously since its founding. Indeed, the culture of the agency favored the development of individualistic adaptations to management needs and the performance of all administrative functions on overtime. These examples can be contrasted with institutes or agencies of equal or smaller size that provided some clear structural support for all administrative components of the tasks mentioned previously.

Figure 1 presents the typology of centers that emerges when the two leadership dimensions — technical focus and administrative support — are trichotomized as high, medium, and low and cross-tabulated. In the remainder of this chapter, the organizations on the diagonals — the Grand Master Center, the Visionary Band, the Research Shop, the Empty Shell, and the Facilitative Center — will be discussed, and their positive and negative implications for project management will be highlighted.

The Grand Master

The main characteristic of the Grand Master Center is strong central leadership both in technical and in administrative matters (Sieber, 1972). Project directors had less autonomy in this type of organization than in most other types, both in choice of topics to investigate (topics had to be consistent with the vision of the technical leader) and in other technical areas, such as choice of staff (staff were typically selected by the director or by a senior staff member whose views were consistent with the director's). Few senior staff had much knowledge of the administrative aspects of the center: Resources for writing proposals and completing their work were always made available, but

Figure 1. Management-Based Typology of Center Corporate Support

Technical Focus	Administrative Support		
	High	*Medium*	*Low*
High	Grand Master		Visionary Band
Medium		Facilitative	
Low	Research Shop		Empty Shell

neither accountability nor control was vested primarily in the project director. For the Grand Master Centers in university settings, research activities were highly integrated with training of advanced graduate students, who typically were among the best and the brightest in the relevant department and who had been drawn by the organization's visibility, research experience, and professionalism.

All Grand Master Centers were described as highly charged environments, where staff members had enormous commitment to the center's mission and worked very hard. Typically, it was expected that most staff would be junior faculty members or research associates, who would "make their bones" in the center but not necessarily remain there for their entire career.

For the project director, the Grand Master Center has several advantages. The project director enjoys almost complete buffering from administrative roadblocks and red tape, a relatively secure position (although all centers operated at least partly on soft money, in no case did project directors seem to feel that making ends meet was a problem; negotiating funds was typically the responsibility of the director), and a highly stimulating, sharing environment that provided great social support for the completion of research projects and rapid publication. One respondent described his experiences in a Grand Master Center as what every young researcher ideally hopes for in a collegial research setting.

Other aspects of the Grand Master setting have potentially negative consequences for research management. One individual who spent most of his career in such a setting indicated that he had come to view intellectual stimulation and constant sharing as exchange among true believers. The pervasive influence of the director make the homogeneity of staff a constraint on the development of real breakthroughs. Intellectual homogeneity can be increased by social homogeneity, since Grand Master settings can be less comfortable for minorities and women. Thus, over the years, the research from such settings may decrease both in utility and in technical quality. In addition, senior staff who remain for a long time can come to chafe at their inability to gain administrative and fund-raising responsibilities, since these represent marketable skills in the general research environment. The Grand Master Center is also sensitive to fluctuations in relationships between the director and major funding agencies. Since only one individual moderates the relationship with the funding agency and since that individual represents a particular perspective, the relationship can become catastrophically unstable.

The Visionary Band

In this type of organization, the charisma of the founder permeates the organization and helps to set the research agenda, but the day-to-day operations depend largely on the efforts of project directors. Administrative structures barely exist, and those who staff them are often inexperienced, since administration per se tends to be devalued by the leader. As one informant put it, "The management information systems were very primitive. All the necessary information was in the head of the project director. There was a sense that, if we were doing our job as we should—for example, with the appropriate commitment and concern for quality—it would all work out in the end."

To work as a project director in a Visionary Band has its rewards and its drawbacks, depending on what the director most values in the work setting. Respondents who worked in this context mentioned the same organizational characteristics: the absence of bureaucratic procedures, which permitted project directors to operate with great flexibility; strong commitment by staff to the work and the content, which meant that extra effort could always be relied on to complete a given task; and the very high quality of junior staff, who often were drawn to the organization by the charisma of its leader. To summarize the positive qualities of the Visionary Band, it combines the cohesiveness that characterizes the Grand Master Center with an openness and autonomy in carrying out activities that is particularly appealing to young project directors.

The drawbacks of the Visionary Band have to do with poor resource management procedures, which often involve shifting staff around on short notice to complete reports, data collection activities, or new proposals. Respondents indicated that they often felt that they had little control over the time of staff who were supposed to be working on their project. Overwork was another major issue. One respondent said, "The director knew that we would always come through in producing a good report or paper, and that meant that no one ever had to worry about whether the resources were really adequate. Too much came out of our hides." Another, who had relatively little experience with fiscal management, pointed out that only "reactive assistance" (that is, when there was a clear financial problem) was available from the minimal accounting staff. Most of the substantial overtime went to fulfill the vision of the leader, and some projects benefited more from staff cohesiveness than others. Project directors whose project had low priority could feel frustrated and unsupported. Finally, technical quality support was minimal, not because it was devalued, but because projects always ran short of funds, and the entire organization depended on large amounts of overtime simply to complete required work. One respondent suggested that Visionary Bands function well only when staff are young. More skillful, experienced project directors might be unwilling to join the cycle of overtime and commitment to the director's vision.

The Research Shop

Whatever its actual legal foundation, the Research Shop is based on the assumption that the organization's main purpose is to provide good support for the effective completion of whatever research project can be funded. There is no technical vision, although there is frequently an organizationwide emphasis on technical skills. The funding agency does not buy an organizational perspective when it works with a Research Shop nor does it necessarily find a commitment to the furthering of scientific or social goals, as opposed to production of immediately applicable knowledge. The organization allocates serious attention and resources to ensure that a project director can get the project's work done with a minimum of interference. The support begins at the proposal-writing stage, where specialists are available to ensure that the proposed budget and staff are actually matched to the proposed activities. It includes flexible hiring and consulting procedures, which facilitate putting together a staff to do the work. It provides extensive technical support, ranging from budget-monitoring activities to twenty-four hour typing services. Often, it emphasizes organizational responsibility for the quality of documents produced under its auspices. Thus, the Research Shop aims at the Holiday Inn model for research: There should be no excuses (and no surprises) inside or outside the center.

For the project director, the Research Shop offers several advantages. First, despite the view that such organizations are project-based, not staff-based, most Research Shops prefer stringent conservation of personnel resources that sometimes approaches what academic circles know as administrative tenure. This statement must be tentative, given current funding policies. Louis (1982) discusses some career advantages and disadvantages. In any case, for a reasonably well-established project director, the Research Shop can provide a relatively secure career position. Second, the Research Shop provides resources for obtaining funding, including formal proposal budgets, and accounting support. Third, planfulness can reduce the unexpected overcommitments that are often found in less management-oriented agencies, including unanticipated budget crises in the organization as a whole or in particular projects. One informant who went to a Research Shop from a more traditional academic center said that the management information system was of great value: "I would give it five stars. For the first time, I felt protected by a center against budget problems. I really could trust the budget printouts that I got." The cosmopolitan orientation has beneficial impacts of staff recruitment and retention and on the technical quality of the work, which often is subject to external as well as to internal reviews as a matter of procedure (Pelz and Andrews, 1976). Finally, the Research Shop typically views one of its roles as creating a buffer between the project director and the funding agency, if and when friction arises. Often, such buffering is carried out in the name of contract compliance, but the allocation of a senior administrator's time to negotiation of expectations or resolution of disagreements was reported by several people as a positive feature.

The Research Shop also presents some managerial disadvantages for the project director. First, the Research Shop's management system not only supports but makes demands. One respondent indicated that as much as twenty-five percent of a project director's time can have to be spent meeting the center's internal management requirements. The same individual indicated that it would be easy to spend even more time than that but that she was buffered from greater intrusions by her immediate supervisor. As a consequence, the individual project director typically experiences some tension between organization-based management tasks and technical or research management tasks. Second, although the Research Shop can be cosmopolitan in its intellectual orientations, promotions to top management positions depend more often on management skills than on technical qualifications and publications. Thus, the incentive system can inhibit motivation to produce the very best research. Third, technical quality control mechanisms within the corporation often stress what is acceptable to the funding agency, not to the research audience. While most Research Shops encourage publications and support technical quality, they rarely back up their verbal support with adequate resources, and professional writing typically takes place at nights and on weekends. Finally, one respondent indicated that obtaining new work often receives more emphasis than carrying out existing projects. Because the Research Shop is prepared to support any funded project, the pressure to write many proposals is more than subtle. Such activity can drain the best talent from project staff. The pressure to write proposals can also result in projects that are not technically or substantively interesting to any staff member. A favorite in-house joke in one Research Shop is this: "The good news is that our proposal was funded. The bad news is that we now have to do it."

The Empty Shell

On the face of it, the Empty Shell is an improbable institution—one that provides neither technical nor management support. However, a surprising number of both university and nonuniversity-based research centers qualify as Empty Shells. The major characteristic of the Empty Shell is that it is exclusively project-based: It provides office space for projects that have funding, but it does not have a corps of professional staff who commit a fixed percentage of their time to the center. When funds for a project are exhausted, project staff leave, unless they obtain additional funding. The Empty Shell provides some expense accounting, but other support services are minimal.

The Empty Shell is not typically a place where one has a career or even a permanent job. Thus, the Empty Shell cannot rely on staff commitment. Instead, it has to use a variety of extrinsic incentives to ensure that project funds are sufficient to keep it alive. These incentives include proximity to a major university (which encourages faculty members to take grants through the center to augment their salaries), facilitation of projects that involve individuals from two or more institutions, and a prestigious name that attracts potential project directors. One individual who reported on an experience with an Empty Shell indicated that he, like most people, joined the agency because he had a half-written proposal, and no other appropriate setting in close proximity to his residence would provide him with office space.

The Empty Shell serves some important functions within a university setting, for it provides space for research assistants and accounting help that is not available through individual departments. Where the research involves faculty members from two or more departments, the value of an Empty Shell can be considerable. Outside the university, it provides a setting that is particularly useful for well-established project directors who value autonomy over all other job characteristics. Working through an Empty Shell can be preferable to working as an independent consultant or single-person corporation, because even limited organizational support reduces the administrative headaches that one encounters on one's own, while the minimal collegial and organizational demands do not constrain the individual entrepreneur. As one satisfied occupant of an Empty Shell commented, "This is a place for grown-ups."

The disadvantages of the Empty Shell can be severe. First, the organization provides little or no support for proposal writing, and its resources become active only when funding is actually available. Thus, it is difficult to recruit and retain high-quality staff. Graduate students may come to supplement a stipend or to make ends meet, but they often leave as soon as they are able. Because staff turnover at middle and junior levels is high, it can be difficult to maintain programs of research or coordinated capabilities for investigating particular topics. Collegial interaction is usually low, since most researchers are not associated with the center for long periods of time. Since the center has few formal mechanisms for ensuring the quality of research, projects are typically no better than the individual who serves as principal investigator.

It can be hypothesized that the claim that universities provide poor settings for evaluation research is based on the performance of academic Empty Shell centers, which by definition have few mechanisms to motivate principal investigators to complete their projects on time, on budget, or even on the topic specified by the funding agency, since their salary is covered by their department. However, given the inexperience of many academic principal investigators with management of policy and evaluation research, it is not surprising that some should fail if there is no support structure.

The Facilitative Center

A relatively large proportion of my respondents viewed at least one of the agencies for which they had worked as a Facilitative Center, meaning that it provided moderate technical leadership and moderate organizational support for management tasks. Of the five agencies that respondents perceived as Facilitative Centers, two were independent agencies (one for-profit, one not-for-profit), and three were university-based centers. The key to being classified as facilitative seemed to be a matter of balance. As one individual put it, "The center seems to exist primarily to ensure that the staff can get their work done well, in the way that they want to do it." Another characterized his agency as one that provided "respect, autonomy, and support for principal investigators."

All Facilitative Centers had a permanent staff (hiring was not done on a project basis except for the most junior employees) and a mission that encompassed many social scientific interests but clearly emphasized some substantive or technical areas over others. Each Facilitative Center also had a director or management team that viewed the organization's development and the staff's careers as clearly connected. Another key characteristic of Facilitative Centers was their relative financial autonomy and stability. In universities, such centers tend either to keep at least part of their own overhead or to have generous university funding, while centers outside universities tend to have a relatively stable fiscal situation for one reason or another. As one respondent put it, "Our big grant allowed us a cushion. We never had to worry about letting a good person go when a particular project was finished, because there was always work to do on it."

People in Facilitative Centers described several positive features. First, the leadership encouraged them to believe, as one respondent put it, that "we were going to be able to do what we wanted to do. There was opportunity." Second, there was little or no pressure to become involved in projects that were not congruent with staff interests or that were technically unsound. One academic remarked, "The director occasionally tried to get us involved in state projects that were not very interesting, but there was never any real pressure." Another individual at a private nonprofit center said, "At first, some people hoped that my research would serve some of the other departments. But, that was ironed out quickly. Now, they pretty much leave me alone." Third, Facilitative Centers were described as attractive to very high-quality staff. Facilitative Centers worked well because they were able to retain people who could get funding for high-quality projects. One individual commented that, even when his organization was shrinking in some departments, he always felt that his superior would fight for his right to recruit and retain only the best staff. As a consequence, this respondent reported, his project expanded, while the rest of the agency became smaller. Fourth, autonomy is complemented by administrative support. An academically based respondent indicated that his center had a staff person who spent a great deal of time in Washington ensuring that funding agencies were aware of the center and that the center was aware of funding opportunities. Another respondent, the director of the center, said, "The first thing I did when I started the center was to hire a full-time business person. Our center is a valuable resource to a researcher, because we can act as a buffer between a bureaucracy and individual researchers."

The quality control procedures in Facilitative Centers are typically collegial rather than formal. Sharing and peer review are most often the norm, but like the Research Shop or the Empty Shell, the Facilitative Center encourages a cosmopolitan external review process and development of cross-institutional collaborative arrangements. Nevertheless, most directors of Facilitative Centers appear to act as if the organization had an interest in monitoring the research.

Are there debits to the Facilitative Center? Respondents perceived tensions in balancing the two types of leadership. One respondent indicated that the director of his center occasionally tried to convert the organization into a

Visionary Band, recruiting staff to his own research program and raiding budgets to support that work. Another said, "I've seen the downside of our stability, and it may be stagnation. The center has allowed us to build up a terrific research team, but where will the new ideas come from in five years?" A third respondent indicated that the Facilitative Center had become a Research Shop when its financial stability was shaken by decreases in research grants, while a fourth said, "There's always a tension between serving the research concerns that have no strong interest and getting service projects that will keep our field staff busy."

Conclusions

The preceding discussion suggests that the technical and managerial leadership provided by the top administrators of a research center have a significant impact on the resources available to project directors to carry out middle management tasks. This suggestion was illustrated by descriptions of five common types of centers revealed by interviews with full-time researchers who had experience in multiple settings. The discussion is summarized in Figure 2.

Both the typology and the discussion are tentative, since the data base is quite small. Other factors not discussed here, such as the age of the organization and whether it conducts only social science research or other activities as well, also affect the project director's role as middle manager. In addition, it should be emphasized that individual departments in the large center can operate quite independently, which makes it difficult to characterize the organization as a whole. Organizations also evolve over time. A center that was a Visionary Band at one point in its history can become an Empty Shell in tight times. Despite these problems, however, several tentative conclusions can be offered.

Researchers in Facilitative Centers tend to be most satisfied with their ability to carry out middle management tasks as project directors and to further their own professional careers as evaluators and policy researchers. However, other settings can be more useful for certain individuals and certain projects. For example, a project director may be in a better position to obtain the concerted energies of colleagues in a Visionary Band, at least when the project is central to the organization's mission. Cohesive support can be critical for the younger project director or for a project that involves some difficult intellectual or technical issues. Similarly, a politically sensitive evaluation study can best be performed in a Research Shop that provides high levels of cosmopolitanism and mechanisms that buffer project directors from funding agencies.

The project director's own management strengths and weaknesses can affect his or her ability to function in a given setting. Directors who have well-developed abilities to manage timelines and budgets can find that their own

Figure 2. Corporate Support for Middle Management Research Tasks

Organizational Types	Getting Resources	Recruiting and Retaining Staff	Managing Resources	Maintaining Technical Quality	Maintaining Relations with Funding Agency
Grand Master	very strong support, director obtains	strong support, little diversity, limited career paths	strong support	strong support, with major emphasis on quality control	variable support, most external liaison provided by the director
Visionary Band	very strong support, director obtains	support, but staff burnout causes turnover and staff energies are diffused	little or no support	support in theory, but limited by poor resource management	variable support, most external liaison provided by the director
Research Shop	strong support in time, money, and ancillary services, but too much emphasis on proposal writing	considerable support, but best staff diverted to management	very strong support	procedures exist, but emphasis on technical quality is moderated by utility and acceptability to client	very strong support, including specialized roles for negotiation with funding agencies
Empty Shell	no support	no support	limited support	peer pressure, but no procedures or norms	no support
Facilitative Center	support in time and limited ancillary services	very strong emphasis, both at project director and lower levels	modest support	emphasis on both internal and external review	some support, generally the responsibility of the project director alone

methods conflict with the management controls offered by the Research Shop. Directors who are less well established may function most effectively in a Visionary Band or Grand Master Center, since their energies will not be distracted by the effort to obtain research monies. The director who prefers the traditional professor-with-graduate-students model will work better in an Empty Shell than the director who flourishes in a collaborative research team.

Thus, the project director should consider his or her own professional strengths and weaknesses when choosing a research setting. Once that choice has been made, the research director should attempt, insofar as possible, to plan projects to compensate for research needs that cannot be filled in that setting. In addition, the design of management structures for evaluation and policy research projects must take into account what is feasible or practical in the given setting. On the whole, if the gaps between what is needed and what is available are large, it can be easier to move to another organizational setting to conduct one's research than it is to restructure one's current setting in any radical way.

Finally, there are some implications for funding agencies. When proposals are being reviewed, current practice tends to emphasize the professional qualifications of the principal investigator and the center's track record on research in the particular topic area. However, if the different kinds of center do create distinctive environments for management, then funding agencies should attend to the match between the research process and product that they desire and to the agency's ability to support that match.

References

Bernstein, I., and Freeman, H. *Academic and Entrepreneurial Research.* New York: Russell Sage Founation, 1975.

Campbell, J., Dunnette, M. D., Lawler, E. E., and Weick, K. E. *Managerial Behavior, Performance, and Effectiveness.* New York: McGraw-Hill, 1970.

Coleman, J. *Methods of Policy Research.* Morristown, N.J.: General Learning Press, 1972.

Kahn, R., Wolfe, D., Quinne, R., and Snoek, J. *Organizational Stress: Studies in Role Conflict and Ambiguity.* New York: Wiley, 1964.

Louis, K. S. "Social Policy and Evaluation Research: Sick Giant or Healthy Baby?" In R. G. Corwin (Ed.), *Research in Sociology of Education and Socialization.* Vol. 3. Greenwich, Conn.: JAI Press, 1982.

Pelz, D., and Andrews, F. *Scientists in Organizations* (Rev. Ed.) Ann Arbor: Institute for Social Research, 1976.

Pfiffner, J., and Sherwood, F. *Administrative Organization.* Englewood Cliffs, N.J.: Prentice Hall, 1960.

Rossi, P. H., Wright, J. D., and Wright, S. R. "The Theory and Practice of Applied Social Research." *Evaluation Quarterly,* 1978, *2* (2), 171–191.

St. Pierre, R. "Management of Federally Funded Evaluation Research." *Evaluation Review,* 1982, *6* (1), 94–113.

Sieber, S. *Reforming the University: The Role of the Research Center.* New York: Praeger, 1972.

Sieber, S., and Lazarsfeld, P. *Organizing Educational Research.* New York: Prentice Hall, 1964.

Karen Seashore Louis is associate director and senior research fellow at the Center for Survey Research, a facility of the University of Massachusetts/Boston and the Joint Center for Urban Studies at Harvard and M.I.T. She has conducted policy and evaluation research since 1968.

Evaluation management requires a system for measuring, improving, and accounting for quality. The Institute for Program Evaluation in the U.S. General Accounting Office is developing such a system.

The Definition and Measurement of Evaluation Quality as a Management Tool

Eleanor Chelimsky

What do we mean by quality in program evaluation? How can we define and measure it so that we can see if it is improving? These are basic questions of evaluation management, which managers and staff at the U.S. General Accounting Office (GAO) and elsewhere raise continually, but which have yet to receive satisfactory answers, largely because there is no clear consensus on the subject and no adequate operational definition of what constitutes evaluation quality.

Evaluation management requires some sort of system for measuring, improving, and accounting for the quality of evaluations, and definition is at the heart of any such system. But definitions are not easy to make, both because quality is relative to the observer (what is quality in one place or for one person is not always quality in another place or for another person) and because it is relative to the conditions imposed on the work being examined.

Nonetheless, evaluation managers must develop a way of defining and measuring the quality of their products, both to maintain the excellence and usefulness of these products and to ensure that they continue to improve. Evaluation staff resist managerial edicts that a piece of work took too long or cost too much or was lacking in quality. They point out that such criticisms do little

R. G. St. Pierre (Ed.). *Management and Organization of Program Evaluation.* New Directions for Program Evaluation, no. 18. San Francisco: Jossey-Bass, June 1983.

either to identify what went wrong or to explain what should be done differently next time. Put another way, such criticisms do not generate objective measures that can describe current performance or ensure future progress.

In arriving at a definition of quality, then, it is important to understand and take into account the dynamic relations among the quality, the time spent, and the costs of a job. It is the nature of this relationship that allows us to develop both an overview of the evaluation process that can provide information to managers and staff about what is strong in their performance, what is weak, and what needs improvement and measures that can track changes in performance over time.

At the Institute for Program Evaluation (IPE) in the GAO, we have been working to develop a management system based on a definition of this type, not on a definition that treats quality as strictly a methodological issue. This is because we do our work for the Congress and because the factors of time and information conclusiveness (and hence costs) are crucial to our usefulness. In addition, we had three other purposes in setting up this management system: to give IPE staff and supervisors information on the criteria to be used in appraising their performance; to develop information about the definition, measurement, and assessment of quality that the rest of the GAO can use; and to ensure that the key phase of any evaluation, evaluation design — which so often is truncated or abridged in haste to move rapidly toward implementation — receives adequate emphasis.

Defining Evaluation Quality

To define evaluation quality, it is necessary to process several elements of information simultaneously. For example, the technical soundness of a report can be determined as a function of the time allocated for its performance, the costs required to produce it, and the adequacy of the approach, methodology, or procedure employed. Yet, the quality of an evaluation report is not exclusively a matter of technical soundness. Indeed, if the purpose of an evaluation is to inform policy — this is typically the case for evaluation performed by the IPE — then the evaluation needs not only to be technically sound but also to be useful, to have impact. Therefore, the definition of evaluation quality proposed here necessarily includes two components: technical adequacy and usefulness.

Technical Adequacy. The technical adequacy of an evaluation depends on the constraints placed on the work, including the type of information to be produced (that is, the kind of question posed), the available funds, and the date when results are needed. There is no such thing as absolute technical adequacy, and so, in order to draw proper conclusions about technical adequacy, one must take the constraints just stated into account. For example, not all questions are researchable. Some are so broad that they cannot be answered. Some involve assumptions that are difficult to test in the field. Some presume expertise that is beyond the state of the art. Yet, even the most rigorously planned and executed evaluation is inadequate if it addresses the wrong question — a question that is not the question posed. Similarly, a technically sound evaluation that comes two years late and that costs more than its topic justifies indicates that the design chosen was more ambitious than necessary.

The point is that technical adequacy, like evaluation quality, is relative, and so the definition of technical adequacy requires a balance among various elements. The first factor to be considered in defining technical adequacy is the appropriateness of the evaluation design for answering the question posed within its time and cost parameters. The design process refines and operationalizes the evaluation question and resolves the problem of meeting an information need within time and cost constraints at the very start of the evaluation. Managers should measure technical adequacy at the end of the design phase, examining such issues as these: Was the evaluation question well defined? Was it researchable, or did it need modification? Was the evaluation question renegotiated with the sponsor? Is the design as it now stands powerful enough to answer the evaluation question posed? Is it too powerful? Does it call for collection of massive amounts of data that are not really needed to answer the question? Does it involve unnecessarily elaborate procedures, which may be elegant but which will increase the cost and take too long? It is feasible to perform?

Managers who review these issues with staff at the end of the design phase build considerations of quality, time, cost, and feasibility into the job very early and set up a baseline of expectations with which the finished evaluation can be compared.

The definition of technical adequacy does not stop with preparing the evaluation design, however. A second factor is also involved: the appropriateness of the evaluation's execution to the design selected and the resources available. In assessing the implementation of an evaluation, the manager addresses such issues as these: How well did the design work? Did staff have problems applying it in the field? If so, how were these problems resolved? Did the site or case selection process make sense in terms of the evaluation question asked and the resources available? How conclusive is the evidence obtained relative to what was expected (based on the design) and what was needed (based on the question)? Were the data that were collected the data that were required by the design? Was the instrumentation formatted with forethought regarding the analyses to be performed? Were appropriate statistical tests applied? Do the conclusions and recommendations flow from the design and from the work performed?

In reviewing technical adequacy, it is important to remember the number of viable options and correct approaches that can be employed with respect both to design and to execution. There is no perfect strategy; many strategies are possible for almost every question. However, it also is true that every option implies a trade-off with another option. Getting something means giving up something else. This is the main reason for considering the advantages and disadvantages of various design and execution strategies in the job's initiation phase and for returning to them during the course of execution, if need be.

Although both of these factors are defined as relative, managers and staff can use them to reach fairly precise judgments about technical adequacy. In the case of design appropriateness, each design option is compared with others to determine time to completion (especially if the customer needs results fast), cost (when two designs can answer the question in roughly the same length of time), likely feasibility (data availability, for example), and information conclusiveness (the relative power of each design). In the case of execution appropriateness, performance is compared, first, with expectations at the end of the design phase about time, cost, and evidence obtained and, second, with other evaluations that involve similar problems of execution.

The final factor in defining technical adequacy is the absence of major conceptual errors, inappropriate technical procedures, and improper conclusions or inferences. Although there are many correct approaches to evaluation design and execution, there also exist some patently incorrect approaches that can degrade evaluation quality. Therefore, in addition to monitoring the appropriateness of the evaluation's design and execution, managers need to be alert to some general problems that can crop up during the design, conduct, or reporting of an evaluation. Did staff generalize from a case study? Did they use inappropriate statistical procedures? Did they fail to note that there was a sizable number of nonrespondents to a questionnaire? Did they unintentionally duplicate another study or miss an important issue because an adequate literature review was not performed? Did they attribute observed changes to a program without ruling out other possible causes? Did they make conclusions and recommendations not warranted by the power of the design or the work performed? Did they omit returning to modify the evaluation design (or, if necessary, the evaluation question) when serious problems arose in the course of execution? Any of these problems—and there are many others—can sharply erode technical adequacy and influence evaluation quality.

In summary, the three factors of technical adequacy assume that, if an evaluation features a design appropriate for answering the question posed within the time period and funding allocated; if that design is executed rationally and defensibly; if it obtains the evidence needed or expected; and if no major errors are made in design, performance, or reporting; then it can reasonably be argued that the basic requirements of technical adequacy have been fulfilled.

Usefulness. Usefulness is the second component of evaluation quality. It, too, is a relative concept, since usefulness can exist only with respect to a user and a use. Four factors of usefulness to the congressional customer have been distinguished by the GAO (Staats, 1981): relevance, timeliness, presentation, and impact. While other aspects of usefulness certainly exist, some— such as lucky circumstances, which unexpectedly can make a report very timely—are not controllable by managers or staff; hence, they lie outside the scope of this discussion.

The relevance of evaluation findings to an information need is a critical contributor to usefulness. The findings that are used generally address the questions that policy makers want answered for a specific purpose. Relevance is defined here as a close logical relationship with and importance to a matter under consideration. The timeliness of evaluation findings is equally crucial to usefulness. A relevant report can have no use at all if it is delivered too late. Timeliness is defined here as delivery of pertinent findings at a date that makes them most likely to be of help to the user. The presentation of a report is important, because results must be communicated in a form that the user finds comprehensible and congenial. If presentation is faulty, even relevant and timely reports may not find their audiences. Presentation quality is defined here as the organization of material—according to the conventions of logic, clarity, balance, and good writing—that is most appropriate to the user's needs.

These three factors of usefulness can be controlled by staff, but they can be assessed only by the user. Therefore, it is important for managers to ensure that staff, during the negotiation phase of the evaluation, build in a clear agreement with the sponsor not only about the precise nature of the question posed and the level of confidence required in the answer, the relevance of that question to the user's needs, the date by which the information must be available, and the presentation aspects of information delivery but also the manner in which the information is to be used. Post hoc tracking of evaluation use typically yields only limited information if expectations for use have not been discussed so that relevant measures can be planned and developed. This is especially true when the kind of use involved has been intangible (for example, to develop a concept, to persuade others, to negotiate a policy); that is, when the use is not clearly reflected in the end result.

Relevance, timeliness, and presentation are relative concepts, defined by their appropriateness to the user's needs. All three can enhance the likelihood that evaluation findings will be used. Therefore, the manager needs to ensure at the design stage that all three have been built into the evaluation's performance and at the end of the execution stage that the user has reviewed and assessed the evaluation's usefulness in terms of timeliness, relevance, and presentation.

The impact of the evaluation report is the fourth factor of usefulness. Impact is complementary to the first three factors in that it refers to actual, validated use. At the GAO, impact is defined in terms of accomplishments; that is, in terms of the demonstrable use or influence of a report's findings and recommendations in or on legislation, agency decision making, administration, or management (for example, savings achieved as a result of the report). Impact, then, is evidence of actual use. The notion of impact strengthens the definition of usefulness in that it provides at least one indicator independent of the user's opinion that evaluation findings have in fact been used.

The third factor of the definition of technical adequacy discussed earlier in this section—the absence of major conceptual errors, inappropriate technical procedures, and improper conclusions or inferences—has the same function for the technical adequacy component of evaluation quality as impact does for usefulness: It serves as a nonrelative indicator of technical adequacy. Such indicators are needed in our overall definition to ensure that we will find the "smoking gun"—in this case, a serious technical failure despite appropriate design and execution or nonuse despite glowing customer satisfaction.

Measuring Evaluation Quality

Evaluation quality has been defined as having two components, technical adequacy and usefulness. Each component itself has several factors that must be measured. A first effort at measurement—still under development at the IPE—is shown in Table 1.

Some of the measures for technical adequacy in the design phase must of necessity be approximate, since they are planning estimates. For example, the cost of implementing an evaluation design can only be roughly projected; therefore, the measure invoked in Table 1 is one of the difference in cost between one design and another (for example, a short case study and an outcome evaluation or survey). Feasibility and time to completion must also often be guessed at. However, the adequacy of the design for answering the question posed can typically be ascertained, as can agreement on user needs.

With regard to technical adequacy of execution, the first measure—adequacy in terms of design—seeks to establish the degree of match or mismatch between the front-end planning phase and conditions in the field. It can be determined by managers and staff by comparing what the design anticipated with what was achieved. The second measure—adequacy in terms of execution—speaks to the way in which mismatch problems were resolved. Here, feedback from field staff to evaluation managers provides the necessary information. The third measure—adequacy in terms of costs and milestones—involves two comparisons: of final cost and time to completion with projected cost and milestones, and of cost and time to completion with cost and time to completion in other evaluations that used a similar design. This allows managers to pinpoint the reasons for delay, the locus or loci of delay, and the elements of unexpected cost increases for each evaluation. Once these problems have been identified across a number of evaluations, progress can be tracked over time. The fourth and fifth measures—adequacy of monitoring and adequacy of tracking—address goals of early warning. The sooner that problems with evaluation performance or with customer satisfaction are discovered, the more likely it becomes that they can be resolved. Thus, these measures compare the dates at which problems appeared with the dates when they were identified, either through performance monitoring or through tracking of use.

Measures for the third factor of technical adequacy — absence of conceptual errors, inappropriate procedures, and improper conclusions of inferences — are not included here. Knowledge in this area is widespread, and the list of measures is long. For example, using correlational analysis to make conclusions about cause-and-effect relationships or overlooking the importance of a defined universe reduce the technical credibility of any report. Such errors should draw the attention of evaluation managers to needed training for staff.

The measures of usefulness factors depicted in Table 1 all seek to reinforce the performance of specific up-front negotiations with the customer and formal tracking of customer satisfaction and use. Feedback from the user to the evaluation manager provides the critical information.

Discussion

The effort to define and measure evaluation quality depicted in Table 1 is a first attempt to deal with a difficult management problem. As they undergo testing and development in the IPE, the various concepts included in Table 1 will be amended, revised, refined, and improved. But the overall approach affords several advantages.

First, it moves managers out of the realm of static, ad hoc criteria informally applied. The approach is both formal and dynamic. It tries to ensure that all elements directly affecting the development and measurement of evaluation quality are included and documented and that their interrelations are accounted for. Other elements can be added to this framework, and the individual evaluation manager can accommodate his or her views of what is most important by giving each element a different weight.

Second, this approach allows the manager to find multiple measures of progress in evaluation quality over time. For technical adequacy, this is accomplished by incorporating into the assessment not only the soundness of the design from the methodological viewpoint but also the question posed, the design's feasibility, and the time and funds available. For usefulness, it is accomplished by incorporating into the assessment a consideration of user need, user satisfaction, and use itself.

Third, this approach can help to control resources and improve productivity by pointing up the requirement for technical design review by managers early enough to ensure that the design can be effective in terms both of cost and of the time required for performance. Evaluation quality can never be equated with time and high cost. Rather, quality is achieved when a design is the best possible one, given the time and funding available. This is a matter of common sense: It is no more true that a long, costly effort generates high quality than it is true that low-cost, rapid efforts must necessarily result in poor quality. Thus, the approach promotes attention to resource expenditures by making them a function of evaluation quality.

Table 1. Definition of Evaluation Quality: Seven Factors and Their Measurement

Technical Adequacy		Usefulness	
Factors	*Measures*	*Factors*	*Measures*
Appropriateness of design to evaluation question, cost, and time	• Adequacy of selected design for answering the question posed • Feasibility of implementing the design in required time frame • Minimization of costs with respect to the question posed • Specification of agreement with user on what the question is, how the report will be used, when it is needed, and how use will be measured	Relevance to user information needs	• Prior agreement of user with regard to questions that report will address • Prior awareness by user of report limitations (conclusiveness, and so forth) • User satisfaction after report delivery
Appropriateness of execution to question, design, cost, and time	• Adequacy of execution in terms of the design requirements • Appropriateness of design revisions to conditions in the field • Adequacy of execution in terms of projected costs and milestones • Adequacy of monitoring and reporting on design, time, and cost problems • Adequacy of tracking of customer satisfaction and impact	Timeliness	• Prior agreement with user • Information delivery by due date • User satisfaction after report delivery
		Presentation	• Adequacy of logic, organization, and writing • User satisfaction after report delivery
Absence of major technical errors in design, execution, and reporting	• Adequacy with respect to technical and methodological soundness • Adequacy with respect to the accuracy of what is reported	Impact	• Prior agreement with user on how the report will be used and how use will be measured • Evidence of policy use • Increased productivity • Improved management • Achieved savings

Finally, by separating technical adequacy from usefulness, the approach avoids confounding the two, which can impede the effort to improve either one. Technical adequacy alone does not ensure usefulness. Many excellent studies have gathered dust on policy makers' shelves. In the same way, usefulness cannot speak to the question of technical adequacy. Many useful evaluations have been technically mediocre. Put another way, customer satisfaction is an excellent way of measuring usefulness but not technical adequacy, and methodological review is an excellent way of measuring technical adequacy but not usefulness. Care was taken in developing this approach to allow separate assessment of technical adequacy and usefulness; to link the two components, since both are essential in determining evaluation quality; and to lay the foundation for developing a better understanding of the relationships between them (for example, by including the specification measures of use in the managerial review of technical adequacy).

The preceding discussion of evaluation quality takes the position that it is reasonable to define evaluation quality as composed of two components, technical adequacy and usefulness. Three factors figure critically in the manager's review of technical adequacy: the appropriateness of the evaluation design to the question to be answered and to the time and the resources allocated for answering it; the appropriateness of the evaluation's execution to the design selected and to the time and costs required; and the absence of conceptual errors, inappropriate technical procedures, and improper conclusions or inferences from evaluation design, execution, and reporting. Four factors figure critically in the manager's review of usefulness: relevance, timeliness, presentation with respect to user need, and impact or evidence of actual use. Finally, progress in improving evaluation quality can be monitored by using this definition, these factors, and the resulting measures in evaluation management.

The definition considers design to be the dominant factor not only in improving evaluation quality but also in controlling costs, in minimizing the time required for performance, and in tracking the use made of reports. Such use of design could expand the repertoire of methodologies employed in evaluations. In the same way, the manner in which the usefulness component considers relevance, timeliness, and presentation could lead to changes over time in the ways in which findings are organized or presented.

Improving Evaluation Quality over Time

Evaluation staff need to know whether their efforts to improve performance have resulted in something measurably better. Evaluation managers also need to be able to track results so as to account for the productive use of resources allocated to evaluation. Therefore, one major use of the definitions and measures discussed in this chapter is to enable evaluators and managers to look back some years hence and trace the progress that they have made. At the

Institute for Program Evaluation, our development of a system to track such progress uses indicators derived from these definition, factors, and measures.

Some indicators for tracking change will be obvious by now. Review measures for individual evaluations have already been presented. With regard to measurement of collective change across a set of evaluations, there are many ways in which we expect to measure improvement. Five of these will be discussed here, using a ten-year comparison period: changes in the diversity of product types and methodologies; changes in the average cost and time periods required to perform jobs; changes in efficiency, as measured by product rejections; changes in response capacity, as measured by diversity of reporting formats and improvements in timeliness; and changes in the impact of products, as measured by support to primary users.

The expectation of improvement in evaluation quality is, of course, the basis for the positive changes described in the figures that follow. With regard to Figure 1, product diversity, it would be logical for a new emphasis on design appropriateness (relative to the question posed and to time and cost constraints) to produce an increase in product types and methods. Evaluations in the 1980s could be expected to make use of perhaps six methodologies, where evaluations in the 1970s used only one or two.

Figure 2 shows that increased effectiveness in terms of time and cost is reasonable to expect, because time and cost reductions should accompany diversification in methods. In many past evaluations, a long, slow, and very costly approach has often dominated. Increased diversity is likely to uncover faster, less labor-intensive methods. Further, increases in design efficiency should also reduce costs.

Figure 3 shows that the incidence of product rejection should decrease, because new product types and methods and increased relevance to user needs should improve customer satisfaction.

Figure 4 shows that increased sensitivity to presentation possibilities and to timeliness can also be expected to increase user satisfaction.

Finally, Figure 5 supposes that attention to all these factors should result both in greater credibility and in greater impact.

Summary

This chapter describes a definition of evaluation quality that involves two components, seven factors, twenty-four measures, and various tracking indicators to help evaluation managers account for their performance. The definition incorporates methodological soundness and attention to time lags and costs as well as to use and user needs. The measures assume a managerial review process both at the design phase and at job end that focuses on methodological soundness, cost, and time; feedback from field staff on design implementation; review of customer satisfaction with report relevance, timeliness,

Figure 1. Diversity of Product Types and Methodologies Employed

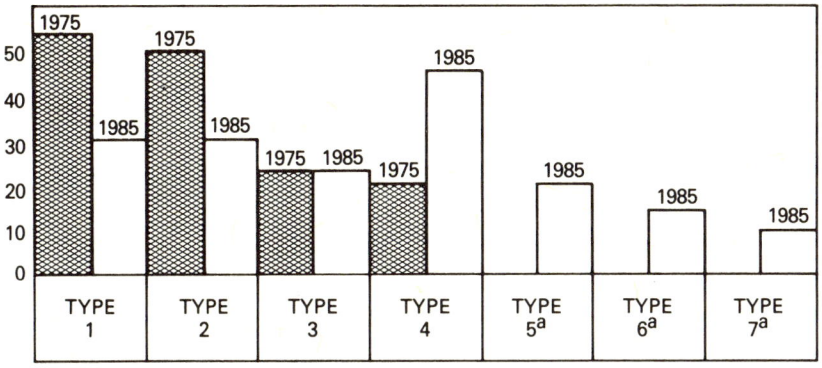

Diversity of Product Types

aNew product types developed and implemented in the 1980s.

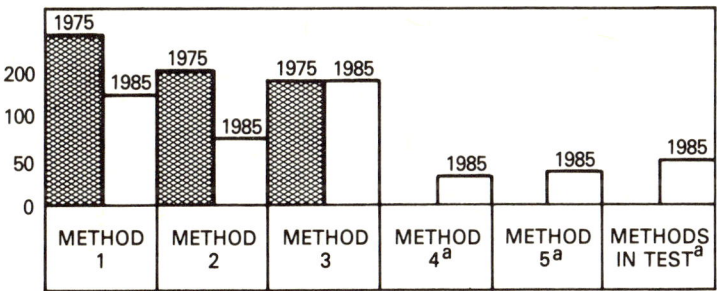

Diversity of Methodologies Employed

aMethods developed and implemented in the 1980s.

and presentation; and documentation and review of the use made of the evaluation.

Hypothetical tracking indicators were also described. These indicators take into account such elements as the information needed, the design, time to completion, cost, feasibility, absence of major errors, relevance, timeliness, presentation, and impact. The presumption is that careful managerial attention over time to all these elements should increase evaluation quality, lower costs, improve timeliness, increase the diversity of methods, increase customer satisfaction, and broaden impact.

The Institute for Program Evaluation will begin testing the system in the 1982 fiscal year. We expect that it will allow us both to track the soundness, efficiency, and usefulness of the evaluations that we perform and to measure changes in our effectiveness over time.

Figure 2. Average Cost of Jobs and Average Time for Delivering Jobs

Average Cost of Jobs

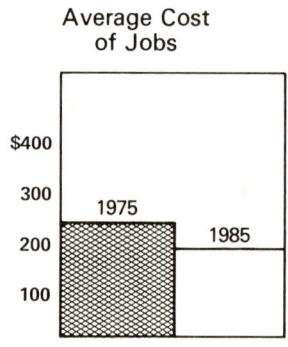

Average Time for Delivering Jobs

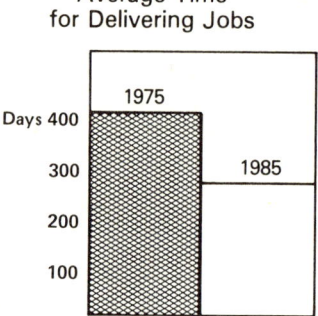

Figure 3. Improvements in Efficiency

Improvements in Efficiency as Measured by Product Rejections

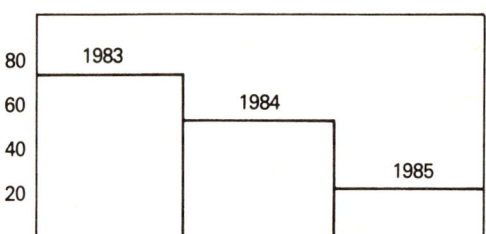

Figure 4. Response Capacity and Timeliness

Response Capacity as Measured by Different Types
of Reporting Formats

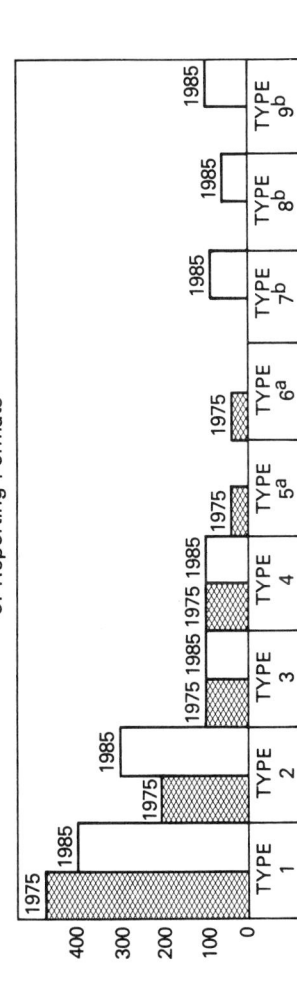

aDiscontinued formats.
bFormats developed and implemented in 1980.

Timeliness as Measured by the Frequency
of On-Time / Behind-Time Deliveries

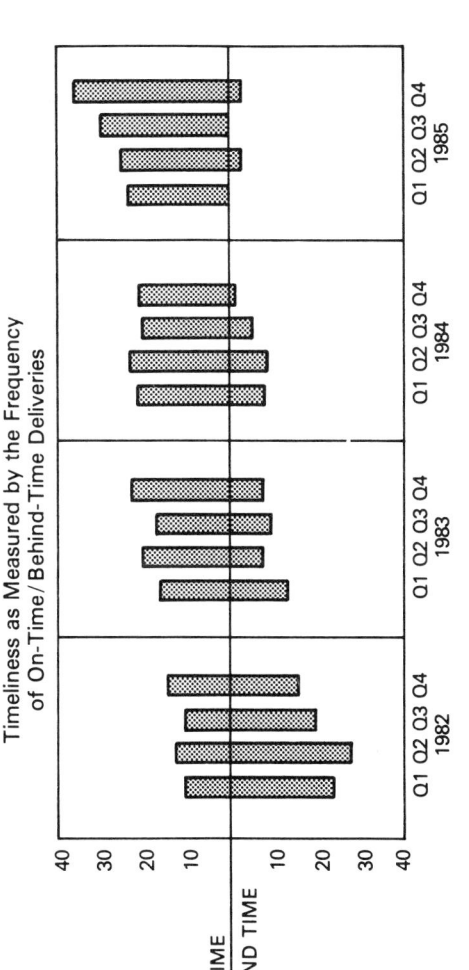

126

Figure 5. Evaluation Impact

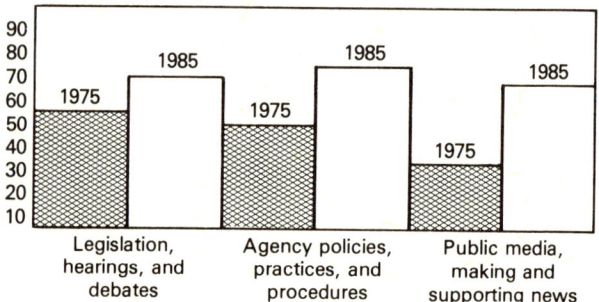

Impact of Evaluation Products as
Measured by Support to Primary Users

Percentage of all reports
that impact
on each category

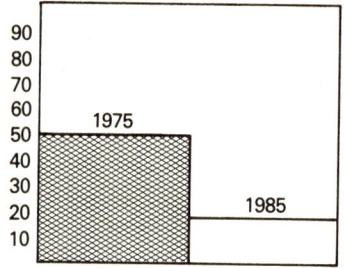

Reports Failing to Impact
on Measured Areas

Percentage of all reports

References

Staats, E. B. Remarks to the annual convention of the Evaluation Research Society, Austin, Texas, October 1981.

Eleanor Chelimsky is director of the Institute for
Program Evaluation in the U.S. General Accounting Office.

Index

127

EW DIRECTIONS
PAPERBACK
SOURCEBOOKS

ractical problem-solving
for busy professionals

eal educational and training
urces for seminars, work-
ps, and internships

SINGLE COPIES
$7.95 each

n payment accompanies or-
*Payment must accompany
e copy orders under $25.00.
ifornia, New Jersey, New
, and Washington, D.C.,
ents please include appro-
te sales tax.) For billed or-
, cost per copy is $7.95 plus
age and handling.

BULK PURCHASE
DISCOUNTS

bulk purchases (ten or more
es of a single sourcebook)
following rates apply:
0–49 copies $7.15 each
0–100 copies $6.35 each
ver 100 copies *inquire*
s tax and postage and han-
g charges apply as for single
y orders—see above. Return
ileges not extended for
cebooks purchased at bulk
r discount rates.

SUBSCRIPTIONS

00 per year for institutions,
ncies, and libraries.
00 per year for individuals
*n payment is by personal
ck*. (No institutional checks
accepted for the $21.00 sub-
ption.) Subscriptions begin
the first of the four quar-
y sourcebooks for the cur-
subscription year. Please
cify if you prefer your sub-
ption to start with the *com-*
year.

ORDER CARD

Please read ordering information in the left margin before filling out
this order form. Other sourcebooks in this series are listed at the
front of this book, along with additional details for ordering. *Prices
subject to change without notice.*

Name (or PO#) _____
(please print clearly)

Address _____

City _____

State _____ Zip _____

☐ Payment enclosed.   ☐ Bill me.

SINGLE COPY ORDERS. Enter sourcebooks by code (such as
HE#2 or CD#5) and title (first two words).
Example: HE#2, Strategies for . . .

_____

_____

_____

_____

☐ **FREE CATALOGUE** describing sourcebooks in all sixteen
New Directions series:

New Directions for Child Development
New Directions for College Learning Assistance*
New Directions for Community Colleges
New Directions for Continuing Education
New Directions for Education, Work, and Careers*
New Directions for Exceptional Children*
New Directions for Experiential Learning*
New Directions for Higher Education
New Directions for Institutional Advancement*
New Directions for Institutional Research
New Directions for Mental Health Services
New Directions for Methodology of Social and Behavioral Science*
New Directions for Program Evaluation
New Directions for Student Services
New Directions for Teaching and Learning
New Directions for Testing and Measurement

*Publication suspended for these series. However, individual sourcebooks
are still available.

SUBSCRIPTIONS. Enter series titles and year subscription is to
begin. Example: New Directions for Higher Education, 1983.

_____

_____

☐ Institutional, agency, and   ☐ Personal. Each series:
library. Each series: $35.00 $21.00 per year *(payable
per year.   only by personal check).*

JOSSEY-BASS INC., PUBLISHERS
433 California Street • San Francisco 94104

BUSINESS REPLY MAIL

FIRST CLASS   PERMIT NO. 16103   SAN FRANCISCO, CA

POSTAGE WILL BE PAID BY ADDRESSEE

**Jossey-Bass Inc., Publishers
433 California Street
San Francisco, CA 94104**

NEW DIRECTIONS
FOR PROGRAM
EVALUATION

Number 10 • 1981

NEW DIRECTIONS FOR PROGRAM EVALUATION

**A Publication of the
Evaluation Research Society**

A Quarterly Sourcebook
Scarvia B. Anderson, Editor-in-Chief

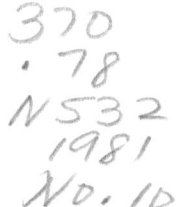
Number 10, 1981

Evaluation of
Complex Systems

Ronald J. Wooldridge
Editor

Jossey-Bass Inc., Publishers
San Francisco • Washington • London

EVALUATION OF COMPLEX SYSTEMS
New Directions for Program Evaluation
A Publication of the Evaluation Research Society
Number 10, 1981
     Ronald J. Wooldridge, Editor

New Directions for Program Evaluation (publication number
USPS 449-050) is published quarterly by Jossey-Bass Inc., Publishers.
Subscriptions are available at the regular rate for institutions,
libraries, and agencies of $30 for one year. Individuals may
subscribe at the special professional rate of $18 for one year.

Correspondence:
Subscriptions, single-issue orders, change of address notices,
undelivered copies, and other correspondence should be sent to
New Directions Subscriptions, Jossey-Bass Inc., Publishers,
433 California Street, San Francisco, California 94104.

Editorial correspondence should be sent to the Editor-in-Chief,
Scarvia B. Anderson, Educational Testing Service, 250 Piedmont
Avenue, Suite 2020, Atlanta, Georgia 30308.

Library of Congress Catalogue Card Number LC 80-84297

International Standard Serial Number ISSN 0164-7989

International Standard Book Number ISBN 87589-857-2

Cover design by Willi Baum

Manufactured in the United States of America

Contents

Multi-program systems are burdensomely multidimensional, and are complicated by the predominance of political variables. Evaluation at the systems level requires a broad paradigm and powerful analytical techniques.

Editor's Notes

In planning this volume, I was motivated by the view that the evaluation profession must move rapidly to integrate the several "types" of evaluation into a unified approach, especially when one is confronting a complex system. Lopsided evaluations that emphasize one type of approach or kind of data and neglect all the rest are ultimately a disservice to the audiences they address. Even if completely accurate, such studies invariably generate fallacies and misconceptions of the most insidious and indelible kind: errors based on fact. Once an error based on fact has taken root, subsequent data and analysis will only make the error grow.

The challenge, clearly, is for evaluators to confront the full, debilitating complexity of the systems that they examine. Each of the contributions to this volume addresses how this challenge may be met. The emphasis throughout is on concepts and methods that are especially appropriate to a multiprogram, multipurpose scope of analysis, for this is where complexity becomes extreme.

The order in which the chapters are arranged is significant. They progress from the general and the abstract to the specific and the concrete. Moreover, the logical flow is roughly aligned with the sequence of thought by which evaluation is designed and performed: values–conceptual model–organization–methodology–data–report. Nevertheless, each chapter is an independent piece, and there is no necessary order in which they must be read.

A mental calisthenic to enhance the reader's appreciation of the following chapters is to consider the many dimensions of system complexity. It is a common and apparently simple observation that the input–process–output schema of general systems theory can be applied to the analysis and evaluation of any program. Yet as soon as this simple schema is invoked, we are on the verge of terrible complexity. Even the simplest situation of one process, one flow of input, and one flow of output is confounded by variations of tempo, heterogeneity of inputs and outputs, interactions of attributes and timing, change over time, and the interplay of deterministic and stochastic mechanisms. Moreover, one input, one process, and one output are never quite enough. Even the most parsimonious description of a program will ordinarily require that multiple interacting processes and flows be considered. Every process can be disassembled into subprocesses. For every flow, there are counterflows, crossflows, and parallel flows that are mutually interdependent. Every process is an output of some higher order or prior process. Every change changes everything. The structural and dynamic complexities of real program systems can scarcely be enumerated. But this is nothing to be discouraged about; this is what makes evaluation interesting and worth doing.

Ronald J. Wooldridge
Editor

Ronald J. Wooldridge is director of forecasting and modeling, New York State Office of Mental Health, Albany.

Only an evaluation design that encompasses genuinely universal principles can be applied to services in different categories and still produce valid comparisons.

The Primacy of Values and Ideologies in Human Services Evaluation

Wolf Wolfensberger

Human services walk on three legs: ideology, legal practices, and implementation. Our efforts toward developing adaptive services can be greatly facilitated and supported by laws that concern themselves with service structure, funding, consumer rights, and so on. However, even the best laws will be perverted if implementation is not characterized by profound, positive ideologies and values. After all, law is a discipline that reflects higher ideals and, without these ideals, the course inevitably leads to violence and abuse. Thus, not only human service behavior but almost all human behavior is fundamentally determined by ideology. *Ideology* is a combination of beliefs, attitudes, and interpretations of reality that are derived from one's experiences, knowledge of what one presumes to be facts, and values.

Ideologies can be "big" or "little." Religions, political systems, and philosophies of life are all "big" ideologies or conglomerates of ideologies. "Little" ideologies concern how we function in our private and human-service lives. We have many such ideologies in education, psychology, psychiatry, rehabilitation, and social work. We even have agency ideologies, that is, ideologies held by personnel in certain agencies, such as welfare offices and sheltered workshops.

Unfortunately, agency ideologies are often agency myths or agency dogmas, and there is a point where an ideology, a myth, and a dogma merge into one. Today, we recognize that the once prevalent ideology of welfare agencies in regard to foster and adoptive placement of retarded infants ("Everybody knows that you cannot place severely handicapped children") was a dogma and, since it was false, also a myth. But this ideology was very powerful, and it determined what was done for many decades. Few people remember today that infant intelligence scales had a major impetus through attempts to prevent the adoption of handicapped young children.

Ideologies are extremely powerful forces that rule and determine a host of behaviors, both important and unimportant ones. Even scientists who pride themselves on the purely empirical nature of their scientific work are ruled by ideologies. Thus, scientific theories come and go, although they are never provable and only occasionally disprovable. They come and go because of the prevailing scientific ideologies. The history of science is replete with situations where a formidable body of evidence was ignored or denied because the prevailing ideology could not account for such evidence. The evidence against bloodletting was overpowering, yet it was practiced for hundreds of years. Today, one of the most widely practiced psychiatric techniques, namely, psychotherapy, is virtually devoid of carefully controlled evidence despite more than fifty years of practice. We all have our transempirical scientific ideologies. For instance, I am skeptical about extrasensory perception, although the evidence for it is very strong. My scientific ideologies find it difficult to account for such evidence. Therefore, I dismiss the evidence. As Anatole France once said (1908, p. 10), "It is true that the scientific reasons for preferring one piece of evidence to another are sometimes very strong, but they are never strong enough to outweigh our passions, our prejudices, our interest."

Thomas Kuhn (1970) has analyzed how scientists are affected by fundamental evidence and assumptions, which he calls paradigms. He discusses how we work to strengthen paradigms, how we conduct research and gather empirical support for them. Then someone comes along with a better paradigm, and we do not even disprove the old one; we simply leave it and go on to another, which better fits the world view, the spirit of the time.

Is it a bad thing that ideologies are so powerful and that they can override facts and empiricism? Perhaps it is in the physical sciences, but not in human services. Here, I hope that values will forever be supreme over facts. Values are valuable, and our lives should be ruled by them. But at the same time, we must strive toward three goals: good ideologies rather than bad ones, ideologies that transcend empiricism and are not inconsistent with it, and conscious ideologies rather than unconscious ones. I shall elaborate each point.

Good Ideologies Rather than Bad Ones

Some ideologies are obviously more adaptive than others, as ideologies differ in the degree to which they are consistent with one's other and higher-order ideologies. Yet, it is only by wisdom or hindsight that we can differentiate between good and bad ideologies. Otherwise, there would be no bad ideologies, because everybody would embrace only the good ones.

Unfortunately, there are probably only two ways to improve the quality of our ideologies. One way is to strive with sincerity to root out all unconscious ideologies, which usually are unconscious only because they are "bad." A second way is to realize that there are times when we can apply, from decision theory, the principle of minimizing risk. For instance, some ideologies may be redundant but they will do no harm, while others can do much harm; some ideologies may increase our options, while others will reduce them. The theory that mental retardation is primarily hereditary leads logically to treatment nihilism, while an environmental theory impels treatment activism. Now, if the hereditary theory is wrong and we adopt it, we lose all human value by doing nothing where much could be done. That is what we did for many decades. However, if we adopt the environmental theory and it is wrong, we may lose money and material resources but we lose little in human value. If retarded infants can be placed in foster homes but we do not try to place them because we do not believe that it can be done, we have thrown away a valuable option and harmed many children. If it cannot be done but we try and fail, we have only wasted a little effort and money, and the children are no worse off than they were before. These are good examples of the application of decision theory.

A contemporary example of the application of decision theory is the situation in residential services in mental retardation and mental health. We have behind us more than fifty years of failure, and we cannot possibly do worse now than we have with our past patterns. Some people say that we should not try new patterns, because they are unproven. In actuality, the worst that can happen is that we will do as badly as we have in the past, while the best that can happen is a partial or full breakthrough to a new way of serving people. Thus, decision theory alone sometimes dictates that we should embrace a new ideology, tried or not.

Ideologies That Transcend Empiricism and Are Not Inconsistent with It

Let us compare two ideologies. One holds that as many handicapped people as possible should engage in work that is as culturally normative and valued as possible. The other holds that severely handicapped children who are homeless should be institutionalized because no one will foster or adopt them. The first ideology transcends empiricism. It states a principle and leaves it up to the future and to empiricism to determine what *as many as possible* and *as culturally valued or normative as possible* mean. We may not know what the limits are; that, empiricism may determine; but we can sketch the directionality. In contrast, the second ideology is so phrased as to be directly empirically determined. There is nothing wrong with an empirically based ideology, but it should not be inconsistent with empiricism, and the second ideology is.

The following is an example of an empirically based ideology that is consistent with empiricism: Most severely retarded adults, and even many profoundly retarded adults, can perform work that, although sheltered, is culturally normative in quality, though perhaps not in quantity. Although this statement is thoroughly consistent with the empirical evidence, it is not generally accepted by vocational personnel. The reason why they reject this ideology is not the lack of evidence but that they so devalue severely or profoundly mentally retarded adults that they cannot bring themselves to accept the reality of their growth potential.

Conscious Rather than Unconscious Ideologies

One very bad thing about our ideologies is that, more often than not, we are not aware of them. Sometimes, we so take them for granted that we lose sight of their existence. People's attitude toward air provides an analogy. We so took it for granted that we discovered its existence only 300 years ago. At other times, we simply are not bright enough to formulate our ideologies in words. At still other times, our ideologies are so bad that we cannot consciously face up to them.

For example, we all claim to believe in equality, and then we practice gross discrimination. But we deny it, because we cannot admit it, and therefore we do not realize that we discriminate. In our human services, we claim to render treatment, and then we dehumanize, yet we deny that we do. Our educators call for segregated special education of the mildly retarded, and then the evidence shows that even with specially trained teachers, small special classes, and special materials, the special children learn less than they would if left in large classes with regular teachers and classmates years ahead of them. But we first deny the evidence, and when we can no longer deny it, we ignore it, repress it, and keep doing what makes us feel comfortable with our ideology. When finally we are forced to integrate, we make sure it will fail, and then we prove our point, which was an ideological one to begin with.

Once an ideology has taken hold of us, it will express itself not only in all aspects of our clincial practices but also on all other levels of our functioning, including the highest systemic level of societal and service organization and structuring. How could it be otherwise? Individuals' values do summate, and there can be even more unconsciousness in the summation of individual ideologies than in the expression of a personal ideology. After all, some sytems are so complex that those who have made small individual contributions to their totality can maintain splendid anonymity.

Ideology and Evaluation

The ideological base that underlies evaluation designs is often both unrecognized and unconscious. For example, the underlying assumption in the accreditation system of services to elderly citizens is that nursing homes for aged persons are legitimate services and that, once a certain level of technical adequacy is introduced, the service is justified and good. Similarly, the underlying assumption in the accreditation system for sheltered workshops is that workshops are a good answer to the needs of their clients. The accreditation process does not address the relation of the workshop to a comprehensive vocational continuum.

There is a difference between a value system's being a poor one and its values being unrecognized. The ideology that old age is a disease is a bad one, but it is often consciously advanced. That is why a majority of services for the elderly are medical in nature, why the language and symbolisms associated with services for the elderly are so often medical, why the services themselves are often placed close to hospitals and cemeteries, and why they are staffed by nurses, physicians, therapists, and so on.

It is a big advantage for an evaluation design to be *consciously* ideological and theoretical; such designs tend to be more cohesive. Designs that lack structure are, by contrast, relatively mechanical, fractionated, incoherent, and of narrow scope.

Only an evaluation design that encompasses genuinely universal principles can be applied to services in different categories and still produce valid comparisons. Yet, too many human service workers are unconscious of the universals underlying their services and practices. During the process of socialization into their professions and service roles, human service workers are generally taught to be particularistic. Thus, they tend to view their own profession as having skills and concerns that no other profession has, their local services as having problems unlike those of services elsewhere, their own agencies as unique, the times as unique, and their communities as unique. Believing this, evaluators have produced studies of astonishing specificity and little or no general utility.

If every subject of evaluation requires a unique approach, then we have defined the total work so that enough of it to matter will never be done. Evaluation must teach precisely the opposite, that there are enduring universal desiderata that apply over a wide range of places, times, and services.

A further ideological dimension is how an assessment approach views current service structures and even entire service systems. Widespread implementation of ideologically sound evaluation would do much to do away with the current patterns of service provision, while most evaluation procedures take the existing service system ideology and status quo very much for granted. That is, many evaluators legitimize current patterns by taking for granted that they should exist (the case of nursing homes has already been mentioned). Accordingly, their efforts consist entirely of examining how efficiently (sometimes, how least destructively) the pattern operates. In the case of work and work training settings, for example, the Commission on Accreditation of Rehabilitation Facilities (CARF) has concentrated on operating better sheltered, isolated, segregated workshops, rather than on specifying an alternative vocational services system continuum as the ideal toward which services should strive.

In contrast, an ideology-based evaluation would study the relevance of current practices to the needs of the people whom an agency serves. In effect, it would ask the complex question, "Are the right clients properly grouped, are they being worked with by the right people, and are these people doing the right things and using the right methods consistently?" This question is concerned with a program's *raison d'être* and with the capability of the service to fulfill it. An orientation toward the attainable ideal rather than to the status quo is fundamental if the evaluator's responsibility as a change agent is to be fulfilled.

As an illustration of how faulty ideology can affect evaluation practices, consider the numerous scales that purport to assess the quality of services but that in actuality are clinical measures of the functioning and progress of individual clients. These scales measure whether and how well clients can walk, talk, tie their shoelaces, and so on. These are clinical measures of competence, and the sum of these clinical measures is supposed to constitute an appropriate measure of the quality of the whole service. For example, a measurement instrument used in Colorado to assess the quality of group homes is really an assessment of the competencies of the residents of the home. This kind of preoccupation with clinical progress springs from an interpretation of deviancy as clinical, not societal or systemic in nature. As a result of this perspective, problems are phrased in terms of victims' inadequacies: whether there is brain damage, whether the individual is sick or old or poor. In fact, some people claim that almost every social problem is due to the people who display the problem. Obviously, if one views human societal problems as problems of individuals who are inferior, handicapped, or incompetent, then one will naturally seek only clinical measures of service quality and success.

In contrast, a systemic orientation does not require one to deny the clinical reality or source of certain behaviors, but it does require one to recognize the societal interpretation in determination of deviancy. In reality, it is the service system that needs to be tested for retardation, incompetency, lack of discipline, disorder, irrationality, hallucinations, delusions (of grandeur, and so on), addiction (for example, to power and money), physical handicap (such as building inaccessibility and function incongruity), destructiveness, or threat to society.

As a society or political subdivision approaches an ideal system, it will become more important for service systems to be assessed as systems, because as the clinical growth of clients becomes asymptotic and as the returns of what one can do on the clinical level diminish, it will become more important for services as a whole to be of high quality.

As the systems approach is incorporated into the field of evaluation, the primacy of ideological considerations will become clearer and more generally accepted, because service systems typically consist of many separate components over which there is no single conscious plan or policy framework.

References

France, A. *L'Île des Pingouins* [Penguin Island]. Paris: Calmann-Lévy, 1908.
Kuhn, T. A. *The Structure of Scientific Revolutions.* (2nd ed.) Chicago: University of Chicago Press, 1970.

Wolf Wolfensberger is a professor at Syracuse University, where he directs the Training Institute for Human Service Planning, Leadership, and Change Agentry.

Evaluation has generally incorporated the scientific method into its paradigms. However, systems thinking, which considers not only individual programs but also the relationship of programs and their overall direction, is just beginning to emerge in the field.

The Organizational Imperative

Ronald J. Gerhard

This chapter will discuss the need for and applicability of general systems theory concepts in the evaluation of human services by describing the role of evaluation in human service agencies and by demonstrating the necessity of combining the programs to be evaluated and the evaluative process itself in a single unifying conceptual model.

Human service delivery systems attempt to improve the quality of life by meeting specific human needs. Misunderstanding, which may occur as either ignorance or confusion, is a significant obstacle to the achievement of this purpose. (*Ignorance* may be defined here as the absence of information, and *confusion* as the misapplication of information.) Problems resulting from ignorance are dealt with by the scientific method, which recognizes and formulates problems, collects data through observation and experimentation, and formulates and tests hypotheses. Problems resulting from confusion are dealt with by general systems theory, which organizes resources, focuses behavior, and assesses outcomes. Evaluation has generally incorporated the scientific method into its paradigms. However, systems thinking, which addresses not only individual programs but also the relationship of services and their overall direction, is just beginning to emerge in the field. This chapter will concentrate on the problems created by confusion and on the use of conceptual models to reduce confusion.

Conceptual models are used by concrete operating systems in the formulation and integration of plans that design goals, characteristics, and schedules; control techniques that monitor and adjust performance; and review procedures that assess and evaluate the utility and worth of the operation. A conceptual model of an organization is a description of how these three stages of organizational life — design, performance, and review — relate to one another and to the environment in which they function.

The Organizational Imperative

Changes in human service delivery systems are linked to changes in other, broader systems. Alterations in political, economic, and technological systems have an enormous impact on social systems and their human service delivery components. The current wave of reform and innovation in human services is linked, in part, to the revolutionary changes now under way in the fields of telecommunications, data processing, and general systems theory. Martin (1978) observes that these changes are both massive and fundamental and that they will transform society even more profoundly than the industrial revolution of the eighteenth century. In order to benefit from improvements in technology, human services and delivery systems must be receptive to changes. This attitude is itself a change, a change that systematically rationalizes, orders, and structures the elements of service delivery systems. These are the changes that represent "the organizational imperative," for these are the changes that make organizations amenable to the advances being made in other fields.

In recent years, human service agencies at federal, state, and local levels have experienced wave after wave of new managers, new techniques, and new directions. As costs have mounted and morale declined, services have deteriorated. As analyzed by Hardin (1968), bureaucracies have proliferated, but to little avail. Any amount of random tinkering with or expansion of unsystematic activities can only produce greater confusion and randomness. Insights into the nature of these problems and their solutions, no matter how revealing, will not help the services to meet their full potential to serve people until the services are organized in a way that allows for maximum control and predictability.

Managing Change

Conceptual models enable organizations and individuals to predict and control complex behavior by helping them to understand, maintain, and modify simple behavior. Models do this by simplifying, rationalizing, focusing, and constraining behavior to control the direction of change. The rate of change can be controlled by establishing schedules. Table 1 depicts the relationship between controls over the rate and direction of change.

The conceptual models used to control the direction of change are ways of looking at programs or systems that are complex enough to reveal the impact of decisions yet simple enough to be readily understood and used by decision makers. The result is a clarification of direction such that fear of change does not prevent change and the glamour of change does not accelerate it. Models provide courage in the form of ideals and restraints in the form of goals.

Models enable decision makers to construct an instant replay, as it were, of significant events and, equally important, to construct an instant preplay of planned actions. While the instant replay is useful for problem analysis, the instant preplay is useful for problem avoidance. At issue here is not the technological capacity to illustrate graphically, pictorially, or tabularly the outcome of simulation modeling. Rather, it is the mental capacity to participate in a simple form of time travel by structuring information into patterns of change. Conceptual models make systematic anticipation possible.

Conceptual models are the most comprehensive way to focus system behavior, but they are not the only way. Plans, policies, regulations, and standards also focus behavior, but they do not provide for internal consistency. A properly functioning system will have an appropriately balanced mixture of focusing techniques (although imbalances seem to be the standard). For example, frustration resulting from a lack of the general guidance that a conceptual model provides is often manifested in the proliferation of detailed guidance in the area of individual performance. Often, such guidance takes the form of increased regulation by control agencies in an effort to prescribe personal behavior with real or imagined standards of outcome or performance. The overuse of these techniques can be compared to the writing of ever more detailed procedure manuals for carpenters in the hope that, if the carpenters could learn to cut truer or nail firmer, then the outcome of

Table 1. Managing Change

Rate \ Direction	Controlled Direction	Uncontrolled Direction
Controlled Rate	Management	Evolution
Uncontrolled Rate	Revolution	Chaos

their work would resemble the building desired, even though they were not provided with a blueprint.

Although improved personal performance is a worthwhile goal, it is not a substitute for clear direction. The lack of a holistic control mechanism at the conceptual level creates a need for totalistic control mechanisms at the operating levels. Organizations, like people, can be incapacitated by uncertainty about their identity. Order and control, the basic fail-safe mechanisms of managers, when achieved by improving system identity, can greatly reduce the need for demoralizing regulations and procedures. A clearly articulated purpose produces conformity by providing a clear and rewarding alternative to personal deviations. When control techniques are not related to a clear purpose, they produce stagnation by limiting all forms of personal behavior and by escalating personal risks without also providing predictable successes.

The blueprint analogy applies well to situations of known dimensions. However, in innovative situations, a conceptual model is more appropriately likened to a compass. Both blueprint and compass use the available information to control direction. The model's level of detail should reflect the level of understanding of the problem, but where knowledge fails, ideals serve as general guides. Without an ideological base, models soon become useless descriptions of past experiences with limited utility in innovative situations. Whether they are used as a compass or as a map, models provide behavior-constraining or -defining ideations which facilitate the transition from theory to practice.

The real dilemma in modern human service complexes lies in having to choose from among too many alternatives, not from among too few. Our ability to rationalize must be constrained by observing the boundaries of that rationality. One role of conceptual models is to help to bound rationality.

At this point, some further clarification of the term *system* is necessary. System has been defined many ways. Perhaps the most general definition can be paraphrased from Ackoff (1960) as unity consisting in mutually interacting parts. Many contemporary writers invoke the "health delivery system," the "education system," and so forth, then add parenthetically the word *nonsystem* to indicate that their use of the term has been strictly nominal. These authors are trying to convey the fact that such systems are not rational but confused. Perhaps we should speak instead of "the human service complex" until such time as the complex has been rationalized to the degree that it not only meets the nominal definitions of a system but is in fact clearly systematic. The distinction is important, because it is quite possible to discuss a system of totally random, totally irrelevant, and totally misunderstood events.

Substitution of *complex* for *system* allows us to make the required distinction between rational and irrational systems.

Figure 1, based on Miller (1970), orders many standard definitions of system elements to reveal that systems are unified by their structure to transmit power in order to maintain identity and to achieve their desired ends.

The Problem

The confusion referred to above results in numerous organizational malfunctions that greatly reduce our ability to understand or to manage the service complex. Schein (1965) has defined four evaluative

Figure 1. Characteristics of Systems[a]

I. *Structure* (Patterned Arrangements)
    A. *Organizational*—patterned arrangements of responsibility and authority
    B. *Physical*—patterned arrangements in time and space
    C. *Communication*—patterned arrangements of interactions
II. *Transmissions* (Utilization of Power)
    A. *Inputs*
        1. Resources (land, labor, capital, time)
        2. Information
        3. Values
    B. *Processes* (changes in patterns, over time)
        1. Reversible (functions)
            a. primary, goal-seeking
            b. cybernetic, constraint-producing
        2. Irreversible (history)
    C. *Outputs*
        1. Outcomes—primary effects of processes
        2. Impacts—effects of outcomes or wastes on other systems
        3. Waste—residual outputs
III. *Power* (Ability to Effect)
    A. *Energy* (Capacity for or exerted physical force)
    B. *Command Signals* (Behavior defining controls)
IV. *Identity* (Distinguishing Attributes)
    A. *Boundaries*—Discontinuity with environment[b]
    B. *Environment*—All objects which cause or receive system impact[c]
        1. Physical
        2. Cultural
        3. Technological
V. *Direction* (The Ends to be Achieved)
    A. *Purpose*—Specification of rationale for ends
    B. *Goal*—Specification of characteristic of ends
    C. *Objectives*—Specification of means of achieving ends

[a]Miller, 1970.
[b]Chin, Gregory, and O'Brien, 1970.
[c]Schein, 1965.

criteria for organizational health: adaptability (the ability to solve problems and to react flexibly to changing environmental demands); sense of identity (knowledge and insight on the part of the organization as to what it is, what is goals are, what it should do, and the degree to which the goals are understood and shared by its members); capacity to test reality (the ability to search out, perceive accurately, and interpret correctly the real properties of the environment); and integration (the ability to ensure that organizational subparts are working at common purposes).

Table 2 relates some typical classes and types of organizational malfunctions to an inability to meet these four criteria. It further subdivides these malfunctions into three levels of impact: industry (multi-agency), agency, and individual (worker).

Many of the items that appear in Table 2 are taken from material presented by Wolfensberger at a March 1980 workshop.

Table 2 uses known organizational problems as a basis for model building. When this matrix is applied to a specific industry, agency, or individual, it provides a problem-identifying model free from the expediencies that so often reduce priority statements to crisis-oriented reactionary comments. The matrix can be easily expanded by adding dimensions for functions, product lines, regions, or other needed subdivisions. The choice of dimensions should be guided by characteristics of the problems. This approach allows generic solutions to be applied to each row or column, specific solutions to each cell, and unique solutions to each item. Without such a structure, all problems require unique solutions that greatly reduce the opportunities for developing an organization with internally consistent, mutually enhancing, and reciprocally supportive activities.

Construction of Conceptual Models

Principles for the construction of conceptual models will be illustrated in this and succeeding sections by examples. The effort to analyze these examples will reveal more about modeling than any single set of principles or guidelines. Accordingly, I will rely heavily on charts and tables. Models are only rarely capable of full expression in prose.

Structure. The macrostructure of a generic conceptual model for human services is shown in Figure 2 as a network of interacting and intercommunicating systems: the political system, which empowers operations; the service system, which performs the desired operations; the consumer system, which receives the outcomes of operations; the information system, which reports on operations; and the social system, which receives the impacts and secondary outputs of the operations.

Table 2. Organizational Malfunctions

Criterion \ Level	Industry	Agency	Individual
Adaptability	*Uneconomicalness* Inequitable distribution of resources Excessive resource expenditure	*Inefficiency* Inflated unit costs Parochialism	*Ineffectiveness* Defensiveness Fixation on process rather than outcome
Identity	*Weak Role and Mission* Overregulation Unclear external boundaries Conflicts of interest	*Weak Policies, Practices, and Goals* Poorly defined functions Poorly defined target populations Confused structures	*Weak Ideologies and Commitments* Stagnation Amorality Risk avoidance
Reality	*Inadequate Constituency* Weak consumer advocacy Poor political support	*Insensitivity to Human Needs* Segregation and congregation of atypical people "Distantiation" of atypical people	*Defeativeness* Low clinical outcome expectations Prolongation or production of consumer dependency
Integration	*Inadequate Regionalization* Limited strategic planning Unclear internal boundaries Inertia	*Fragmentation* Lack of coordination Inadequate referrals	*Isolation* Impersonality Ignorance of proven techniques Reduced accountability

Figure 2. Macrosystem Interactions

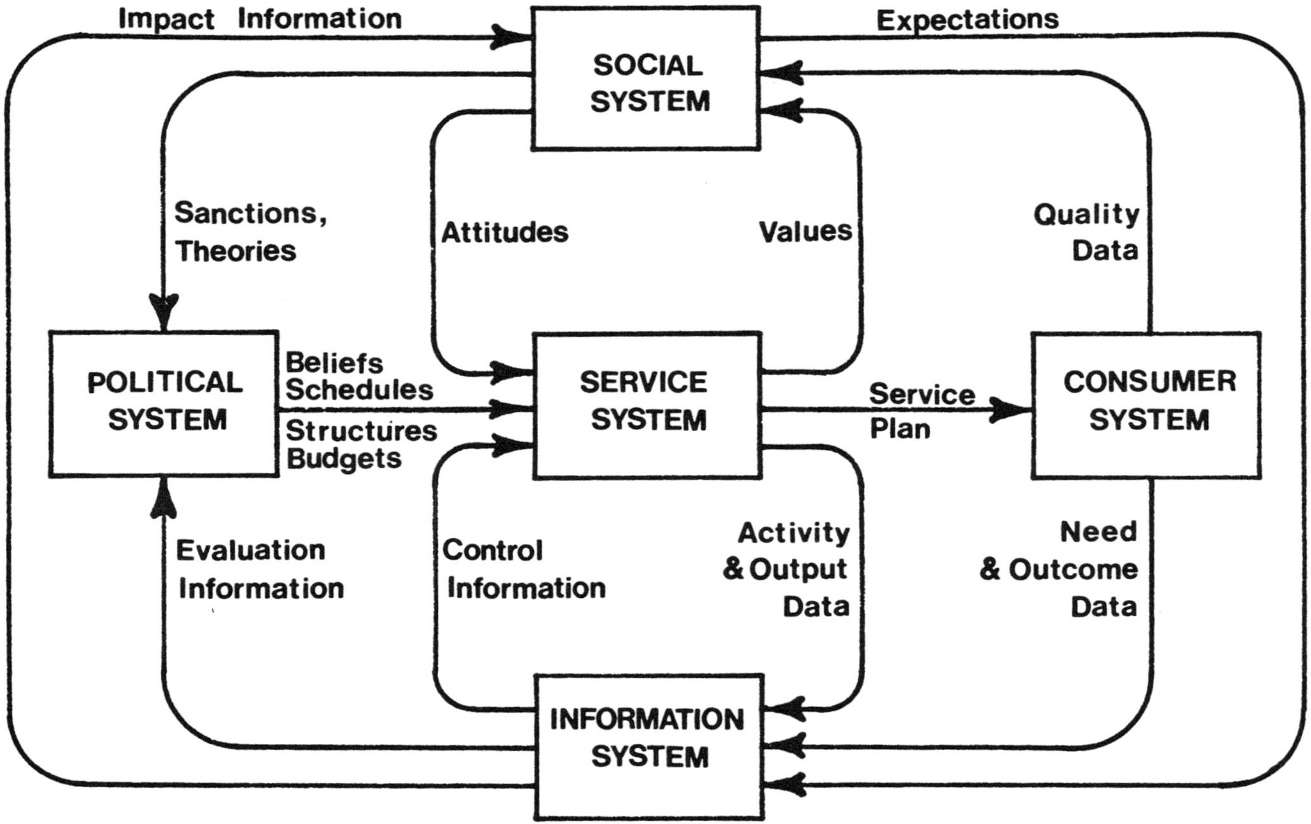

The two figures that follow show two further levels of conceptual modeling. Each subsequent level expands the center cell of its predecessor.

Figure 3 focuses on the service component of the macrosystem as a distinct system. The inputs shown animate the model by establishing the essential linkages to the technological/theoretical data base, the sociopolitical power base, and the ideological value base of the organization. If these relationships are not included, the model is in grave danger of being unwanted, incorrect, or impotent. The inputs must also be linked with the model's outputs via three types of feedback processes: deductive processes, which infer specific acts from general principles; inductive processes, which infer general theories from specific acts; and reductive processes, which consolidate complex data to concepts, especially those of a subjective, intuitive nature. The remaining process, productive behavior, contains all the activities that produce the system's outputs.

Figure 4 focuses on the productive behavior process of the service system as a system in its own right. This figure divides the process into five functional areas or divisions of labor. Typical interactions between each pair of functional areas are identified to indicate the complex intrasystem relationships required of a totally comprehensive conceptual model. Obviously, a model does not have to include every detail of operations in order to be useful. Indeed, it should include only those items that are needed to describe or predict the consequences of a particular decision.

Taxonomies. For every conceptual model, there is an associated taxonomy of terms. The taxonomy is to a conceptual model as a dictionary is to a language system. However, just as language systems are structured by means of a logical and functional classification of words into verbs, nouns, adjectives, and so on, so must the taxonomy be structured into a logical, hierarchical classification of system elements. A taxonomy should possess the following characteristics: mutually exclusive classes that eliminate ambiguity by providing intraclass homogeneity and interclass heterogeneity; jointly exhaustive classes that cover all required elements; and hierarchically ordered classes that can be aggregated in several dimensions. In addition, customs or rules for usage must be established. Such rules are what distinguish a recipe from a grocery list. Both can contain the same elements, but the former also provides instructions necessary to achieve a desired outcome.

Functions of Conceptual Models

Conceptual models have one overriding goal: to help organizations to achieve and maintain organizational health. They have four

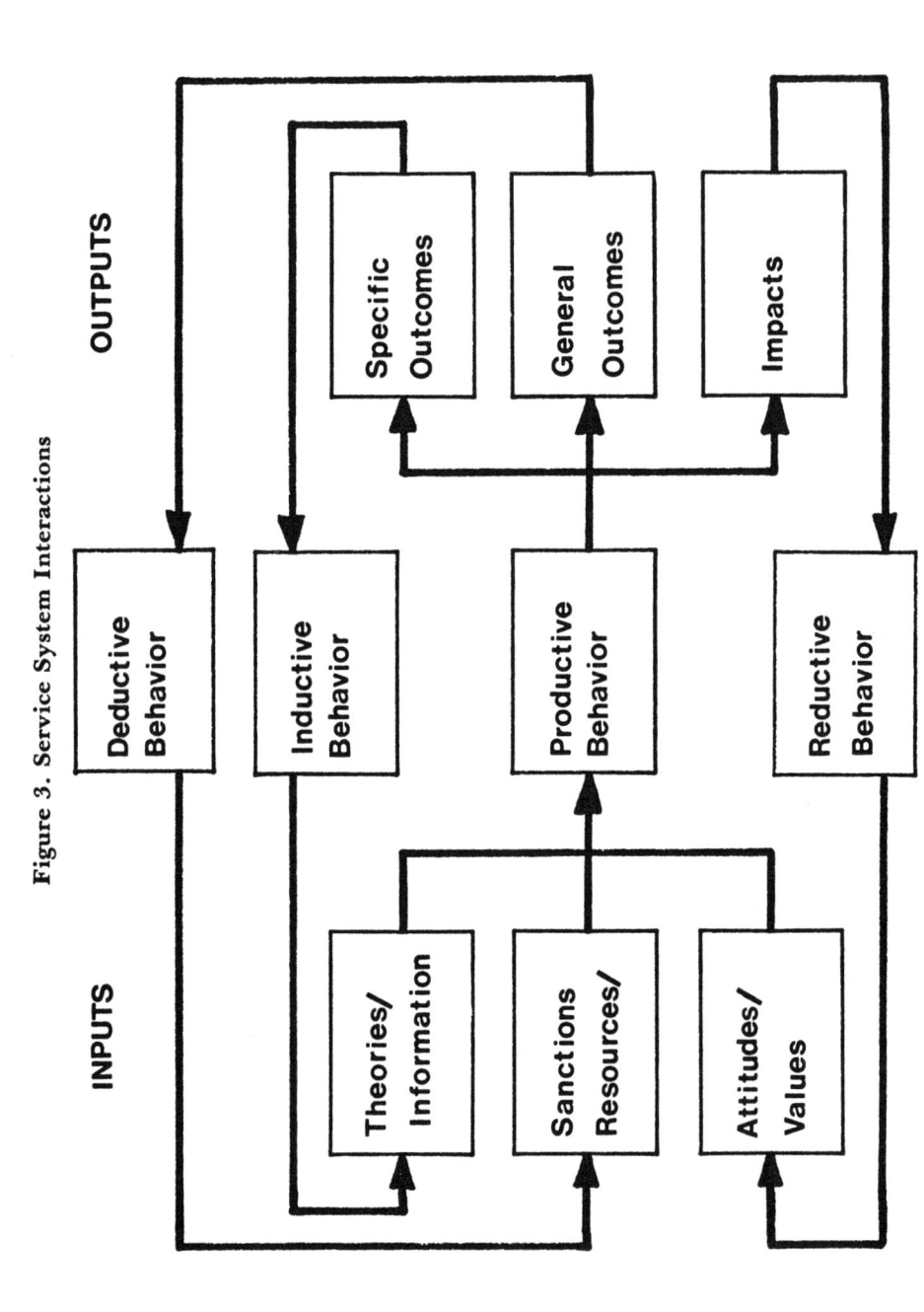

Figure 3. Service System Interactions

Figure 4. Microsystem Interactions

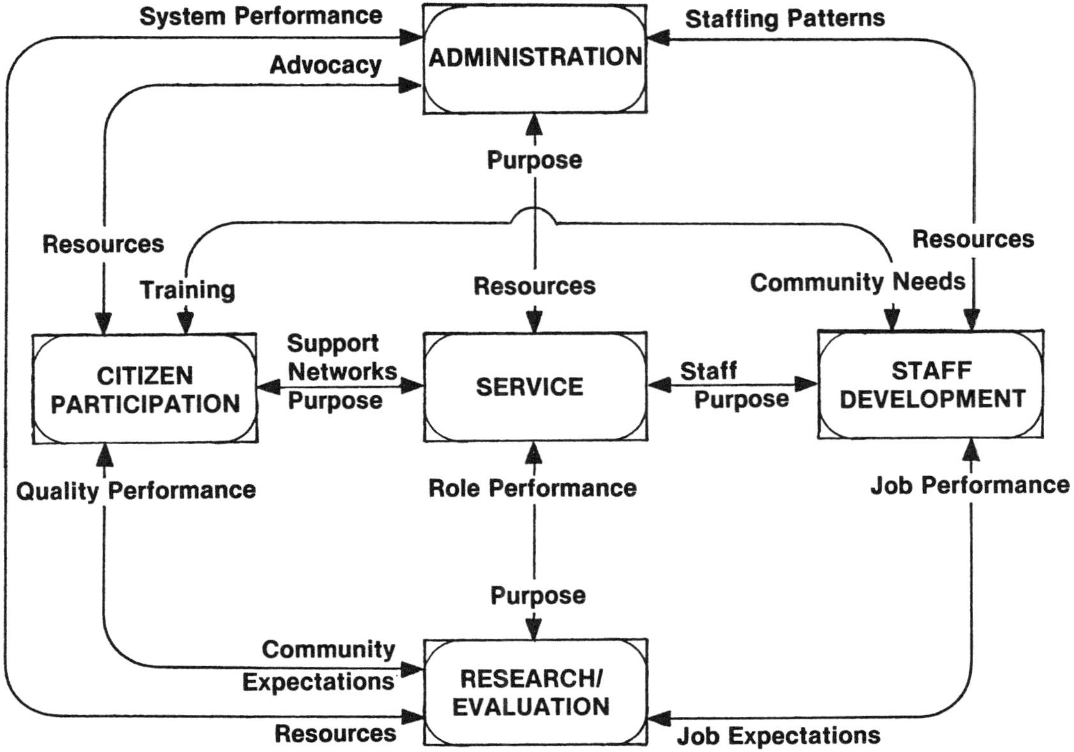

major functions to achieve this goal; that is, they help organizations to develop and maintain adaptability, to establish and maintain identity, to keep in touch with social realities, and to integrate all required resources and activities. Let us now describe these four functions in greater detail.

The *adaptability function* provides an order that allows problems not merely to be identified but also to be solved. Table 3 compares systematic and conventional approaches to the adaptability function. The *identity function* provides a clear purpose and general direction from which goals and objectives may be drawn. Figure 5 illustrates how a conceptual model answers the general identity question in terms related to the specific concerns of each of its components. The *reality-testing function* provides a framework for gathering and analyzing information about the environment. There is an old story about the operators of a buggy-whip shop who welcomed construction of a new auto plant next door. Confined by a narrow conceptual model, they regarded their new neighbor as a boon to their business, since it would generate additional traffic right by their doors. It is no less difficult for organizations to stay in touch with reality than it is for individuals. The *integrating function* provides a structure and an ethos within the system that are capable of assimilating many diverse problems, issues, and perspectives. As illustrated in Table 4, this function contains and productively resolves the tensions that arise from system diversity.

Table 3. Adaptability Function

Area	Systematic Approach	Conventional Approach
Time Horizon	Future-oriented anticipatory planning and training	Present-oriented reactive planning and training
Focus	Objective, purposeful, and goal-oriented	Subjective, random, and process or clinically oriented
Specificity	Differentiated problems, goals, structures, functions, and outcomes	Confused problems, goals, structures, functions, or outcomes
Problem Solving	Multipath, policy-based, proactive, cause-directed	Single-path, crisis-based, reactive, manifestation-oriented
View of Change	Painful but essential, done openly	Lack of commitment to bear pain causes defensive, resistant, or secretive behavior
Integrity	Services are part of coherent network	Services function in isolation
View of Issues	Interrelated and universal, attributed to lawful processes	Unique and specific, attributed to change or specific persons

Figure 5. Identity Function

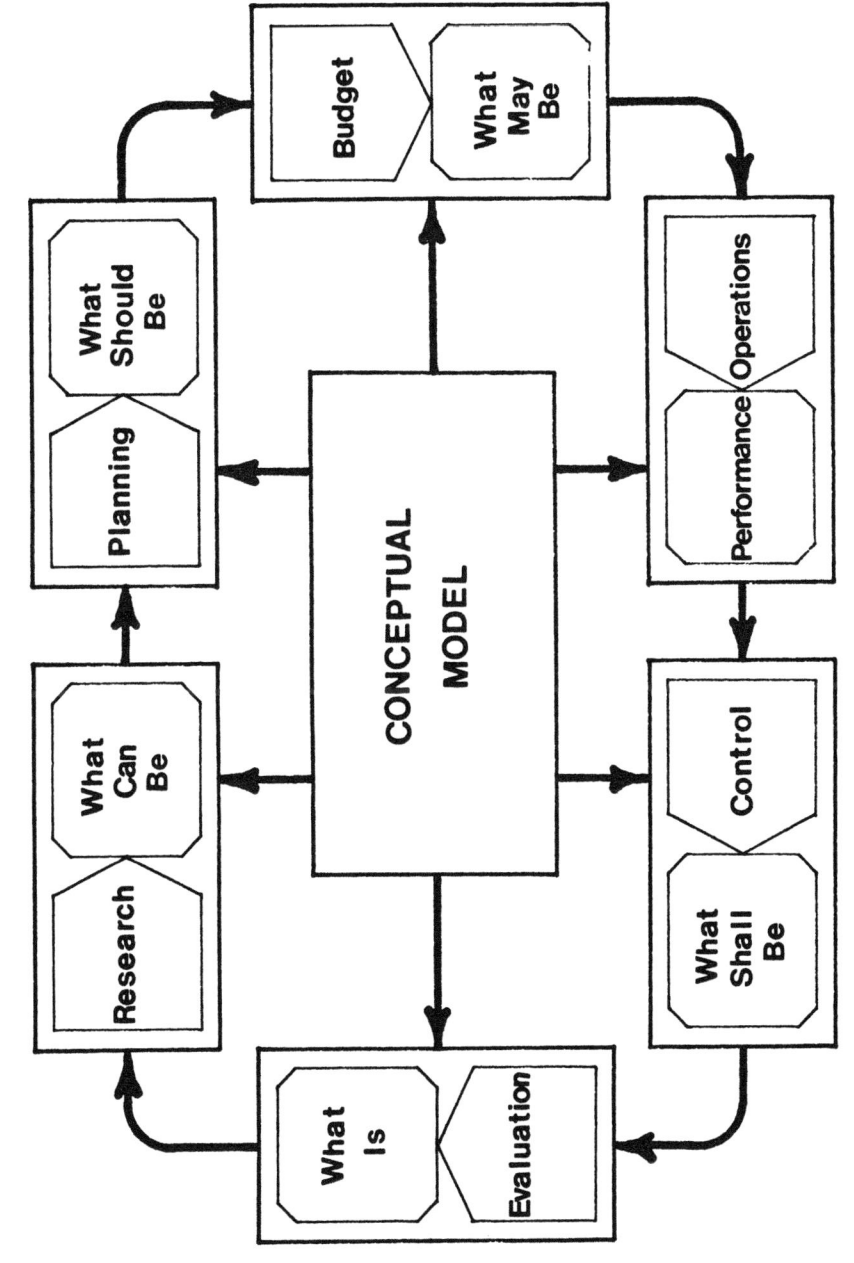

Table 4. Integrating Function

Domains of Integration	Perspective
Theory–Practice	Academic
Attitudes–Beliefs–Behaviors	Clinical/Service
Goals–Structures–Functions	Planning
Organization–Delivery–Financing	Corporate Management
Planning–Management–Control	Operations Management
Input–Process–Output	Systems Theory
Design–Performance–Review	Evaluation

Applications of Conceptual Models

Table 5 summarizes how the design, performance, and review stages of systems operations are conceptually integrated with one another across the three organizational levels: corporate, operations, and service.

Design. Conceptual models assist those who must design an operating system in four ways: by providing a clear sense of purpose; by providing a format for integrating diverse beliefs, values, and sanctions; by defining and organizing the elements of the system; and by providing a systematic and hierarchical planning function. Table 6 arrays three types of planning against three organizational levels of planning. The three levels of planning are: *strategic* — a process to obtain resources and create the social, political, and economic conditions necessary for success; *tactical* — a process to deploy resources and to schedule the achievement of general administrative objectives; and *individual* — a process to arrange and expend available resources and to carry out specific actions for individual consumers. The three types of planning are: the *technological applications process* — the utilization of the technological/theoretical data base in the development of plans that are objective statements about the quantitative aspects of service delivery; the *value-driven process* — the utilization of the ideological value base in the development of plans which are subjective statements about the qualitative aspects of service delivery; and the *consensual validation process* — the utilization of the sociopolitical power base in the development of plans that are expedient statements about the political aspects of service delivery. The three types of planning process rarely exist in a pure state both because they are not mutually exclusive and because each is necessary but alone not sufficient for most planning. These processes

Table 5. Summary of Applications

Organizational Levels	Planning Levels (Design Stage)	Control Levels (Performance Stage)	Evaluation Levels (Review Stage)	Emphasis	Time Frame
Corporate Level	Strategic Planning	Financial Control	System Evaluation	Availability of Services (Inputs)	5 Years!
Operations Level	Tactical Planning	Management Control	Program Evaluation	Provision of Services (Processes)	12–18 Months
Service Level	Individual Planning	Quality Control	Outcome Evaluation	Consumption of Services (Outputs)	6 Months

are linked to the organization's data base, value base, and power base. As a result, many organizations find themselves with a suboptimal mix of processes at any given time, depending upon current administrative priorities.

Figure 6 depicts the hierarchical nature of the planning function and its relationship to the feedback process that provides the basis for the control and evaluation functions.

Performance. Conceptual models assist in improving system performance by identifying control points and adjustment mechanisms and by providing a systematic and hierarchical control function. The control function is differentiated from the other feedback-oriented function of evaluation by the fact that control results directly in routine adjustments of day-to-day performance. In contrast, evaluation results in judgments that can be used to make changes at either the design or the performance stages. Table 7 relates the three general types of control mechanisms to three levels of organizational control.

The three levels of organizational control are *financial* — mechanisms used to regulate the distribution, utilization, and flow of fiscal resources, such as budgets and cash reporting procedures; *management* — mechanisms used to regulate the distribution, utilization, and flow of nonfiscal resources, such as personnel practices and occupancy rates; and *quality* — mechanisms used to ensure the degree of excellence of service delivery, such as credentialing and utilization review. The three general types of control mechanisms are illustrated in Figure 7. Reduction in the amplitude of deviation is measured by comparing the preaction indicator A to the postaction length of indicator B. Reduction in the frequency of deviation is measured by comparing the width of the typical preaction tempo indicator C to the width of the typical post-

Table 6. Planning Matrix

	Types of Planning		
Levels of Planning	Technological Applications Process	Value-Driven Process	Consensual Validation Process
Strategic			
Tactical			
Individual			

Source: Neufeldt, 1973.

action tempo indicator D. Shift in the locus of deviation is measured by comparing the location of the preaction indicator E to the postaction indicator F.

Review. Conceptual models assist in the review of organizational performance in two ways: by providing an organization with known structures, objectives, schedules, protocols, budgets, and values that provide the standards of comparison to be applied by the evaluation process; and by providing a comprehensive description of the evaluation function that uses these standards to produce assessments. Table 8 relates five major types of evaluation to three organizational levels of evaluation.

The purpose of evaluation is to determine the consistency of the goals, values, and actions taken in order to meet the needs of target populations. To achieve this, evaluation determines the utility and

Table 7. Central Matrix

	Types of Control		
Levels of Control	Locus of Deviation	Scope of Deviation	Frequency of Deviation
Financial			
Management			
Quality			

Figure 6. Planning Process

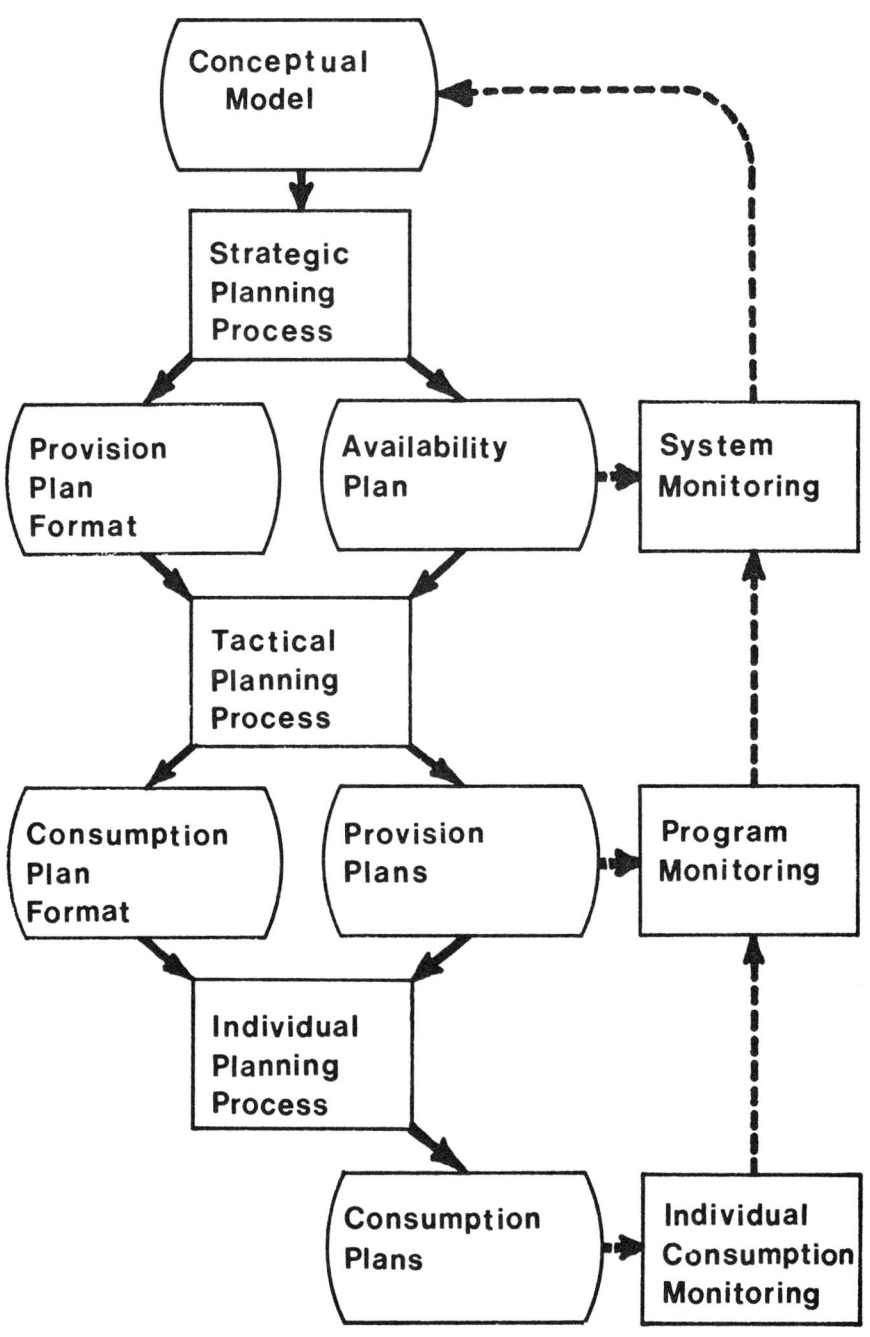

worth of each activity. Utility is determined by comparing processes and outcomes to planned objectives, schedules, and policies. Worth is determined by comparing processes and outcomes to held values and principles. Therefore, evaluation must be linked to both the planning process, which provides objectives, schedules, and policies, and to the ideological basis of the organization, which provides the values and principles that become the standards of ideological coherency. These standards are combined to form the organizations' review plan, which is merely another case of provision planning, as shown in the section on

Figure 7. Control Mechanisms

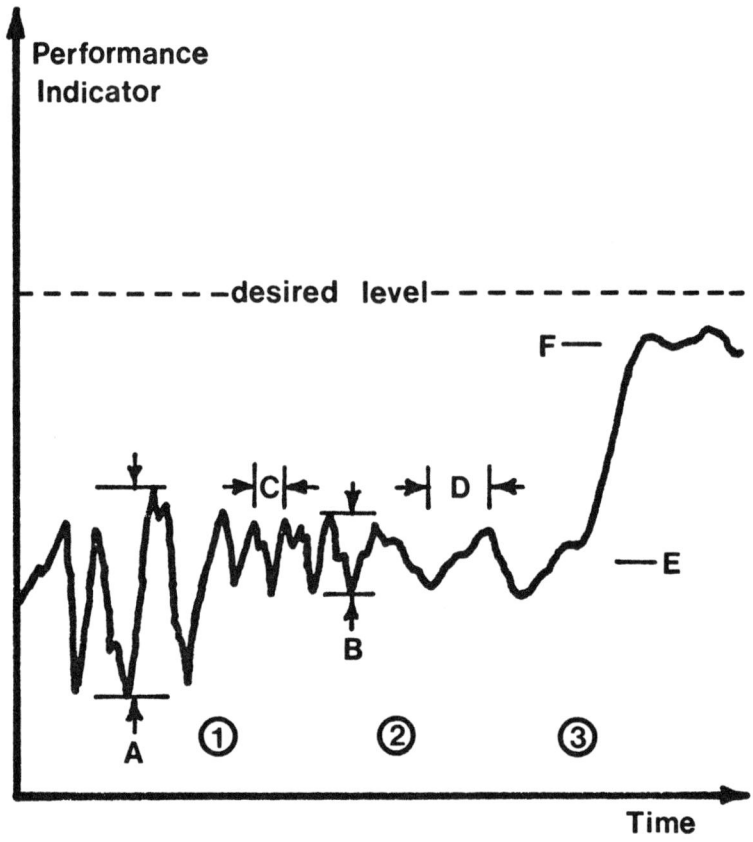

① Narrow Amplitude of Deviations

② Reduce Frequency of Deviations

③ Shift Locus of Deviations

Table 8. Evaluation Matrix

		Levels of Evaluation		
Types of Evaluation		*System (availability)*	*Program (provision)*	*Outcome (consumption)*
Utility	*Rate of Change* Progress versus Schedules			
	Direction of Change Achievements versus Objectives			
	Methods of Change Procedures versus Protocols			
	Cost of Change Expenditures versus Budget			
Worth	*Value of Change* Schedules, Objectives, Protocols, and Budgets versus Values			

Source: Gerhard, 1979.

planning. In this case, *provision* refers not to provision of service but to provision of management support.

The three levels of evaluation are: *system* — assessment of the long-range availability, distribution, and utilization of systemwide inputs; *program* — assessment of the annual provision of services by each organizational component; and *outcome* — assessment of the periodic effect of services on individual consumers

The development of the evaluative paradigm is continued in Table 9, which adds evaluative areas and evaluative determinants to the notions of type and level developed above.

The next step, in which Tables 8 and 9 are combined into a larger matrix, is left to the interested reader. Gerhard and others (1976) give a more complete development of evaluative principles for use in evaluating mental health programs.

Figure 8 depicts the flow of evaluative information and the relationship of the evaluation process to the planning and operating processes. Evaluation stands between the multitiered planning and operating processes and makes comparisons among the information that they generate.

Unlike the control process, which focuses on specific benchmarks, there are no limits placed on the evaluation process, and while the coherence of actions and goals is stressed, the coherence of agency goals to higher-order goals and values is also assessed. However, the

Table 9. Model Coherency

	Model Coherency: Consistency of Goals and Values with Target Population	*Evaluative Areas*	
		Plan Coherency: Consistency of Goals and Values Across Planning Levels	*Performance Coherency:* Adherence of Actions and Outcomes Across Operating Levels
Evaluative Determinants	*Goal Coherency (Utility):* Consistency of Goals and Adherence of Performance with Goals Across Organizational Levels	*Goal/Plan Coherency:* Consistency of Goals Across Planning Levels (Goals to Goals)	*Goal/Performance Coherency:* Adherence of Actions and Outcomes to Goals Across Operating Levels (Actions and Outcomes to Goals)
	Value (Worth): Coherency Consistency of Values and Adherence of Performance Across Organizational Levels	*Value/Plan Coherency:* Consistency of Values Across Planning Levels (Values to Values)	*Value/Performance Coherency:* Adherence of Actions and Outcomes to Values Across Operating Levels (Actions and Outcomes to Goals)

broad scope of the evaluation process itself is not a reason to shift the evaluative function to an outside agency. Such a move almost always guarantees that this major function will be guided by a different conceptual model or by none at all. The periodic need for external accountability and advocacy should not be mistaken for a reason to disarm continuous internal guidance and review functions.

Conclusion

Conceptual models provide a means for untangling a complex and confusing reality. They provide a context for understanding and order, and they incorporate a content of values and precepts. In human service agencies, this promotes system capacity to improve the quality of life. For evaluation, it promotes internal and external validity of evaluative judgments.

As Ackoff (1960) indicates, a system should be a unity consisting in mutually interacting parts. The discussion contained in this chapter has attempted to foster an awareness of how conceptual models can help service systems to evolve toward a level of precision in their operation that Ackoff was able to achieve in their definition. Unity is achieved when an organization has goals that promote accord, structures that provide symmetry, and functions that operate with consis-

Figure 8. Evaluation Process

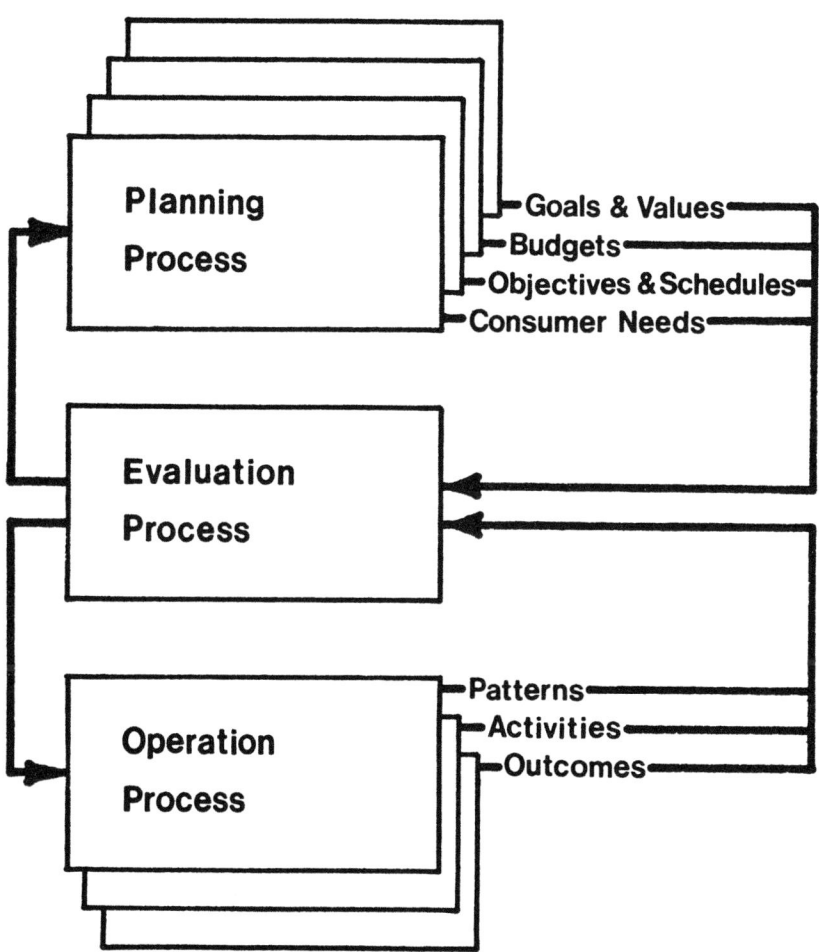

tency. Systems achieve unity when these simple principles have become intrinsic characteristics that are patterned, as though by genetic code, in their complex designs. The resulting designs are themselves the cause of mutually reinforcing and adaptive behaviors performed by the organization's interacting parts. This degree of deliberate and rational behavior can occur only under the influence of some unifying agent. An agent is needed not only to set the stage for change by imposing an adaptive structure but also to ask the questions "Use toward what ends?" and "Use on what basis?" A conceptual model is such an agent.

References

Ackoff, R. L. "Systems, Organizations and Interdisciplinary Research." In *General Systems Yearbook,* Vol. 5, Part 1. 1960.

Chin, R., Gregory, M., Sr., and O'Brien, L. "General Intersystem Theory." In A. Sheldon, F. Baker, and C. P. McLaughlin (Eds.), *Systems and Medical Care.* Cambridge, Mass.: M.I.T. Press, 1970.

Gerhard, R. J. "Source Book for Planning." Prepared for the New York State Office of Mental Health, Albany, 1979.

Gerhard, R. J., and others. "The Balanced Service System." In *Principles for Accreditation of Community Mental Health Service Programs.* Chicago: Joint Commission on Accreditation of Hospitals, 1976.

Hardin, G. "The Cybernetics of Competition: A Biologist's View of Society." In W. Buckley (Ed.), *Modern Systems Research for the Behavioral Scientist.* Chicago: Aldine, 1968.

Martin, J. *The Wired Society.* Englewood Cliffs, N.J.: Prentice-Hall, 1978.

Miller, J. G. "A General Systems Approach to the Patient and His Environment." In A. Sheldon, F. Baker, and C. P. McLaughlin (Eds.), *Systems and Medical Care.* Cambridge, Mass.: M.I.T. Press, 1970.

Neufeldt, A. H. "Considerations in the Implementation of Program Evaluation." Paper presented at the fifth Banff International Conference on Behavior Modification, March 1973.

Schein, E. H. *Organizational Psychology.* Englewood Cliffs, N.J.: Prentice-Hall, 1965.

Wolfensberger, W. "Retreat to Examine Moral Issues in Human Services from a Judeo-Christian Perspective." Sponsored by the Greater Louisville (Kentucky) Alliance for the Promotion of Judeo-Christian Values in Human Services, March 10–13, 1980.

Ronald J. Gerhard is policy analyst at the New York State Office of Mental Health, Albany.

*The evaluation activities of a large organization must be more
than a set of individual projects. Coordination, leadership, and
a long-term strategy are essential for overall success.*

Organization and Management of the Evaluation Function in a Multilevel Organization

Mark A. Abramson
Joseph S. Wholey

There is no single way to organize and manage the evaluation function
in a multilevel organization. Within the federal government, each of
the thirteen cabinet agencies has developed a different approach. A
variety of other arrangements for evaluation have been established at
state and local levels. This chapter examines the issues of organization
and management of evaluation in multilevel organizations, presenting
the experience of the U.S. Department of Health, Education and Welfare as a case study.

　　The Department of Health, Education and Welfare (HEW) was
the largest cabinet agency in the federal government. Managing evaluation in a department as large as HEW was a complex task. In its final

　　This chapter is adapted from a paper originally delivered at the 1980 Meeting
of the American Society for Public Administration, San Francisco, April 13–16, 1980.

fiscal year (1980), the Department had a budget of nearly $210 billion, employed 145,000 individuals, and spent approximately $50 million on evaluation. In May 1980, the Department of Health, Education and Welfare became the Department of Health and Human Services (HHS). *In order to acknowledge this reorganization, our discussion will employ the past tense throughout, even though much of what we will describe continues as present reality in HHS.* The Office of the Assistant Secretary for Planning and Evaluation continues in HHS and is presently implementing many of the activities discussed in this chapter.

The premise of this chapter is that the evaluation function in a multilevel organization should be more than a set of individual evaluation projects conducted in different offices at different levels. To make it more than a set of individual projects, it is necessary for some unit to assume an oversight, coordination, and leadership role. We will discuss one such unit, HEW's Office of the Assistant Secretary for Planning and Evaluation (ASPE).

Our primary interest is in the tools that can be used by a central evaluation management office in a department that is managed on a decentralized basis. The management tools presented here enabled a small central evaluation management unit to give direction and meaning to the evaluation function in a very large, highly decentralized department. The chapter focuses on how evaluation may be organized, planned, and managed; on the dissemination and utilization of completed evaluation studies; and on how the evaluation function can be assessed.

Organization and Management of Evaluation

The Role of a Central Evaluation Management Unit. A *multilevel organization* is defined as an organization that consists of several hierarchical levels, each of which has different responsibilities. Each level needs its own evaluation information. As a consequence, separate evaluation offices for each level have become the norm. Such offices operate under names such as the following: Office of Program Planning and Evaluation (OPPE), Office of Planning, Evaluation, and Legislation (OPEL), and Office of Policy, Research, and Evaluation (OPRE). While the OPPEs, OPELs, and OPREs of the bureaucratic world all have slightly different names, the functions of each are roughly the same, regardless of level or programmatic scope.

As evaluation units multiply within an organization, problems of coordination grow. It becomes more and more difficult to identify the roles of the different units, each of which attempts to serve the interests of its own level of management. As former HEW Secretary Joseph A. Califano once stated (United States Senate, 1979a, p. 69):

"They [evaluation offices] are sprinkled around HEW like holy water in a church, and we are trying to do an analysis of them to see how they ought to be organized and what they should do." This sprinkling of evaluation offices around the organization is likely to exist in any multilevel organization. Frequently, the evaluation unit at the top of the organization plays a leadership role, attempting to give direction to the counterpart units within the hierarchy.

Roles that a central top-level evaluation office can perform include allocating evaluation resources, coordinating evaluation through a planning/plan review process, providing substantive and technical guidance to the organization's evaluation efforts, disseminating new evaluation techniques, providing training and technical assistance, disseminating information about completed evaluation studies, and responding to outside requests for information. Given the fact that subordinate evaluation units will each attempt to serve their own level of management, tensions are inevitable if the central evaluation unit attempts to give any real direction to the evaluation units at lower levels within the organization. Foot-dragging and paper compliance are likely. Clear objectives and sustained interaction are necessary if the central evaluation unit is to be a positive influence on other evaluation units within the organization.

The HEW Experience. As noted earlier, HEW was a prime example of a multilevel organization. An organization chart of HEW (Figure 1) makes this point very clearly. The Department of HEW consisted of the Office of the Secretary (OS), and five Principal Operating Components (POCs): Office of Human Development Services, Public Health Service, Health Care Financing Administration, Social Security Administration, and the Education Division.

To understand the complexity of the evaluation function in a multilevel organization, it is useful to examine the organizational levels in HEW that conducted evaluation. The most striking fact about evaluation in HEW is that evaluations were conducted in approximately forty different organizational locations within the Department. Evaluation studies were conducted, both intramurally and under contract, by the Office of the Secretary and at the Principal Operating Component, agency, and bureau levels. Each level is briefly described below.

Office of the Secretary. A number of evaluation studies were supported by staff offices within the Office of the Secretary: Office of the Assistant Secretary for Planning and Evaluation (ASPE), the Office of the Inspector General, and the Office for Civil Rights. These evaluations, undertaken principally by ASPE, frequently addressed policy questions posed by the Secretary or the Under Secretary.

Principal Operating Components (POCs). POC evaluation units had two main functions: coordinating evaluation in the POC (a role similar

Figure 1. Department of Health, Education, and Welfare

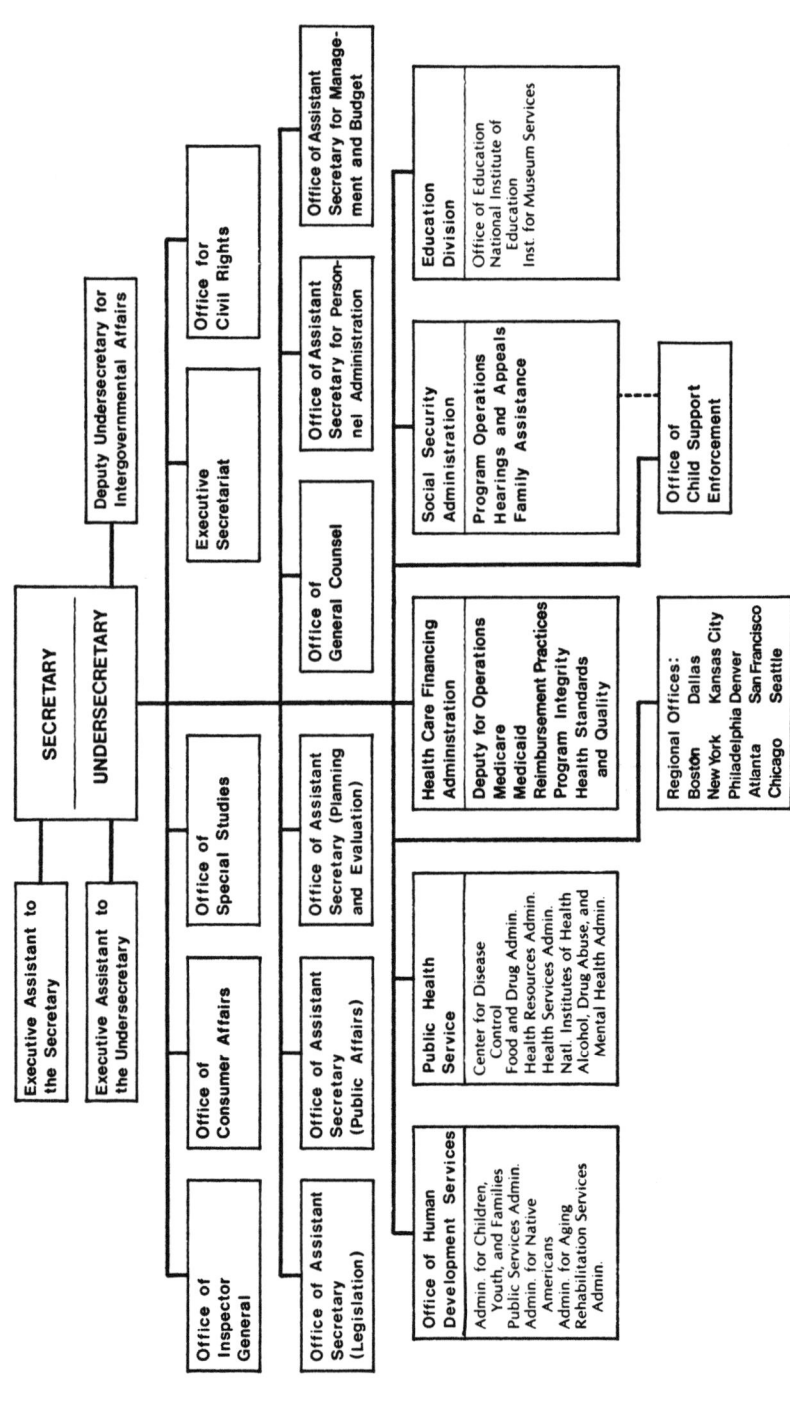

to that of the Office of the Assistant Secretary for Planning and Evaluation as described in this chapter) and conducting evaluation studies. Three POCs—the Social Security Administration, the Health Care Financing Administration, and the Education Division—performed most of their evaluations in a centralized evaluation unit and therefore performed a smaller coordinative role. The other two POCs—the Public Health Service and the Office of Human Development Services—performed most of their evaluations at agency and bureau levels, but they also conducted a small number of evaluation studies at the POC level.

Agency. Many agencies within Principal Operating Components, such as the Administration on Aging (Office of Human Development Services) and the Health Resources Administration (Public Health Service), had their own evaluation offices. These offices frequently supported evaluation projects of interest to agency heads or program managers.

Bureau. Within agencies, some evaluation projects were managed by bureau evaluation offices, such as the Bureau of Health Planning in the Health Resources Administration. Many bureau evaluation studies addressed questions of program efficiency, rather than program impact.

Thus, there were evaluation studies conducted at various levels throughout the Department. In fiscal year 1980, these studies cost approximately $50 million. As the number of evaluation studies grew during the 1960s, it became obvious to some that there was a need to coordinate evaluation within the department. In 1967, responsibility for management of the Department's evaluation effort was placed in the Office of the Assistant Secretary for Planning and Evaluation (ASPE). During the past thirteen years, successive HEW secretaries have assigned lead responsibility to ASPE for the coordination and functional management of evaluation within the department. Eight different Assistant Secretaries for Planning and Evaluation have performed that role.

In addition to a need for coordinating an increasing number of evaluation studies, there was another driving force behind the strong ASPE coordinating role. HEW evaluations were largely funded from 1 percent set-aside funds. The term *set-aside* refers to programs whose authorizing legislation permits funds—usually up to 1 percent of the program's budget—to be used for evaluation of those programs. Authority to spend the 1 percent set-aside funds was given directly to the secretary. In 1969, Secretary Robert Finch issued a directive setting forth guidelines on the use of set-aside funds. Twenty-five percent of the funds were made available to ASPE to conduct projects of Secretarial interest. The Secretary also requested ASPE to develop and coordinate a department-wide evaluation planning process to oversee the remaining 75 percent of the evaluation funds, which would be spent by the POCs and agencies. Since the funds were authorized to the Secretary for evaluation, there was clear rationale for assigning a stewardship role over the expenditure of those funds to ASPE.

Drawing upon the way in which ASPE performed the role of coordinator, leader, and functional manager of evaluation in HEW, we have identified three roles for a central evaluation office: coordinating evaluation in the organization through an evaluation planning and plan review process; providing leadership and direction through issuance of evaluation guidelines and by serving as an example to evaluation units throughout the organization; and disseminating information about completed evaluation studies. Using ASPE as a prototype, we shall discuss each of these roles in detail below.

We note in passing that ASPE filled other functions that will not be discussed here: the allocation of evaluation spending authority among the Principal Operating Components and agencies, the development and dissemination of effective evaluation techniques, the stimulation of actions to reduce the time required to complete evaluations, and the provision of training and technical assistance to POC and agency staffs.

Planning for Evaluation

The Need for Planning. As noted above, the premise of this chapter is that evaluation should be more than a set of unrelated projects carried out by different offices in one organization. The previous section showed how the need for a coordinating office arose in the Department of Health, Education and Welfare. As a method of coordination, ASPE developed an evaluation planning process. The major purpose of an evaluation planning process is to ensure that the evaluation projects conducted throughout an organization are more than discrete, unrelated projects.

It can be argued that, since *evaluation* is a poorly defined term, an evaluation planning process, managed by a central evaluation overseeing office, is needed in any multilevel organization. Such a planning process enables a central office to influence agency and bureau evaluation priorities to reflect the policy concerns of the central office; weed out duplicative and frivolous projects; and ensure that proposed evaluation projects are technically sound. Via a planning process, the central overseeing unit may be able to instill a sense of purpose into an organization's evaluation program. A communication vehicle is, however, needed to set forth this sense of purpose. In HEW, a document entitled "Guidance for Evaluation, Research and Statistical Activities" was issued each year by the Secretary or Undersecretary. The purpose of that document was to give a sense of direction to evaluation offices in the department. In the absence of such guidance, evaluation tends to be a free-for-all, with each evaluation unit pursuing its own ends.

The establishment of an effective planning process is no easy task. Gaining recognition and acceptance for a central evaluation planning office that provides guidance on types of evaluation to be undertaken, review and approval of other units' evaluation plans and projects, and allocation and reallocation of evaluation spending authority does not come easily. Other units within the organization are reluctant to accept such direction and control from any central overseeing office. Friction among evaluation units is common.

As noted below, the keys to an effective planning process appear to be clear guidance on the types of evaluations to be given priority, face-to-face interaction between central and subordinate evaluation units when evaluation plans are developed, and central office assistance to subordinate units in the design and execution of evaluation projects.

Another key to a successful planning process is continuity and stability on the part of the central evaluation unit. If the central evaluation unit shifts direction annually, it is much more difficult to establish a credible planning process in the eyes of the subordinate evaluation units. Aside from having continuity and demonstrating some stability of direction, the central evaluation unit must have adequate resources to exercise effective leadership over subordinate evaluation units that have competing goals. The central evaluation unit must have sufficient resources, both in quantity and in quality, to provide worthwhile review comments in a timely fashion. Indeed, it can be argued that mediocre oversight is worse than no oversight at all.

The HEW Experience. While each Assistant Secretary for Planning and Evaluation has viewed his or her evaluation role somewhat differently and placed organizational responsibility for evaluation coordination in various locations within ASPE, a constant thread throughout the last decade was the implementation of Secretary Robert Finch's 1969 memo directing the annual issuance of a departmental "Guidance for Evaluation Activities." In this document, the Office of the Secretary set forth detailed instructions for the development of agency evaluation plans, which were then to be reviewed by ASPE. The amount of ASPE resources devoted to implementing this document has varied from year to year; the quality of ASPE reviews has varied accordingly.

Since 1978, responsibility for overseeing HEW evaluation activities within ASPE has been placed in the Office of Evaluation and Technical Analysis (E&TA). With the creation in 1978 of a new position, Deputy Assistant Secretary for Evaluation, ASPE returned to an organizational arrangement similar to that of the 1967–1971 period, when evaluation coordination was first the responsibility of a director of evaluation and then the responsibility of a deputy assistant secretary for evaluation and monitoring. Between 1971 and 1978, evaluation coordination was performed in other parts of ASPE.

In implementing the "Guidance for Evaluation Activities," E&TA has worked closely with other ASPE units, including the Office of Health Planning, directed by the Deputy Assistant Secretary for Planning and Evaluation/Health; the Office of Education Planning, directed by the Deputy Assistant Secretary for Planning and Evaluation/Education; the Office of Social Services Policy, directed by the Deputy Assistant Secretary/Social Services Policy; the Office of Income Security Policy, directed by the Deputy Assistant Secretary/Income Security Policy; and the Office of Program Systems, directed by the Deputy Assistant Secretary/Program Systems. In reviewing an agency evaluation plan, E&TA coordinates a joint review with the appropriate ASPE office. The other offices participate in all meetings with agency evaluation staff.

It should be noted that there have been critics of ASPE's coordinating role. As part of the Office of the Secretary, ASPE was criticized for being still another layer in a top-heavy hierarchy that often placed unreasonable demands on Principal Operating Components' and agency evaluation personnel. It was sometimes argued that, because of their proximity to programs, agency and bureau staff knew their programs better and that the ASPE evaluation plan review role added little — other than lengthening an already long evaluation process. It is in this creatively intense environment that ASPE functioned. During its bureaucratic life, ASPE attempted to serve the role not of a bureaucratic kibitzer but of a constructive critic.

In reaction to criticisms that the evaluation planning process was too cumbersome and lengthy and had become a "paper process" in the worst sense of the term, ASPE attempted to make evaluation planning and evaluation plan review a more interactive, face-to-face process. ASPE was also able to speed up approval of evaluation plans and projects by starting earlier in the year and providing quicker turnaround in reviewing agency evaluation plans.

In FY 1980, ASPE began implementing a two-phase evaluation plan review process. This two-phase plan worked fairly well in its first year and was used again by the new Department of Health and Human Services in the FY 1981 evaluation plan review process, which was structured as follows.

April–May: Agencies prepare Part I of their evaluation plan — brief ten- to fifteen-page "evaluation strategy statements" that will have priority in the forthcoming fiscal year, and paragraph-length descriptions of proposed evaluation projects. Meetings were held among

ASPE, POCs, and agency staff in which the strategy statements were discussed and ASPE provided guidance on the topics likely to be of major interest during the forthcoming year. Some agencies' proposed evaluation projects were dropped as a result of this initial review process, before much effort had gone into project design and development. On the basis of these meetings, agencies then developed Part II of their plan, consisting of detailed descriptions of each proposed evaluation project.

June–August: During this three-month period, agencies submitted detailed project descriptions in Part II of their evaluation plans. Meetings were held at which ASPE and POC reviewers asked questions of agency evaluation staff concerning proposed projects. Projects were reviewed for their relevance to departmental decision making, relevance to program management concerns, soundness of methodological approach, and avoidance of overlap with other departmental evaluation projects. On the basis of these meetings, formal review comments and memoranda approving or disapproving proposed evaluation projects were transmitted to the appropriate agencies.

Although it was not perfect, the evaluation planning and review process did work. Potentially duplicative evaluation projects were identified and not funded. Related projects were often combined. Substantial changes were frequently made in the design of proposed projects. Some studies were revised to answer additional questions of interest to the Secretary. Other studies were revised down in scope and their questions were more precisely targeted. Proposed evaluation projects were weeded out if they appeared to ask questions of little potential relevance to policymaking or program management.

The major drawback to the two-stage evaluation plan review process was that it was very time-consuming. Review staff were obliged to put in the hours required to make the process meaningful. Much time was spent in meetings. Nevertheless, the review process did improve the quality and relevance of agency evaluation projects, and, on balance, the process appears to have been worthwhile.

Providing Leadership for Evaluation

The Need for Change from Past Directions. The usefulness of evaluation is frequently questioned by policymakers, program managers, and evaluators. After evaluations are completed, government policymakers and program managers often find that evaluations are irrelevant to their information needs. Typically, they complain that evaluations are slow, inconclusive, or answer the wrong questions.

Given the complex policy and management environment in which public managers operate—in particular, given the resulting ambiguities in program objectives and information needs — it is not surprising that evaluators have found it difficult to produce useful information. In practice, program evalution has rarely led to more effective programs.

In 1974, the Urban Institute (Horst and others, 1974) assessed some reasons typically given for the failure of evaluation to affect program performance. According to Urban Institute evaluators, the poor utilization of evaluation and its failure to contribute to improved program performance appeared to result from inadequate definition of the program or of the problem addressed by the program, insufficient specification or understanding of the causal links between program activities and anticipated results, and unwillingness or inability on the part of management to act on the basis of evaluation information. As a result of research on program evaluation, Horst and her colleagues concluded that evaluation is likely to lead to better program performance only if the program design meets three key conditions: Program objectives must be well defined; that is, those in charge of the program have agreed on a set of realistic, measurable objectives and program performance indicators in terms of which the program is to be assessed. Program objectives must also be plausible; that is, there must be evidence that program activities are likely to achieve measurable progress toward program objectives. Finally, intended uses of information must be well defined; that is, those in charge of the program must have agreed on how program performance information will be used to achieve improved program performance. Evaluation resources can be used for pre-evaluation activities that help programs to meet these three conditions. In the next section, we will show how HEW attempted to establish a new direction for evaluation that would produce greater use of evaluation studies.

The HEW Experience. Using an analysis of why evaluation studies have not been previously used, HEW's central evaluation unit attempted to move the department in a new direction. In the "Guidance for Evaluation Activities," the Office of the Secretary had a vehicle in which it could state the directions in which agency evaluation offices should move. In 1979 and 1980, the Undersecretary made it departmental policy to place more emphasis on management use of evaluation to document and improve program performance. It was departmental policy that evaluation resources should increasingly be used to clarify program objectives, to assess what program activities could realistically be expected to accomplish, to produce evidence on the extent to which HEW programs were achieving their intended results, and to identify changes in program activities that would improve program performance.

In transmitting the guidances for FY 1980 and FY 1981 (U.S.

Dept. of HEW, 1979; U.S. Dept. of HEW, 1980a), the Undersecretary stated that agencies should give high priority to program performance evaluations intended to result in definition of realistic, agreed-upon, measurable program objectives and performance indicators for the department's programs and in evidence on the extent to which the department's programs were operating as planned and producing the results intended by the legislation, as further defined by the measurable objectives and performance indicators agreed upon for the program. The purposes of program performance evaluations were to assist program managers in the management of their programs and to provide policymakers with evidence on the extent to which the programs were achieving specific objectives.

Four types of evaluation activities were subsumed under the term *program performance evaluation: evaluability assessments,* which identify program objectives and performance indicators (types of evidence) that will be used to assess the extent of progress toward those objectives and evaluation/management options for changing program activities, objectives, or uses of information in ways that are likely to improve program performance; *short-term evaluations,* which provide the designs (measurements and comparisons) to be used in monitoring or evaluating program performance and which test those designs by collecting a limited amount of program performance data; *full-scale evaluations,* which evaluate program performance in terms of agreed-upon measurable objectives and performance indicators; and *program performance summaries,* which summarize all available evidence on how programs are performing in terms of a specific set of objectives and performance indicators. Initially, the Department placed the emphasis on evaluability assessment, the first type of program performance evaluation listed above.

Evaluability assessments were designed to serve as the foundation for future full-scale evaluations. In evaluability assessments, the following activities are performed: document program objectives and expectations of central office and regional office program managers, policy makers, and those who deliver services at state and local levels; compare and contrast the expectations of those at different management and policy levels, including policymakers at OMB, in Congress, and in relevant interest groups; examine program reality to estimate the likelihood that measurable progress will be made toward program objectives; document intended uses of information on program performance; identify changes in program resources, activities, and collection and use of information through which program managers could produce a better-designed, more efficient, more effective program; and obtain agreement on realistic, measurable objectives and performance indicators by which the program will be held accountable. In FY 1980, the Undersecretary recommended that at least 20 percent of agency evaluation funds be spent on program performance evaluations. In FY 1981, the Undersecretary directed that at least 30 percent of POC and agency evaluation dollars would be devoted to such evaluations.

In addition to placing greater emphasis on program performance evaluations, the "Guidance for Evaluation Activities" also required each agency to develop a two- to four-year schedule for completion of program performance evaluations for all of its programs. The aim of this requirement was to enable the department to have agreed-upon measurable program objectives and relevant performance information for all its programs. The overall objective of all these activities was to reach a point at which program managers had agreed on the program criteria on which the program would be assessed and managed; had established systems for assessing program performance in terms of the agreed-upon program objectives and performance indicators; and had collected and used program performance information to produce demonstrably efficient, effective, responsive programs.

In addition to trying to influence agencies — via the annual "Guidance" document — to conduct evaluability assessments and other program performance evaluations, ASPE attempted to lead by example. During 1978, 1979, and 1980, ASPE completed approximately twenty-five program performance evaluations. A list of those studies is presented in Figure 2. These evaluations were conducted by in-house teams or by combinations of in-house teams and contractors working under task-order contracts. Agency evaluation staff often were members of the in-house teams. By actually conducting program performance evaluations, ASPE demonstrated that such studies were feasible. ASPE also learned first-hand about some of the problems likely to be encountered in doing such studies and was thus able to offer advice when these problems were encountered by agency staff.

Dissemination of Evaluation Information

The Need for Dissemination. Evaluation efforts can only be justified if they result in products that are used. Therefore, one important role of a central evaluation unit is to encourage the dissemination of evaluation information. One way to accomplish this is to have the central evaluation unit serve as a repository for all completed studies within the organization. This makes it easier for those inside and outside the organization to find out about previously completed studies. High staff turnover among government project monitors often makes it difficult or impossible to locate copies of completed evaluation studies. A central repository allows the organization and the public to capitalize on earlier investments in evaluation.

**Figure 2. Program Evaluations Conducted by the Office of the
Assistant Secretary for Planning and Evaluation**

Office of Human Development Services
Administration on Aging
Development of Head Start Performance Indicators
Development of Head Start Parent Impact/Satisfaction Indicators
Head Start Training and Technical Assistance
Rehabilitation Services Administration: Management of the
    Vocational Rehabilitation Program

Public Health Service
Bureau of Community Health Services: Primary Care Program
Indian Health Service: Financial Management System
National Health Service Corps
State Conditional Educational Support Programs for Medical and Dental Students
Allied Health Professions Grant Program
Community Mental Health Centers Program (evaluability assessment)
Development of Performance Indicators for
    Community Mental Health Center Program
National Institute of Mental Health: Community Support Program
General Internal Medicine and Pediatrics Residency Program
National Institute of Alcohol Abuse and Alcoholism
    State Manpower Development Program

Health Care Financing Administration
Early and Periodic Screening, Diagnosis, and Treatment Program

Social Security Administration
Low-Income Energy Assistance Program

Education Division
Bilingual Education
Vocational Education (initial assessment)
Follow Through (evaluability assessment)
Follow Through (design and test of performance monitoring system)
Bureau of Education for Handicapped: Early Childhood Education Program
Cooperative Education
Institute of Museum Services

Cross-Cutting
Civil Service Reform
Bilingual/Bicultural Services for Ethnic Minorities

While the usefulness of such a repository should not be underestimated, it can be enhanced by four other activities: publication and wide dissemination of a directory listing completed evaluation studies; synthesis of completed evaluation studies; preparation of briefings or briefing memos summarizing evaluation results for top agency management; and reporting to top agency management, budget units, and the legislative branch on the utilization of completed evaluations.

The HEW Experience. ASPE has used three mechanisms to disseminate information about completed evaluation studies:

Evaluation Documentation Center. Created in 1971 to identify, categorize, and index HEW-sponsored health program evaluation studies, the Evaluation Documentation Center (EDC) was expanded and refined in 1974, when education, income maintenance, and social services evaluations were added. In 1976, further development of EDC services brought computerized publication of project descriptions of all HEW evaluation studies. The computer system was further refined in 1979.

The Evaluation Documentation Center maintained a library of completed evaluation studies; compiled executive summaries of completed evaluation studies that described the project, evaluation objectives, evaluation methodology, major findings, and recommendations; produced a description sheet providing a one-paragraph abstract, administrative data (including date of the study, amount of funding, sponsoring agency, agency contact, and performer), descriptive terms that identify subject content, terms identifying the programs evaluated, a document control number, and project status, for each ongoing or completed evaluation study; compiled subject, sponsor, and program indexes for ongoing and completed studies; and developed a computer system that makes specialized searches and special report production possible.

The major publication of the EDC is the *Compendium of HEW Evaluation Studies* (U.S. Dept. of HEW, 1980). This work described HEW evaluation studies conducted in the last several years. Knowledge of these studies was relevant to a broad range of HEW staff and others responsible for policy development, program management, and assessment of program performance. The last edition included descriptions of more than 1,400 evaluation projects. The volume will serve as a valuable resource to staff who must plan new evaluation studies by helping them to know what studies have been funded in the past and what results are available.

Preparation of Evaluation Summaries. In 1978, ASPE coordinated the development of evaluation summaries for thirty-eight HEW programs. Programs were selected primarily on the basis of known future decision points, clear Secretarial interest, or controversy. Each summary attempted to identify what was known and what was not known about program impact, cost-effectiveness, program management, and so on. The principal source of information used was HEW-sponsored program evaluations. Management data, audits, General Accounting Office reports, and various non-HEW studies were also used in preparing the evaluation summaries. These summaries were made available to all policymakers and to staff engaged in development of the department's proposed FY 1980 budget.

Report on Evaluation Utilization. In addition to these two activities, ASPE initiated a series of reports on evaluation utilization (U.S. Dept. of HEW, 1980b). These reports were designed to provide a forum in which the utility of evaluation activities in stimulating program changes and program improvements could be demonstrated. The reports were inspired by criticism from the Senate Appropriations Committee (United States Senate, 1979b, p. 25) that "the Committee is unaware of any significant program improvements that have been brought about by the Department's large annual investment in evaluation contracts with consultant organizations. It seems as though, year after year, the same programs get reevaluated, yet never change."

The ASPE report on evaluation utilization noted that the channels through which program evaluation affected HEW policies and programs ranged from direct use to indirect use. A study that contributes to increasing general understanding and influencing the climate of opinion about a program by better informing the participants in the process of legislative reauthorization is an example of indirect use. Immediate use of study results by program management to modify program regulations is an example of indirect use. The report also illustrated the impact of evaluation findings on the development of legislation, on the development and alteration of regulations and guidelines by which legislation is implemented and programs are administered, and on day-to-day program operations.

Evaluating the Evaluators

A central evaluation unit is an excellent place from which to assess an organization's evaluation process. Again, the goals formed by ASPE are illustrative. It was established as a goal that, over the next several years, there would be an attempt to assess the success of departmental evaluation activities by several criteria. As discussed earlier, a major criterion would be whether program managers had developed agreed-upon measurable program objectives and relevant program performance information for their programs. ASPE proposed to track the progress of all HEW programs with the scale presented in Figure 3. As this implies, the major objectives of HEW evaluations were not to produce reports, however worthwhile and academically sound they might be, but to improve program management and program performance. If program management and program performance were not improved, the HEW evaluation effort was not a success.

While this criterion was dominant in ASPE's assessment proposal, several other criteria can also be used to assess evaluations for specific audiences (see Schmidt and others, 1977; Wholey, 1979). For example, when the customer is an individual consumer, such as a pol-

Figure 3. Scale of Results-Oriented Program Management and Demonstrably Effective Program Performance

Level 0: Program management has defined the program in terms of a set of program objectives and performance indicators (types of evidence) in terms of which the program is currently assessed and managed.

Level 1: Program management has defined and gotten the agency head's agreement on a set of realistic, results-oriented program objectives and program performance indicators to use to assess and manage the program in the future.

Level 2: Program management has developed and gotten the agency head's agreement on an evaluation design or information system design for measuring program performance and intraprogram variations in performance in terms of program objectives and performance indicators identified and agreed upon at Level 1.

Level 3: Program management has implemented a system for measuring program performance and intraprogram variations in performance in terms of the program objectives and performance indicators identified and agreed upon at Level 1.

Level 4: Program management has established and gotten the agency head's agreement on realistic targets of expected program performance in terms of the program objectives and performance indicators identified at Level 1 and the measurement system implemented at Level 3.

Level 5: Program management has achieved acceptable or improved program performance in terms of the performance targets established at Level 4.

icy analyst who has specific information needs, evaluations should be assessed by whether the evaluation product meets the specifications agreed to by the customer and the evaluation office, whether the customer reviews the evaluation product, and whether the evaluation product meets the customer's information needs. When the customer is the management team responsible for implementing and overseeing implementation of specific government programs, evaluations should be assessed by whether program management acts upon the evaluation information to maintain or modify program activities or objectives, and whether program performance improves. When the customer is the large set of policymakers involved in debating and resolving a specific issue over what government will do, evaluations should be assessed by whether policymakers' attitudes, opinions, and positions on the issue are modified.

Conclusion

In this chapter, we have used the evaluation activities of HEW's Office of the Assistant Secretary for Planning and Evaluation as a case study of a central evaluation unit in a multilevel organization. Three of the major ASPE evaluation roles have been discussed in detail: coordinating evaluation within the department, providing leadership and direction, and disseminating information about completed evaluation studies. Other evaluation roles have been mentioned.

We have not discussed the many activities of ASPE on the planning side. That is clearly the material of another chapter. Here, it should be pointed out that, in an age of limited resources, ASPE policy development activities were in competition with ASPE's evaluation activities. The relative emphasis among the multiple ASPE roles shifted many times while ASPE was a unit of HEW and these shifts are likely to continue in ASPE under HHS. Fiscal and personnel resources are clearly going to be limited, especially for staff units such as ASPE. Thus, it is possible that ASPE's evaluation activities may be redirected by a future Assistant Secretary with a different set of priorities.

Whatever the long-term future, the short-term outlook is clearly for limited resources. It is unclear how evaluation in government will fare. Since evaluations are usually funded from discretionary appropriations, there is a real possibility that evaluation funds will be restricted. In our view, the level of resources allocated to evaluation should be related to the extent to which evaluations contribute to demonstrable improvement in program management and program performance. Thus, it is critical that the manner in which evaluation is organized and managed should be based on consideration of how such improvements may be fostered.

References

Horst, P., and others. "Program Management and the Federal Evaluator." *Public Administration Review*, 1974, *34* (4), 300–308.

Schmidt, R. E., and others. *Serving the Federal Evaluation Market.* Washington, D.C.: The Urban Institute, 1977.

U.S. Department of Health, Education and Welfare. *Fiscal Year 1980 Guidance for Evaluation, Research, and Statistical Activities.* Mimeograph. Washington, D.C.: U.S. Department of Health, Education and Welfare, April 1979.

U.S. Department of Health, Education and Welfare. *Compendium of HEW Evaluation Studies.* Washington, D.C.: U.S. Department of Health, Education and Welfare, 1980.

U.S. Department of Health, Education and Welfare. *Fiscal Year 1981 Guidance for Evaluation, Research, and Statistical Activities.* Mimeograph. Washington, D.C.: U.S. Department of Health, Education and Welfare, February 1980a.

U.S. Department of Health, Education and Welfare. "Evaluation Utilization in the Department of Health, Education and Welfare." Mimeograph. Washington, D.C.: U.S. Department of Health, Education and Welfare, April 1980b.

United States Senate, Senate Committee on Appropriations, Subcommittee on the Departments of Labor and Health, Education and Welfare, 95th Congress, Second Session. *Hearings on the Departments of Labor and Health, Education and Welfare Appropriations for 1979.* Part 2. 1979a.

United States Senate, Senate Committee on Appropriations. *Senate Committee Report 92-247, Departments of Labor and Health, Education and Welfare, and Related Agencies Appropriation Bill, 1980.* July 13, 1979b.

Wholey, J. S. *Evaluation: Promise and Performance.* Washington, D.C.: The Urban Institute, 1979.

*Mark A. Abramson is a program analyst in the Office of
the Assistant Secretary for Planning and Evaluation,
U.S. Department of Health and Human Services.*

*Joseph S. Wholey is professor of public administration at the
University of Southern California's Washington Public Affairs
Center and from 1978 to 1980 was deputy assistant secretary for
evaluation in the U.S. Department of Health, Education
and Welfare.*

*Evaluation is an information-gathering process, and it can unravel
in much the same way as a detective story. Just as Sherlock Holmes
redirects his crime-solving activities as new clues arise, evaluators
should be committed to adapting their evaluation activities as
new information is obtained.*

Decision-Oriented Approaches to Program Evaluation

Richard C. Larson
Edward H. Kaplan

Regardless of one's particular definition of evaluation, there can be no
doubt that it is a process that produces information. This information
may pertain to the extent of program compliance with contractual obligations, to managerial aspects of program operation, or to a test of
some hypothesis about program functioning. Whatever the specific
form of the information obtained from an evaluation, we would argue
that the information is useful only to the extent that it informs decisions. For example, information that exists as data on a computer tape
is of no value until and unless it is analyzed and used in some way. In
just the same way, information not acted upon is no more valuable
than no information at all.

The work of the first author was supported in part by grants nos. 78-91-AX-
0007 and 80-IJ-CX-0048 from the National Institute of Justice of the U.S. Department
of Justice to the Operations Research Center of the Massachusetts Institute of Technology. The work of the second author was supported in part by Public Systems Evaluation, Inc., 929 Massachusetts Avenue, Cambridge, Massachusetts.

Any decision can be viewed as an irrevocable allocation of resources. This definition of decision comes from Howard (1966), who explains that "irrevocable" implies not "for all time" but for the next short time interval that an allocation of at least one resource has been made. "That is, a decision is not a decision to make a decision but rather the concrete action implied by the decision. After any time interval, a decision may be replaced by another decision, perhaps as a result of updated information." Thus, if evaluation is a process that produces information useful in decision making, then evaluation is a process that produces information to assist in the allocation of resources. While this line of reasoning does not define the particular form that evaluation should take, we claim that it helps to clarify much of the debate over the various definitions of evaluation. Evaluation for compliance, evaluation for programmatic change, or evaluation for scientific inquiry — all can be reconciled by considering the decision makers who intend to use the information that comes from the evaluation.

The potential allocation of resources associated with an evaluation must be considered broadly. It can range from obvious programmatic changes (for example, shifting staffing patterns or operating procedures) to congressional authorization to spend more (or less) money on similar programs nationally or to a change in research efforts by one or more researchers who may want to devote more (or less) of their resources to that programmatic area. The allocation of resources can even refer to decisions by members of a program's client group to increase or decrease participation in the program.

Evaluation has a rich and diverse history. It seems rooted not only in substantive areas of concern, such as education, psychology, and mental health, but also in methodological areas of concern, such as classical statistics and experimental design. In the late 1960s and during the 1970s, the expanding role of government in providing services placed heavy demands on evaluation as a way of testing alternative ways for providing services. The demands on evaluation are not likely to diminish during the 1980s, but their nature may change as a result of increased interest in the accountability and productivity of service-providing agencies. Yet, these demands are being placed upon a field that amalgamates methodologically and substantively distinct areas of inquiry. Thus, there is a strong need for constructs and theories that serve to unify the heretofore disparate elements of evaluation. Evaluation for decision making is, we believe, one very useful framework in which to consider existing evaluation approaches and to identify the need for new approaches. It is our purpose in this chapter to review currently popular evaluation paradigms in their relation to decision making and to describe some new approaches that seem to contribute to the decision utility of evaluation.

We begin by reviewing the classical approaches of input, process, and outcome evaluation. Next, we will focus on three complementary quantitatively oriented methods for evaluation that can be used in conjunction with one or more of the classical approaches. We categorize these complementary methods as Bayesian approaches, adaptive methods of evaluation, and model-based methods. We will end with a brief summary and some conclusions.

Classical Approaches to Program Evaluation

Any operating public program is a process that acts on inputs to create outcomes. Many, perhaps most, classical evaluation paradigms for public programs have focused separately on program input, program process, or program outcome, so it is convenient to classify evaluations according to the program element being evaluated.

Evaluations that examine the resources or inputs dedicated to a given program are referred to as *input evaluations*. Perhaps the most limited type of evaluation, input evaluations are concerned with the inventory of personnel, facilities, and other resources assembled for the program; the proposed client or target group; and the program design. As a rule, primary attention is directed at compliance questions—for instance, whether program inputs as assembled and deployed comply with governmental or contractual regulations. One type of input evaluation is the program audit, which simply seeks to compare planned program expenditures for staff, facilities, and equipment with actual expenditures. Recently, such program audits have been extended into the area of program operations, and program managers have been required to fill out periodic reports of program activities and workloads, comparing and contrasting these with those planned in the approved contract or grant. Input evaluations are usually commissioned by program funding agencies or regulatory agencies; their findings are usually not directly useful to program personnel, except in cases where operations must change in order to achieve compliance. The decision makers who most often use the results of input evaluations are program funders, governmental regulatory agencies, and their equivalents.

While input evaluations focus on the resources directed to a given program, *process evaluations* examine the actual utilization of these resources by studying what the program physically does. A process evaluation of a program seeks to understand the causal mechanisms that translate the program inputs into program outputs or outcomes. If data about program outputs are unobtainable, a process evaluation tries to understand the mechanisms whereby program inputs are translated into action. Process evaluations use a mixture of qualitative and quantitative techniques to understand the usually multifaceted nature of the program process. These include analysis of process-related performance measures; utilization of participant observers, interviews, and questionnaires; and other methods for understanding the total environment of the program. The outlook is Bayesian rather than statistical, meaning that impressionistic information can play a role which equals that of statistical information. Process evaluation can yield information that helps to establish the degree of program influence on observed outcomes. Process evaluations can also identify unintended side effects of the program. The findings of a process evaluation are often directly relevant to managers of the program being evaluated, but in many cases their usefulness to personnel and similar programs elsewhere is limited, owing largely to the idiosyncratic nature of the program and the specificity of evaluation conclusions.

What process evaluation does not attempt to determine is whether the program achieved its stated goals. This question is addressed by *outcome evaluations*. Several methodologies are available for performing outcome evaluation, but it is clear from the evaluation literature that experimental designs currently constitute the preferred approach. As Rossi and Wright (1977, p. 13) claim, "There is almost universal agreement among evaluation researchers that the randomized controlled experiment is the ideal model for evaluating the effectiveness of a public policy." Indeed, if it is possible to conduct a randomized experiment, the programs may be analyzed by the procedures of classical statistics. However, as the design of a test diverges from that of the classical experiment, the rationale for the use of statistical evaluation devices is weakened. In realistic evaluation situations, the requisite degree of rigidity required to apply these statistical methods with any confidence is rarely achieved.

A wide range of decision makers can be interested in the results of an outcome evaluation, including legislators considering the institutionalization of the experimental program across a wider jurisdiction, researchers who wish to test one or more intervention theories, program managers who wish to revise program activities to better achieve ultimate objectives, or program funders interested in learning whether the program is achieving its objectives.

It is ironic that the most widely used statistical method in outcome evaluations — the statistical test of a hypothesis — is itself not decision oriented. Most typically, one poses the null hypothesis that the program had no effect on one or more outcome variables and tests that hypothesis with an experimental or quasi-experimental design. It has by now been well documented in the evaluation literature that this procedure tends to be biased toward acceptance of the null hypothesis (or, shall we say, toward not rejecting the null hypothesis), and neither acceptance nor rejection of the null hypothesis is especially useful in the decision-making context. In addition to asymmetries regarding the likelihood of the emergence of alternative hypotheses, the classical hypothesis test is incapable of including the costs of various types of errors (for example, of accepting the null hypothesis when it is false or of rejecting the null hypothesis when it is true). Such costs or errors are extremely important in a decision-making framework, yet classical statistics has difficulty in dealing with them. Thus, we have a situation in which outcome evaluation, which potentially affects the largest pool of decision makers, is supported by an evaluation paradigm that is largely inconsequential for decision making. In our view, this is one of the major gaps in current evaluation methodology.

Bayesian Approaches to Program Evaluation

As we have argued above, evaluations should be designed and conducted with their relevance for decision making in mind. In fact, the decision to evaluate or not to evaluate is itself an important allocation of resources. Thus, when one seeks to develop a unifying theory for evaluation, one most naturally gravitates toward methodologies that aid in the analysis of decisions. This leads us to the exciting field of Bayesian statistics and decision analysis (see, for example, Keeney and Raiffa, 1976; Thompson, 1975).

The use of the terms *Bayesian method, decision analysis,* and *utility theory* has often been confused and misinterpreted in the evaluation field. In fact, there are several different components to the application of these methods in evaluation. One approach to the use of decision analysis in evaluation is seen in the work of Edwards, Guttentag, and Snapper (1975). These authors proposed to use utility theory to establish numerical preferences on alternative outcomes of a program and its evaluation. By applying simple single-attribute linear additive utility theory to program evaluation, they attempted to derive recipe-type procedures for conducting what they call *decision theoretic* or *Bayesian* evaluations. Another distinctly different application is described by Thompson (1975), who considers the very decision to evaluate as problematic. His application of these methods considers whether or not to evaluate and, if the decision to evaluate is made, which evaluation design to select. He argues that the best performance measure for an evaluation is the expected policy improvement consequence of the evaluation design, minus the expected cost of implementing the design. Here the policy improvement and cost units must be compatible, a requirement which should not be taken lightly in the complex field of evaluation. The mathematical operation of calculating expectation by averaging over alternative outcomes must be done before the evaluation is undertaken. This requires inclusion of subjective probabilities over outcomes as well as the utility of alternative outcomes. Thompson calls the policy improvement component of the averaged quantity the prior information value or PIV of an evaluation. Invoking decision analysis, Thompson argues that the PIV has the following properties: A decision maker should not pay more for an evaluation than its PIV, although expenditure of any amount less than the PIV is justified in the absence of alternative evaluations; among competing evaluations of equal cost, the evaluation with the highest PIV should be preferred; and among competing evaluations of different costs, the evaluation with the highest net PIV — the prior information value less the cost of the evaluation — should be preferred (Thompson, 1975, p. 40). The policy benefits underlying the PIV derive from the possibility that information provided by the evaluation will lead to program improvement.

While we think that the PIV is a useful concept, we believe that it may not be appropriate to advocate its use in actual evaluation settings at this stage in evaluation research. Estimation of the expected policy benefits of an evaluation and standardization of the benefits and costs is simply too difficult a task for all but the simplest situations. This limitation of the PIV concept does not, however, preclude its conceptual utility as a means of answering the question of whether to evaluate and of selecting the appropriate evaluation design.

Other Bayesian or decision-oriented methods relevant to evaluation focus on Bayesian statistical methods. Here, we refer specifically to Bayesian hypothesis testing and Bayesian methods of parameter estimation. One highly desirable attribute of Bayesian statistical methods is the ability of the Bayesian structure to include both impressionistic and hard information compatibly within one parameter estimation framework. Thus, for instance, an evaluator doing both a process and an outcome evaluation may have both process and relative frequency-type knowledge of one or more parameters; the process or impressionistic knowledge can be utilized to create a prior distribution on the unknown parameters, and the relative frequency information can be used to update the prior distribution to obtain a posterior distribution. While this approach may seem to be attractive in an evaluation setting, we are unaware that any completed evaluations have actually used this approach. Critics of the approach argue that the procedure is subject to large abuse, in the sense that prior beliefs and prejudices can be incorporated into a prior distribution under the guise of utilizing process information and bias the evaluation results as the evaluator desires. While this is certainly true, we would argue that the allegedly more scientific classical statistical hypothesis test is subject to equal abuse (for example, one could cleverly select a null hypothesis that would be difficult to reject for small and moderate sample sizes). The Bayesian parameter estimation approach has been used to reanalyze evaluations of time series studies, such as the saturation patrol study reported by Schnelle and others, 1977; Willemain (1978a) has applied Bayesian procedures in a reanalysis of Schnelle's data.

One of the most relevant applications of Bayesian ideas in an evaluation framework is the Bayesian hypothesis test. The Bayesian hypothesis test is, in fact, less a hypothesis test than a procedure for deriving an optimum decision rule. Thus, decision making is its primary focus. In the simplest form of the Bayesian hypothesis test, there are two possible states of nature: state 0 and state 1; and two decisions that one can make are: to say that state 0 is the true state of nature or to say that state 1 is the true state of nature. The idea is to incorporate one's prior knowledge, the costs of various kinds of decisions and their concomitant errors, and recently acquired data into a unified framework for decision making.

Perhaps these ideas are best illustrated by a simple example from the medical field. Suppose we have a patient who is being tested for the presence of cancer; that is, the two states of nature are state 0, representing no cancer, and state 1, representing cancer. The decision to be made by a physician is whether or not to operate on the patient in the hope of eradicating the cancer. The risks are obvious: not to operate in the presence of cancer seems to carry the greatest risk; to operate in the absence of cancer yields unnecessary risk; not to operate in the absence of cancer is clearly the best possible situation. All of these can be summarized succinctly by four costs:

C_{00} = the cost of not operating in the absence of cancer
C_{01} = the cost of not operating in the presence of cancer
C_{10} = the cost of operating in the absence of cancer
C_{11} = the cost of operating in the presence of cancer

Our prior beliefs regarding this patient derive in part from our knowledge of the probabilities for patients from similar populations reviewed in the past. That is, we assign a value of P_0 to the probability that the patient in fact does not have cancer and P_1 to the probability that the patient in fact does have cancer. From past experiences, we have found that a fraction P_0 of similar patients did not have cancer and that a fraction P_1 of similar patients did have cancer.

The physician then carries out a test on the patient, and this test yields a numerical score; for example, the density of abnormal blood cells on a microscope slide. On the basis of this score, the physician will determine whether to operate. The second element of our prior belief is brought into play at this point. It has been found that patients who do not have cancer yield a distribution of score values centered around a particular value S_0 of the score, while individuals who do have cancer yield another distribution of score values centered around S_1. Unfortunately (from the decision maker's viewpoint), the two distributions overlap, and this creates ambiguity in the score results and a potential for decision errors.

A decision rule, which is the outcome of the analysis of the Bayesian hypothesis test, is a partitioning of score values so that one has regions of score values in which the physician decides to operate and regions in which he decides not to operate. Any particular partitioning or decision rule has an associated error of deciding to operate when in fact there was no need, and an associated error of deciding not to operate when it was needed. Suppose for a particular decision rule that we call α the probability of deciding to operate when in fact the patient does not have cancer and β the probability of deciding not to operate when in fact the patient does have cancer. These α's and β's are the same α's and β's that one obtains in the classical statistical hypothesis test. Letting TC represent the total expected cost of a given decision rule,

$$TC = P_0[C_{00}(1 - \alpha) + C_{10}\alpha] + P_1[C_{01}\beta + C_{11}(1 - \beta)]$$

Minimization of the total expected cost is the emphasis of the analysis in a Bayesian hypothesis test.

In this example, if the various costs involved relate to life expectancies, then the largest life expectancy would accrue to the patient who is not operated on and who does not have cancer, while the shortest life expectancy would accrue to the patient who does have cancer but who is not operated on. Since years of life expectancy are a positive good, to translate them into costs we must multiply by -1. As an example, suppose we take the following values for costs:

$$C_{00} = -30 \text{ years}$$
$$C_{01} = -5 \text{ years}$$
$$C_{10} = -25 \text{ years}$$
$$C_{11} = -20 \text{ years}$$

We also assume that $P_0 = 0.65$ and $P_1 = 1 - P_0 = 0.35$. Suppose further that the distribution of test scores for those who do not have cancer is normal with mean 40 and variance 169, while the distribution for those who do have cancer is normal with mean at 60 and variance at 169. The situation is diagrammed in Figure 1.

Utilizing all this information, it is not difficult to evaluate alternative decision rules (see Table 1). The optimal decision rule is a threshold score value equaling 45.95. For score values less than this amount,

Figure 1. Normal Frequency Curves of Test Scores for Patients
With ($S_1 = 60$) and Without ($S_0 = 40$) Cancer

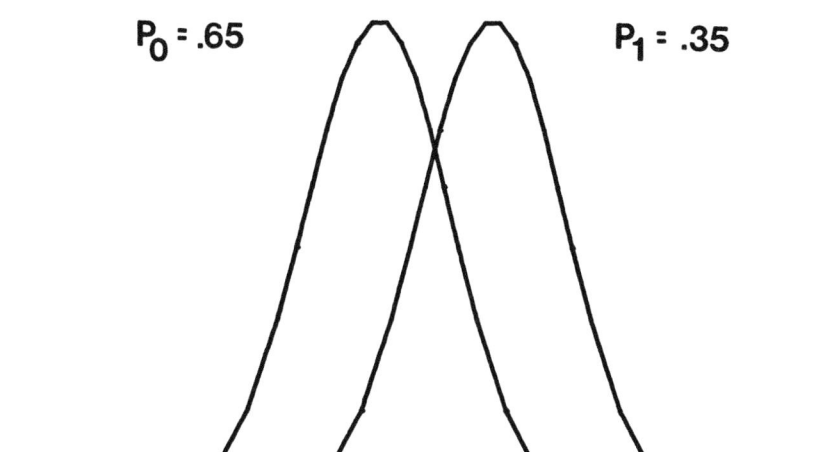

$P_0 = .65$ $P_1 = .35$

40 60
(S_0) (S_1)

the physician decides to operate. This decision rule minimizes the total expected cost of the procedure, where cost, as we have indicated, is measured in years of life expectancy. We may contrast the life expectancy resulting from the optimal policy with that resulting from alternative, sometimes naive policies. The optimal decision rule results in a life expectancy of 24.71 years. However, if the physician is completely risk-averse and always decides to operate, then the life expectancy reduces to 23.25 years, but if he decides never to operate, the life expectancy is reduced to 21.25 years. A physician whose testing procedures left much to be desired might decide at random to operate on 35 percent of the patients; such a policy would result in a life expectancy of 21.95 years. In contrast, if one adhered strictly to α and β values found in the popular statistical tests, one would find that for an α of .05, there would be a corresponding β of .5424 and a life expectancy of 23.49 years; for a β of .05, there would be an α of .5424 and a life expectancy of 24.47 years. We see that blind adherence to any prespecified values for α or β will, in general, yield nonoptimal decisions. This same limitation on α values of .05 arises in many elements of outcome evaluation in which the evaluators attempt to apply statistical recipes to their evaluations which yield decisions that may be far from optimal.

Table 1. Life Expectancies Corresponding to
Alternative Decision Rules

Decision Rule	α	β	Life Expectancy
1. Always Operate	1.0	0.0	23.25 Years
2. Never Operate	0.0	1.0	21.25 Years
3. Operate on 35 Percent of All Patients	0.35	0.65	21.95 Years
4. Fix $\alpha = .05$	0.05	0.5424	23.49 Years
5. Fix $\beta = .05$	0.5424	0.05	24.47 Years
6. Optimal Decision Rule (Minimize Total Cost)	0.3236	0.1399	24.71 Years

Adaptive Evaluation Design

It is our belief that the process of evaluating public programs should often be adaptive rather than fixed. One need for adaptiveness is clear: if the program being evaluated changes, evaluation activities may need to be adjusted, if they can be, to compensate for the change. Another is less obvious. Information gathered during the course of an evaluation arrives in a probabilistic manner, providing evaluators with different knowledge profiles about the program at each intermediate point during the evaluation. Some, perhaps most, knowledge profiles should suggest a change in evaluation activities. Armed with Bayesian decision-oriented concepts discussed in the previous section, one can develop a consistent structure for considering alternative evaluation designs.

To formalize these ideas, evaluation activities are directed by an evaluation design, which we define as a set of rules indicating how scarce evaluation resources are to be allocated over time and task. A fixed evaluation design is one in which the rules are inflexible or deterministic and do not allow for change at intermediate points during the evaluation. An adaptive or flexible evaluation design is one in which the rules are stated in a manner that is dependent on the evaluator's knowledge profile at intermediate points during the evaluation.

One difficulty in developing new methods of program evaluation is knowing when you have something that is in some sense better than what was used before. Thus, we need measures that allow us to compare the evaluative quality of the methods that we develop to the evaluative quality of more standard methods. This problem is not limited to researchers. Practicing evaluators, too, require valid and systematic means for comparing feasible evaluation designs in order to make an intelligent choice. (We do not use the word *optimal* here, because it is too strong for the problem setting.) To our knowledge, the idea of comparing alternative evaluation designs by means of an integrated set of performance measures attributable to the designs is new in the field of public program evaluation.

In a strict decision-theoretic sense, the best performance measure for an evaluation is the net PIV, as argued in the preceding section. Nevertheless, estimating the expected policy benefits of an evaluation and standardizing units of benefits and costs is too difficult a task for all but the simplest situation. Thus, at least in the short term, one should seek performance measures for evaluations that are easier to implement than the PIV. One class of promising evaluation design performance measures consists of measures that focus on particular evaluation performance characteristics, given that it has been decided to perform an evaluation with specified inputs. That is, one would emphasize selection of the preferred design, as indicated by one or more performance measures, within certain operational constraints involving time, money, personnel, or other resources devoted to the evaluation. This strategy is more compatible with evaluation practice, in which many if not most evaluations are commissioned by a Request for Proposal, a process that almost invariably places time and budget constraints on the evaluation.

We have just begun research on adaptive evaluation designs and we are exploring a number of evaluation design performance measures, including the information expected from an evaluation as measured by entropy or other indexes of information content, various measures of parameter variability as indicated by updated Bayesian density functions (for example, the variance of an updated or posterior distribution), and more traditional statistical measures obtained from classical statistics.

Equipped with a set of performance measures for evaluation designs, we plan to apply a number of them in particular evaluation problem situations. One example involves adaptively determining the various time periods of an evaluation. An evaluation is often partitioned into distinct time periods, with each period representing either a different set of evaluation activities or a different program implementation stage. During a three-period evaluation, for example, the evaluator might collect baseline data, during-program data, and post-program data. An important part of any evaluation design is the determination of the length of each period, usually with a constraint that limits the length of the entire evaluation and probably with certain other evaluation resource constraints. For instance, a very simple one-year, two-period fixed design would allot the first six months to the collection of baseline data and the second six months to the collection of new program data (assuming that a revised program is implemented precisely at the six-month mark). While most evaluation designs fix the lengths of the various evaluation time periods, circumstances arise in practice that make it possible adaptively and dynamically to determine the length of these periods. Basically, the purpose of each period is to collect certain information within acceptable tolerances of uncertainty. Evaluation resources devoted to each period result in costs that vary linearly with the length of the period. Here, the problem of adaptive evaluation design is to determine dynamic decision rules for switching times between one evaluation period and the next, where accumulated costs and known information content are balanced against expected costs and information content of future decisions. The problem may even be extended from the adaptive determination of period durations within a given sequence to the optimal sequencing of evaluation periods.

Preliminary work by Willemain (1978b) and Willemain and Hartunian (in press) examines what is probably the simplest design issue for time series comparisons, namely, determining the division of a prospective time series comparison between simple baseline and experimental phases. This work assumes that the aim of experimental intervention is to change the rate of a Poisson process, as the approach grew out of reanalysis of a Nashville experiment with saturation-level patrols which established that the count of serious crimes can be well described by the Poisson probability law (Willemain, 1978a). Because most time series analyses have a retrospective baseline, the length of the baseline is usually determined by the availability of data. We found no guidance in the literature on how to determine the baseline duration prospectively when faced with an overall budget constraint. The analysis produced a method for optimal division of an evaluation budget between the two phases of the time series comparison. The optimal division depends on four key parameters: the budget level, the relative daily cost of the two phases of the experiment, the prior expectation of the baseline rate, and the prior expectation of the experimental impact. When the experiment is poorly funded, the choice of baseline duration becomes critical for obtaining the best possible estimate of the experimental impact, and proper design can greatly improve the efficiency of the evaluation. When this situation is considered to be adaptive, the duration of the baseline is made to depend on the baseline data as they appear. If the empirical results unfold in a way that confirms the prior estimate of the baseline rate, then the baseline has served its purpose and the resources can better be invested in the experimental phase of the study.

Optimal fixed and optimal adaptive designs were considered by Willemain and Hartunian (in press) in very simple two-period situations. Our current work is aimed at extending these analyses to more complex and realistic situations.

Another application of adaptive evaluation design that is responsive to information profiles as they appear at various times in an evaluation addresses adaptive allocation of evaluation resources. Viewed analytically by the methods and performance measures used to study the previous problem, this problem appears to be quite similar. Substantively, it is quite different, and it is applicable to a far broader range of evaluation acitvities, particularly in process evaluation, where analytical guidance has been scant. Recalling that evaluation is an information-gathering process, it can unravel in much the same way as a detective story, and just as Sherlock Holmes redirects his crime-solving activities as new clues arise, evaluators should be committed to adapting their evaluation activities as new information is obtained. Our present work is aimed at such evaluation activities as adaptive allocation of interviewer and participant observers in process evaluation. We anticipate that a report on this work will be available early in 1982.

One other major element of our adaptive evaluation design research focuses on the response of an evaluation to changes in the program being evaluated. We start with the premise that any program operating in a public agency is a dynamic process, with individuals maturing and changing their priorities, with operations evolving over time, and with new constraints imposed by regulatory agencies, new legislation, citizens groups, and so on. Any evaluation design that assumes a rigidly fixed world for any considerable amount of time is likely to experience difficulty as a result of these natural changes over time. Some of these processes have been recognized in the evaluation literature, such as maturation and attrition in Campbell and Stanley's (1963) now famous "threats to internal validity." One of the objectives of randomization is to structure an experiment so as to have these time-varying processes affect the control and experimental groups equally. In this way, measured differences between control and experimental outcomes cannot be attributed to these changes. The issue becomes much more problematic when randomization is not employed, as in time series quasi-experiments.

In our current research, we distinguish between incremental program changes and major changes, which we call fundamental changes. For the incremental type of change, we are exploring various methods and techniques that could be used to correct the evaluation data for the variability caused by incremental program change. Our primary method is based on modeling techniques, as discussed in the next section. For the fundamental type of change, we are exploring the possibility of incorporating the risk of that type of change a priori in the evaluation design process. For the incremental program changes, we believe that the soundest way to ensure the integrity of evaluation is to build simple mathematical models that correct for the gradual or sudden changes that arise in the environment; the assumptions in these models should be stated clearly and, when possible, subjected to empirical testing. An example will be described in the next section.

In our study of fundamental program changes, we note that no evaluation design can stand impervious to all changes in the program or in its environment. One would like to incorporate the possibility of fundamental change in a program or its environment — change so great that the evaluation cannot continue — into the evaluation design process. Our point here is to catalogue the four or five likely causes of such catastrophic change and to assess the probability of each. One could use laws of combining probabilities to obtain a good Bayesian estimate of the probability of failure. If that probability exceeds some threshold, then the evaluation design as originally planned is unworkable. One may ask, "What is the alternative?" As an example, if the original evaluation were to occur at a single site, one clear alternative that appears to warrant serious consideration is multisite evaluation. Due to budget constraints, the cost of multisite evaluation is a smaller sample size at each site. However, the benefit is an increased likelihood that at least some useful information will be obtained by the end of the evaluation.

In general, in this part of our research on adaptive evaluation designs, we seek to identify the institutional, political, legal, and technical factors that create fundamental change in a program, environment, or both. We seek to determine the reliability with which the risks of such changes can be estimated. We seek also to develop probabilistic procedures, borrowing concepts from reliability theory and using relevant performance measures to develop less risky alternatives to single-site designs and other standard approaches.

Model-Based Methods for Evaluation

Closely linked to Bayesian and adaptive evaluations are the methods of model-based evaluation. A model is a conceptualization of a process or part of a process. It represents a hypothesized set of relationships that acts on the set of independent variables to produce values for the set of dependent variables. A model does not need to be mathematical; in fact, verbal or narrative models are often much richer than corresponding mathematical models. In evaluation, models offer aid for evaluation activities by systematically considering the set of causal linkages that acts on inputs to produce outcomes (that is, a model is a hypothesized set of relationships that, through program processes, transforms program inputs into program outcomes); by uncovering the importance of certain performance measures; by discovering the presence, cause, and magnitude of unintended biases in a data sample; by estimating the necessary duration of the evaluation at the design stage in order to assure that equilibrium, rather than transient program behavior, is observed and evaluated; in general, by building an evaluator's insight and intuition, thereby providing a systematic framework for generating and testing hypotheses and assisting in the exploration of counterintuitive or unintended results; and by providing a basis for evaluating evaluations.

The use of modeling in an evaluation is quite compatible with the Bayesian and decision-oriented approaches discussed above. In fact, utilization of Bayesian statistical procedures requires probabilistic models as part of the Bayesian analysis. In a decision tree context, estimation of the probability with which certain events will occur is made easier by the construction and analysis of appropriate models at the appropriate branch of the decision tree. Our recommendation for the use of modeling in evaluation goes further than strict technical application of models; we argue that hypothesized or conjectured relationships, whether mathematical or verbal in nature, should be used throughout the evaluation enterprise to provide a coherent structure for carrying out that enterprise. For example, in process evaluation, without one or more conjectured models that link program inputs through process to program outcomes, one would find it extremely difficult to structure a plan for collecting information in one's evaluation activities; Carol Weiss calls such conjectured models for process evaluation "causal chain" models (Weiss, 1971, p. 140).

The recommendation for using models in evaluation is not new. For instance, Brenner and Carrow (1976) presented views very similar to ours. They argued that proper evaluation must specify the theoretical rationale whereby the criminal justice system ought to affect the crime rate or some other outcome and control for the effects of all significant variables that would of themselves significantly affect the crime rate or other outcomes.

"Recent methodological developments in the social sciences have pointed to the appropriateness of constructing a structural model by which causation is understood to flow from the interaction of a number of different variables. Such a model, resembling those in physical sciences, includes integrating different theories, all of which have a simultaneous effect on the outcome phenomenon" (Brenner and Carrow, 1976).

There are essentially two ways to generate models in evaluation activities: top-down or bottom-up. Top-down implies that underlying theories or hypotheses give rise to the models. Bottom-up implies that the entire universe of models has been considered and that one or more of these are statistically discovered from the evaluation data. There are numerous problems with bottom-up modeling, which in application resembles little more than curve fitting. The flow of causation is hard to determine, and such things as correlations with invisible third variables can confound and confuse results. Our preference is for utilization of top-down or deductive models whenever possible.

Deductive models do not have to be complicated to provide insights. Here are three examples to illustrate this fact:

Institutional Half-Life. Suppose that we are considering the evaluation of a major reform or intervention in a public institution that has a twenty-five year retirement plan for its employees. Suppose further that the institution is in an equilibrium mode with regard to the number of employees; that is, it is neither growing nor diminishing in number of employees. Many major interventions are known to be impeded by institutional memories, which diminish only as the older employees leave to be replaced by new, younger employees. An evaluation designer could argue, then, that any major intervention in such an institution would only reach equilibrium or steady state once a good fraction of the sources of institutional memories has left the agency. One measure of the duration required for such an exodus is the institutional half-life of the institution, which is defined as the time required for a 50 percent turnover of personnel. In the institution just discussed, with a twenty-five-year retirement plan, the institutional half-life would be perhaps five or ten years if most employees stayed until retirement. However, this amount of time is quite sobering to a potential evaluator, who may want to consider an evaluation over a six-month, one-year, or even two-year period. Indeed, the idea of institutional half-life may suggest to the evaluator that any evaluation that is feasible within the short term must of necessity occur shortly after the intervention.

Crime and Streetlighting. Sometimes, simple modeling concepts will suggest alternative interpretations of evaluation performance measures that can change the appearance of failure into an appearance of success or vice versa. As an example, consider a city that is implementing a new strategy for combating street crime along one major street in the city. Suppose that, before the program, the number of street crimes per month along that major street was ten, and suppose that following implementation of the new program, the number of street crimes per month increased to twenty. An evaluator of this program could conclude that the program had been a failure, since the number of crimes doubled following the program. However, these data could be reinterpreted by considering the probability of an individual pedestrian being victimized while on the street. If the pedestrian volume following the new program quadrupled, then the *per-pedestrian* victimization probability would be half what it was before the program. In this light, the program appears successful. We are not arguing here that a single interpretation is correct but that the incorporation of one simple modeling idea — the flow of pedestrians and pedestrian-specific victimization probability — can sharply alter one's view of the success or failure of a program.

Interbeat Dispatch Frequency. Within police circles, a police officer is usually required to respond to as many calls for service within his or her own beat as is physically possible. That is, police administrators require that an officer assigned to a given beat handle as large a fraction of the calls for assistance on that beat as possible. This enhances officer identity with the beat, and it also enhances citizen satisfaction, since citizens get to know the officers assigned to their beat. However, any evaluator evaluating a program involving police patrol forces should be aware of a physical law that limits the dispatch assignments within an officer's patrolling beat. The result of this law is as follows: On the average, if patrol officers in an area are busy X percent of the time, then approximately X percent of patrol dispatch assignments are to officers in beats other than that in which the call for service originated. That is, for officers busy X percent of the time, roughly X percent of their dispatches take them to beats other than their primary beat. Also, citizens see officers responding to their calls for service from other beats roughly X percent of the time. This result is derived from a simple modeling concept. Since calls for service arrive in a completely random and unscheduled manner, if a patrol officer is busy X percent of the time, then X percent of the time a call for service that arrives from his beat will find him already busy. Thus, a dispatcher who requires a rapid response to that call for service must find and dispatch an available unit for that X percent of calls in a contiguous or nearby beat. What is true for one beat is true for all. The law can be modified only by altering the dispatcher's procedures, such as deliberately delaying certain calls for service and entering calls in queue, in order to await the availability of the beat car.

Very simple models such as those illustrated above could greatly enhance the evaluator's insight and intuition into program process and program outcome, and this could lead to improved evaluation designs, executions, and analyses.

As we have demonstrated, informal, back-of-the-envelope models can often be employed in evaluating public programs. There are situations, however, where the degree of program complexity warrants the use of more sophisticated models. To model such large-scale programs can require the aid of a computer.

Computer-based models have recently been used in evaluation of large-scale housing and criminal justice programs. For example, researchers at the Urban Institute developed a detailed simulation model of the urban housing market; this model has been employed to analyze various housing programs, including the HUD-sponsored housing allowance experiments (Carlton and Ferreira, 1977; de Leeuw and Struyk, 1977). This model was used to assess the implications of alternative housing assistance payment formulas, so that the most desirable subsidy scheme could be identified. Also, the model can determine the fraction of income spent on housing under alternative assumptions governing the elasticity of demand for housing; this is obviously quite important in the analysis of housing allowance programs. The computer-based JUSSIM (Justice Simulation) model has been used to examine the entire criminal justice systems of a number of states (Blumstein and Larson, 1972). JUSSIM enables one to trace entire cohorts of offenders through the criminal justice system. Thus, JUSSIM aids in studying court and prison congestion, the effects of sentencing on the size of the prison population, and the timing of various levels of recidivism (for example, time until rearrest versus time until reconviction). Although the models referenced here are quite complex, the rationale for using them is the same as the rationale for using simple models. In the examples that we have cited, researchers were able to examine the likely outcomes of alternative programs in a systematic manner.

Summary and Conclusions

Throughout this chapter, we have argued for the development and utilization of a coherent, decision-oriented approach to evaluation. Many details of what we have proposed have yet to be worked out in complex evaluation settings, and we would be naive to claim that everything we propose could be implemented without difficulty. Yet, it is our contention that there is a clear need for one or more coherent and comprehensive approaches to this amalgam of heretofore disparate fields. We have chosen a decision-oriented approach because we believe that the primary purpose of single-project evaluations is to inform one or more decision makers.

Much of what we have proposed involves formal methods, requiring mathematical modeling, Bayesian statistics, and so on. The literature on operations research alone yields such relevant tools of analysis as probabilistic modeling, decision analysis, Bayesian analysis, and Markov decision processes. Other relevant tools come from the fields of optimal control theory, information theory, and stochastic processes. While these methodologies are indeed powerful, their most successful applications have tended to be in highly technical areas such as process control in chemical plants, oil exploration, space exploration, and operation of communications systems. Only recently have we begun to see successful limited applications of these techniques to more human-oriented areas such as the forecasting of personal career trajectories, the location of human services facilities in cities, the allocation of municipal services resources, the prediction of recidivism patterns, and even the identification of sources of selection bias in criminal justice evaluations.

Analytical techniques such as these work best in precisely structured environments with readily measurable input, process, and outcome variables. They tend to become analytically intractable when imbedded in an imprecisely formulated environment. These attributes would appear to limit the applicability of modern quantitative techniques within the imprecise field of evaluation. We believe that this is a correct conclusion if one judges the results of using these techniques by the infallible "recipes" that they generate for the naive evaluator. However, we believe that a second yardstick is required. We do not propose using these techniques as foolproof recipes in evaluations. Rather, we believe that the careful and judicious use of abstractions in evaluation settings can yield valuable insights to the evaluation designer and implementer that greatly improve one's understanding of the many facets of evaluation. Armed with improved insight and intuition, the evaluation designer will have analytically grounded guidance as to the consequences of alternative evaluation designs that he or she may consider.

The situation is somewhat analogous to that of business school students who are taught decision analysis and Bayesian statistics for use in complex and ill-defined business settings. By working through the analysis of abstractions of business problems, the potential decision maker gains insight into the dynamic, adaptive decision situations that will confront him or her every day as a manager. Yet, rarely as a manager will he or she in fact sit down to diagram a decision tree. The process has to be integrated into one's intuitive decision-making process.

By applying these techniques in an evaluation setting, we hope to develop similar useful abstractions and analyses for evaluators. The alternative is to ignore the need for comprehensive conceptualizations of the evaluation enterprise. Analytically, it is certainly much easier to borrow from other analytical areas, such as classical statistics, when necessary. But to allow the increased difficulty to be the determining argument against decision-oriented comprehensive evaluations would be unfortunate. Decision-oriented approaches show considerable promise for reducing the misallocation of expensive evaluation resources, the collection of redundant information, haphazard responses to unexpected changes in the program, rote performance of statistical analyses without sequentially formulating and testing hypotheses, analysis and display of information without regard to the decisions to be influenced by it, and, most troublesome, the tendency to view rigid experimental design as the ultimate paradigm for evaluation.

References

Blumstein, A., and Larson, R. C. "Analysis of a Total Criminal System." In A. W. Drake, R. L. Keeney, and P. M. Morse (Eds.), *Analysis of Public Systems.* Cambridge, Mass.: M.I.T. Press, 1972.

Brenner, M. P. H., and Carrow, D. "Evaluation Research with Hard Data." In *Criminal Justice Evaluation.* New York: United Nations, 1976.

Campbell, D. T., and Stanley, J. C. *Experimental and Quasi-Experimental Designs for Research.* Chicago: Rand McNally, 1963.

68

Carlton, D. W., and Ferreira, J., Jr. "Selecting Subsidy Strategies for Housing Allowance Programs." *Journal of Urban Economics,* 1977, *4,* 221–247.

deLeeuw, F., and Struyk, R. J. "Analyzing Housing Policies with the Urban Institute Housing Models." In G. K. Ingram (Ed.), *Residential Location and Urban Housing Markets.* Cambridge, Mass.: Ballinger, 1977.

Edwards, W., Guttentag, M., and Snapper, K. "A Decision-Theoretic Approach to Evaluation Research." In E. L. Struening and M. Guttentag (Eds.), *Handbook of Evaluation Research.* Beverly Hills, Calif.: Sage, 1975.

Howard, R. A. "Decision Analysis: Applied Decision Theory." In D. B. Hertz and J. Melese (Eds.), *Proceedings of the Fourth International Conference on Operational Research.* New York: Wiley, 1966.

Keeney, R. L., and Raiffa, H. *Decisions with Multiple Objectives: Preferences and Value Tradeoffs.* New York: Wiley, 1976.

Rossi, P. H., and Wright, S. R. "Evaluation Research: An Assessment of Theory, Practice, and Politics." *Evaluation Quarterly,* 1977, *1* (1), 5–52.

Schnelle, J. F., Kirchner, R. E., Jr., Casey, J. D., Uselton, P. H., Jr., and McNees, M. P. "Patrol Evaluation Research: A Multiple Baseline Analysis of Saturation Police Patrolling During Day and Night Hours." *Journal of Applied Behavior Analysis,* 1977, *10,* 33–40.

Thompson, M. S. *Evaluations for Decisions in Social Programmes.* Lexington, Mass.: Heath, 1975.

Weiss, C. H. "Utilization in Evaluation." In F. G. Caro (Ed.), *Readings in Evaluation Research.* New York: Russell Sage Foundation, 1971.

Willemain, T. R. "Bayesian Analysis of Crime Rate Changes in Before-After Experiments." Report OR 0-75-78. Cambridge, Mass.: Operations Research Center, Massachusetts Institute of Technology, 1978a.

Willemain, T. R. "Analysis of a Contingent Experimental Design: A Before and After Experiment with a Baseline Period of Random Duration." Report OR 79-78. Cambridge, Mass.: Operations Research Center, Massachusetts Institute of Technology, 1978b.

Willemain, T. R., and Hartunian, N. F. "The Design of Time Series Comparisons Under Budget Constraints," in press.

Richard C. Larson is professor of electrical engineering and urban studies at M.I.T., where he is codirector of the M.I.T. Operations Research Center. He is also founder and president of Public Systems Evaluation, Inc., a nonprofit applied research firm.

Edward H. Kaplan is a doctoral degree candidate in the Department of Urban Studies and Planning at M.I.T.

Although the evolution of health program evaluation should keep pace with the parallel evolution of disease patterns and epidemiology, it in fact lags behind.

Disease Patterns, Epidemiology, and Evaluation: An Evolutionary Perspective

G. E. Alan Dever
Rebecca H. Rousseau
Frank M. Houser

In recent years, program evaluation has assumed a high priority for health agencies, such as state departments of health, that are responsible for the distribution of health program funds. Evaluation is regarded by such agencies as a tool for continued improvement of programs in the face of fiscal austerity. Therefore, as federal, state, and local health resources become scarcer, evaluation will continue to gain importance in the health care field. To keep pace with this trend will require accelerated development of new evaluation approaches.

The premise to be developed in this chapter is that although the evolution of health program evaluation should keep pace with the parallel evolution of disease patterns and epidemiology (see Table 1), it in fact lags behind. It is apparent that the emerging trend in health program evaluation is the incorporation of a systems approach. Hence, a systems approach to health program evaluation in state departments of health is proposed in this chapter, and recommendations are made for the essential element in such an approach, namely, an integrated, comprehensive data base.

Changing Disease Patterns

The diseases that constitute the morbidity patterns in a geographical area are necessarily the prime targets for state health departments. The causes, both direct and indirect, of these disease patterns must be investigated, so that appropriate programs can be established. Drawing upon the long-term perspective proposed by Dever (1980), it can be concluded that these patterns evolve over time in accordance with changes in the physical and social conditions of society. In particular, as American society changed from agricultural to industrial, patterns of disease shifted from infectious to chronic.

At the turn of the century, when our society was immersed in the agricultural era, the basic needs of food, shelter, and clothing were of primary importance. High fertility partially compensated for the high infant-to-preschool mortality rates, which resulted from malnutrition and from parasitic and infectious diseases. As a result, 52 percent of the population was less than twenty years of age, and only 3 percent was over sixty-five. The infectious disease cycle is still in effect in today's inner cities and developing countries (Dever, 1980, p. 6).

Table 1. The Evolution of Disease Patterns, Epidemiology, and Health Program Evaluation

Disease Patterns	*Epidemiology*	*Health Program Evaluation*
Infectious Diseases ↓	Single Cause/ Single Effect Model ↓	Goal-Attainment Approach ↓
Infectious/ Chronic Diseases Transition ↓	Multiple Cause/ Single Effect Model ↓	Quasi-Systems Approach ↓
Chronic Diseases	Multiple Cause/ Multiple Effect Model	Systems Approach

With the advent of industrialization, new disease patterns emerged. Affluence, changing values, and changing life-styles also contributed to deleterious social, physical, emotional, and environmental conditions. Roughly since 1925, chronic rather than infectious diseases have held the forefront, and fertility rates have fallen drastically. Thus, in 1970, 40 percent of the population was twenty years old or younger and 8 percent was over sixty-five. Whereas 34 percent of all deaths occurred among the birth to five-year-old group in 1900, 51 percent of the mortality in 1970 occurred in the over sixty-five age group (Dever, 1980, p. 10).

The Evolution of Epidemiology

As the diseases in our society have evolved, epidemiology — the study of the determinants and distribution of these diseases — has changed accordingly. In the late 1800s and early 1900s, the single cause-single effect epidemiological model was sufficient to explain the prevailing patterns of disease. The dominant diseases were those in which a single bacterium or virus was the causal agent. Thus, diseases and their causes were in one-to-one correspondence, and it was appropriate for health programs to be targeted quite narrowly.

As our society began to shift from agriculture to industry in the early 1900s, the patterns of disease entered a period of transition. The incidence of infectious and parasitic diseases began to decline, while the risks of such chronic diseases as cancer and heart disease began to rise. In the course of this transition, a more complex, multiple cause-single effect epidemiological model became more appropriate. The patterns of disease could no longer be explained by single bacterial or viral agents.

Today, when many infectious diseases have been conquered and chronic diseases constitute most instances of morbidity, an extremely complex epidemiological model is required. Our bodies and lives are invaded by a host of society-produced agents such as chemical pollutants in our air, food, and water; radiation; and stress and other social, physical, and emotional hardships. Each of us is affected differently and in ways that are not fully predictable. The chronic diseases of today are associated with a variety of causes, and they may occur concurrently with one another. A multiple cause-multiple effect disease pattern is in effect.

The intricate interrelationships of the multiple cause-multiple effect diseases of our present era make for an equally intricate multiple cause-multiple effect epidemiological model. Causes can be determined but the degree of association of a particular cause with a specific disease or the association between two diseases can only be stated as probabilities.

Health Program Evaluation—Past, Present, and Future

Once the determinants and distributions of diseases are discovered through the methods of epidemiology, the next step is to try to reduce the incidence of these diseases and to ameliorate their effects through specific health programs. These programs are usually implemented with public funds through departments of health. Once such programs are in place, it is necessary to evaluate them in order to determine whether they are working. Thus, the role and the approach of health program evaluation are fundamentally determined by disease patterns and epidemiology; as disease patterns and epidemiology have evolved, so has the field of health program evaluation. However, program evaluation has evolved more slowly.

Past. Perhaps the oldest and most common approach to evaluation of federal and state health programs is the goal-attainment model, in which the degree to which a program has achieved its goals is determined. This approach, however, is limited and shortsighted in that it focuses quite narrowly on the achievement of particular time-limited goals. This narrow approach is the evaluation counterpart of the single cause-single effect model in epidemiology. As already pointed out, the single cause-single effect pattern of health problems and diseases was left behind with the agrarian era and the epidemiological model of 1900. An evaluation method that attempts to measure the success of a health program by determining the extent to which its goals were met without considering related health programs and other influential factors is outdated and may not prove or disprove anything.

Present. A second approach to health program evaluation that has come into being in recent years is the quasi-systems approach. This method goes somewhat beyond the simpler goal-attainment model in that a systems approach of sorts is used to investigate related health programs. Limitations of the quasi-systems approach are that it is oriented toward programs that have a common range of purpose and that are directed at recipients in a limited age range or life stage. In this sense, it is the evaluation counterpart of the multiple cause-single effect epidemiological model. Another common limitation is that environmental factors such as life-style, socioeconomic status, and environmental conditions are seldom adequately investigated, due to a lack of sufficient data. A full systems approach would span all life stages and consider environmental factors as critical variables.

Consider the example of Maternal and Infant (M&I), Family Planning, and Women, Infant, and Children (WIC) nutritional programs. Their common purpose is to improve maternal and infant health status. Evaluations of these programs that illustrate the quasi-systems approach were performed by Dever and Rousseau (1980a, 1980b). These studies were based on a system of linked birth and death records that yielded outcome information. The linked records were then joined with program data that provided information on the program inputs (resources) and throughputs (program processes).

Characteristically, quasi-systems evaluation of these programs analyzes inputs or resources, such as personnel and dollars; processes or activities of each program, such as number of clients seen; and selected indicators of health status to determine outcome. The results of the evaluation then serve as the basis for health policy and program decisions.

The quasi-systems evaluation model is not a full systems approach, because it omits important elements of the overall system. The environment in which programs function is composed of several key determinants of health status, such as life style, socioeconomic status, living conditions, and other environmental conditions, such as air and water pollution. When an evaluator's data base, such as that in the maternal and infant health example, does not contain such environmental data, a complete systems evaluation cannot be accomplished. Further, a focus on only one life stage impairs the relevance of the model to the epidemiology of the chronic disease cycle, in which diseases are decades in the making and have multiple causes.

Future. A proper evaluation of the effect of a state department of health on the health status of its target populations should employ a complete systems approach. Such a model takes into account as many elements as possible of health status, health resources, the processes of health programs, the configuration of the health system, and the effects of environment, including socioeconomic factors. Moreover, the systems evaluation approach encompasses the entire human life span, so that each life stage can be analyzed. Thus, this model of evaluation is consistent both with the chronic disease cycle and with the multiple cause-multiple effect epidemiological model.

Ideally, an infant receiving public health care should be followed through each stage of life. Since chronic diseases are suspected of being twenty or more years in the making and are associated with multiple causes, a prospective systems approach would allow the required process information to be collected and quite specific statements to be made about the effects of public health programs. Although comprehensive health program assessments like the one described here are generally if not totally lacking, departments of health must begin to move toward a full systems approach if the contributions of their programs to favorable changes in health status are ever to be determined.

Prerequisite: A Data Base. Installing the prerequisites for systems evaluation will be a long and complex undertaking in its own right. The core of a systems evaluation model for state departments of health would be an integrated data base that encompassed all life stages from birth to death and all health programs. Judging by our consulting experience in several states, it seems doubtful that any state health agency's information system is designed to provide the necessary data for comprehensive program evaluation. Typically, separate health data bases are set up for each program, and these data bases are conceptually and mechanically incompatible. Moreover, it is the general case that only one life stage is covered, such as the birth and infancy period described in the previous quasi-systems example.

Within the current state of the art in information system technology and design, certain features of an integrated information system can be envisioned. An information system for comprehensive evaluation would center around a basic, common data form containing identifying information on each client, such as name, date of birth, and so on. Each client would receive a permanent identifying number or code so that this basic information would not need to be duplicated at each client encounter.

Data would be initially recorded at the county or primary delivery site level, then transmitted to the district or unit level, where it would be placed in a shared minicomputer system. At this site, the data would be edited and corrected, and various reports would be prepared for local consumption. Then, each district or unit would communicate its data to a master file at the state department of health. In the master file, data on clients, personnel, budgets, expenditures, facilities, and inventory would be comprehensively linked and cross-referenced.

A major barrier to development of an integrated data base for health systems evaluation has been the legitimate concern for safeguarding privacy and maintaining the confidentiality of individual health records. At the federal level, for example, this concern is expressed in provisions of the Privacy Act of 1974 and the Tax Reform Act of 1976, both of which have discouraged such integration efforts. Although data base fragmentation is one form of confidentiality protection, any modern data base management system has a full array of safeguards: passwords, codes, protocols, access monitoring, and so on. As the reliability of alternative safeguards becomes more generally appreciated, it is reasonable to hope that the pressure to maintain file separation will subside. Recent strides in linking data without compromising confidentiality are apparent in the National Death Index of the National Center for Health Statistics, the 1977 report of the Privacy Protection Committee (Privacy Protection Study Commission, 1977), and the

1978–79 Administration bill "Confidentiality of Federal Statistics Records" (Beebe, 1980, p. 1246–1248).

A further consideration is that the cost of an integrated information system would be large. It is our view, however, that the cost would eventually be offset by the benefits. There is little reason to expect a decrease in the information or data required by departments of health. An integrated information system would mitigate the effects of increased data requirements by expediting collection, analysis, and reporting. Furthermore, certain technical problems, such as the widespread exaggeration of morbidity due to duplications of client records, would be eliminated. The systems data base would also provide valuable epidemiological information on the dynamics of health problems and diseases within a state. These findings would serve both administrators and clinicians and provide support for vital policy and service decisions that involved more than one program and more than one life stage. The frustration often felt by program administrators and staff over the lack of coordination among separate evaluations and epidemiological studies would thereby be eliminated.

An important potential benefit of a systems approach to health program data management and evaluation would be improved methods of resource allocation. Ideally, resources are distributed according to an estimated level of need among counties or other geographical health units, as determined by selected health indicators or composite indexes. Where needs are high, resources should correspond; areas with lower needs should receive less funds. However, because of inadequate or inaccurate programmatic data, funds are often misappropriated, so that areas with few problems receive large appropriations and vice versa. A complete and consistent data base would allow simulation and regression modeling techniques to be used to determine the equilibrium levels or break-even points for each region and program. Such techniques would thus make greater efficiency and effectiveness possible for the overall system even if individual programs were not improved.

Although the systems approach is promising, it must be recognized that even the most sophisticated analytical techniques available are insufficient to determine the exact cause and effect relationships involved in the complex health status of a population. Evaluation studies are not performed in a controlled, experimental laboratory setting, but in the sociopolitical environment of a community. Therefore, health program evaluation can never be reduced to a purely technical, scientific process (Schulberg and Baker, 1979, p. 5). Likewise, epidemiology will never revert to the single cause-single effect model used in years past. Health matters today are far too complex, with innumerable interrelated factors.

Conclusion

The health of our society is dominated by a chronic disease cycle. Epidemiologists, health program administrators, and clinicians are drawing upon the multiple cause-multiple effect epidemiological model in an attempt to answer fundamental questions about the proper role of state departments of health in improving health status. However, health program evaluation continues to use outdated approaches and has not yet incorporated the multiple cause-multiple effect viewpoint. If health program evaluation is to keep up with the evolution of disease patterns and epidemiology, a systems approach must be adopted. Otherwise, the wheels of health program evaluation will continue to spin, and valuable energies will continue to be wasted on inappropriate or inadequate analyses.

Advancement of the systems approach in health program evaluation will depend on development of suitable data bases. Thus, there are two alternative investments: to do limited evaluations now, or to build a capacity for more comprehensive evaluations in the future. State health agencies will serve the public interest best if their program evaluation efforts are balanced with respect to these two alternatives.

References

Beebe, G. W. "Record Linkage Systems — Canada Versus the United States." *American Journal of Public Health,* 1980, *70,* 1246–1248.

Dever, G. E. A. *Community Health Analysis: A Holistic Approach.* Germantown, Md.: Aspen Systems Corporation, 1980.

Dever, G. E. A., and Rousseau, R. H. *Maternal and Infant Care Project Evaluation: Georgia 1974–1977.* Atlanta: Georgia Department of Human Resources, 1980a.

Dever, G. E. A., and Rousseau, R. H. *An Evaluation of Mental Retardation — Socioeconomic, Prenatal, and Perinatal Factors: 1974–1978.* Atlanta: Georgia Department of Human Resources, 1980b.

Privacy Protection Study Commission. *Personal Privacy in an Information Society.* Washington, D.C.: U.S. Government Printing Office, 1977.

Schulberg, H. C., and Baker, F. *Program Evaluation in the Health Fields.* Vol. 2. New York: Human Sciences Press, 1979.

G. E. Alan Dever is director of Health Services Analysis, Inc., Stone Mountain, Georgia.

Rebecca H. Rousseau is associate director of Health Services Analysis, Inc., Stone Mountain, Georgia.

Frank M. Houser, M.D., is director of Southeastern Health Care Services, Inc., Atlanta, Georgia.

Small-scale program evaluations cannot discriminate between the flaws of the program and the flaws of the superordinate system.

Evaluating Mental Health Service Systems: A Case in Retrospect

Ronald J. Wooldridge
Jack A. Bernard

As a developing profession, program evaluation is itself a product of its recent practice. Each new study is a further episode of experience in the process of trial and error by which the field is growing. It is important, therefore, for evaluators conscientiously to review their own and others' work as case studies in evaluation. This suggests a need for a specialized form of secondary evaluation (evaluation of evaluation), in which the emphasis is on lessons for the evaluator rather than on corroboration of results. One prototype for such review would be that of a debriefing undertaken jointly by a participant in the evaluation and by an informed but objective nonparticipant. The discussion here is derived partly from an application of this prototype. That is, it comes from a debriefing of one professional evaluator (the second author) by another (the first author) for the purpose of extracting some ideas about evaluation that are exhibited in a specific recent product. Some additional material is also included that represents the logical aftermath of such a review — specific considerations of how the work might have been done differently.

The springboard for our remarks is an evaluation of the Georgia mental health system which was performed by the Georgia State Health Planning and Development Agency under the second author's direction and published in February of 1980 as part of the Georgia Preliminary State Health Plan (Georgia State . . . , 1980). This study is of interest not because it is unique but because it is representative of similar evaluations performed throughout the United States under the auspices of the National Health Planning and Development Act of 1974. Accordingly, our purpose is not to provide a critical or technical analysis but to consider the general issues that are raised by the study's representative aspects. Grounded in these considerations, some ideas for next time are advanced, which take the discussion to a practical level. Our emphasis throughout is on delineating the heuristic principles, attitudes, and opinions that seem to have contributed to the evaluation's utility.

Background: A Description of the Study

Although the mental health system consists of many distinct programs that could be evaluated individually, it was decided to focus the study on the overall characteristics of the system: aggregate costs, availability of service alternatives, geographic accessibility, and continuity of service delivery. In order to convey a sense of the evaluation's scope and approach, several components of the evaluation will be briefly reviewed.

Mental Health Status. To assess health in general, there are three primary types of measures: mortality, morbidity, and disability. However, the mental health field is unique in regard to status measurement in that, quite often, the extent or even the existence of illness cannot be easily established. During the period of the study, there were, in fact, no generally agreed-upon measures of mental health status in use in the Georgia system. It was necessary to employ proxy measures chosen from a limited array of available data.

The indicators most closely examined were rates of unemployment, divorce, suicide, and homicide, with breakdowns for various subpopulations. The decision to look at unemployment rates was supported by the findings of Brenner (1976), which indicated an association between unemployment and such indicators as state mental hospital admissions.

The selected indicators of mental health status revealed a wide variation of status among age groups and geographic regions. This established a frame of reference for subsequent consideration of the prevailing patterns of resource allocation and program differentiation.

The selected indicators also suggested that the mental health status of Georgia compares unfavorably with that of the nation at large.

Least Restrictive Care. At every level of the mental health system, it is declared policy that care should be provided in the least restrictive environment possible. Yet, the system has historically been unbalanced by disproportionate use of hospital-like settings. This imbalance has been costly both in terms of dollars and in terms of the diminished quality of life of the mentally disabled. Hence, it was a major purpose of the evaluation to determine the extent to which a favorable shift in the locus of treatment has been accomplished in Georgia.

In examining service patterns, it was found that the configuration of the system was favorable in regard to the existence of a diversity of programs in noninstitutional settings. However, the relative volumes of service and allocations of resources were not yet consistent with the policy consensus. In particular, it was found that the shift of funds from institutional to community-based programs had not kept pace with the shift in the pattern of service.

Geographic Allocation. While there was no simple consensus on how resources should be allocated across the state, there were several explicit points of view from which the pattern could be considered, so the study investigated the geographic dispersion of per capita funding and its relation to various estimates of local need. No confirmation of any rational pattern was found.

Psychiatric Inpatient Bed Need. Historical trends and future projections of bed utilization at the national and regional levels were employed as a frame of reference for analyzing the Georgia situation. Empty beds are a major component of overall system cost and therefore a major impairment to system efficiency. By even the most conservative standard, it was found that Georgia had an enormous excess of psychiatric inpatient capacity and that this excess was rapidly increasing. Potential savings were estimated at well over $10 million per year.

Work Force. Staffing standards for mental health programs and national statistics on mental health professionals per 100,000 population were adopted as criteria for examining the availability and distribution of mental health personnel in Georgia's system. Differences among the several substate regions and between Georgia and the nation were found to be extreme in every dimension.

The Bottom Line. Even with the most charitable assumptions about the characteristics of Georgia's individual mental health agencies and programs, it is impossible to conclude that the system in which they are embedded is conducive to high levels of aggregate effectiveness and efficiency. Indeed, the practical value of more careful evaluations on a smaller scale is questionable apart from a major change in the operating environment. Small-scale program evaluations cannot discriminate between the flaws of the program and the flaws of the superordinate system.

Integration of Evaluation and Planning

The most basic fact about the study under consideration is that it was performed not as an isolated project but as part of a comprehensive planning process grounded in a public debate of the issues. The study appeared not as a separate report for an audience of program managers but as an integral part of a plan destined for multilevel review and public hearings. Moreover, it was derived in part from similar studies of the substate health planning regions by their respective health systems agencies. The overall process was designed to include consumers of service, private and public providers, and government officials at several levels. Thus, the study should be understood as having come from and as having been done for a process that was predominantly political.

An acknowledgement that political processes were significant in the conduct of an evaluation may have a negative connotation for evaluators who have been influenced by the purist principles of the laboratory sciences. Yet, the political context of an evaluation may do as much to enhance validity as to threaten it. Political sagacity requires, for example, that all legitimate viewpoints should be presented. This protects against the bias of one narrow perspective. Political awareness also dictates that controversial topics should receive a greater share of attention. This ensures greater rigor where the stakes are higher and the questions more difficult.

The politically attuned evaluation is more likely to be respected by policymakers and more likely to be used. Contrary to much of our profession's conventional wisdom, the scientific method does not have a monopoly on truth, and it is not invulnerable to foolishness. Policymakers know this and appreciate the assurance that comes from ample exposure to common sense and public debate. Where else do the underlying values of an evaluation originate if not from the democratic process?

A further virtue of evaluation embedded in a political planning process is the low technical ceiling. The necessity of avoiding advanced methods that may not be understood by the audience is a deterrent against the use of methods that are unnecessarily complex. Striving for methodological simplicity imposes a severe discipline that is conducive to logical elegance. The resulting product tends to be only a syllogism away from action. In contrast, sophisticated methods lead only to a "So what?" response.

Integration of evaluation and planning also promotes a realistic perspective on the role of evaluation in the overall scheme of things. There is a tendency among evaluators to think of their findings as sacred offerings of great import that would result in tremendous progress if only they were taken more seriously. A more balanced view is that evaluation products are added grist for the sociopolitical mill. Our purpose is to support a dialogue that leads toward positive change, not to usurp that dialogue. Evaluation is a support function.

Orientation Toward Issues

Because evaluation tends to be blended in with many other inputs to the policymaking process, it is most influential when it generates a product that will not mix. The payoff for evaluation is when it punctures a prevailing misconception, when it challenges conventional wisdom. This dictates that evaluation should be directed toward vulnerabilities in current thinking. Invariably, these vulnerabilities are already a target of informed dissent, so it is essential for the evaluator to listen for dissent. Testing the bland hypotheses of those who protect the status quo is dull work. A more responsible use of scarce evaluation resources is to focus on the spectrum of dissent and to isolate the issues where evaluation can reasonably be expected to settle a basic question. This was precisely the logic of the study under consideration. That is, the Georgia study was organized around five major issues facing the Georgia mental health system: homogeneity of substate regions with respect to needs for service; homogeneity of substate regions with respect to resource allocation; redistribution of institutional resources to community-based programs; unneeded psychiatric inpatient beds; work force shortages and maldistribution. Issues, by definition, are matters on which opinion is divided and shifting. Hence, evaluation efforts that concentrate on the issues have a greater chance of influencing opinion than evaluations that address other matters.

The merit of doing evaluation that addresses significant issues should be obvious, yet most evaluation is oriented toward determining the degree of compliance with standards or the degree of goal accomplishment. For single programs, an orientation toward standards or goals may be perfectly reasonable. The issues will emerge in the course of the evaluation. However, for multiprogram systems, it can hardly be expected that the several applicable standards and goals will be compatible. Moreover, as a rule there are simply too many of them. The system evaluator is compelled to employ a higher-order, simpler structure. Issue orientation is a neutral alternative that avoids the problem of reconciling conflicting standards and goals.

Practicality

Regarding the general topic of significance in evaluation, it is clear that statistical significance and practical significance are two entirely different matters. This distinction is especially important for large-scale studies. Studies on a statewide basis frequently employ such large sample sizes that failure to obtain significance in statistical tests is rare. Thus, the problem becomes one of considering the importance of effects, not of whether the effects exist. This is not what inferential statistics is for, so some other approaches are required. Development of such approaches is a serious emerging need of the evaluation profession. Our audiences are becoming impatient with studies which only answer the question "What is observable?"

Through exposure to the ideas of statistics and experimental design, an evaluator's judgment is hardened against the fallacies of naive intuition. For most practical purposes, this trained judgment is sufficient to make sense of the available data, and a full formal analysis is not essential. It is practical when confronted with complexity to work more with one's insight and judgment than with statistical tests. This is the approach of the evaluation performed on the Georgia mental health system, and it is the outlook expected of the audience for which it was performed.

Scientific method and formal logic are not the process by which knowledge comes. Rather, they are merely a parallel process that is somehow conducive to the operation of our intuition and insight. Insights thus found are then rendered communicable and credible by science and logic, but this is a separate process from the finding. This is openly acknowledged by mathematicians and physicists but only rarely admitted outside of hard science.

Extensive Use of Graphics

A noteworthy aspect of the final report concerning Georgia's mental health system is that in a mere sixty pages it contains more than thirty bar graphs, maps, and other charts. The philosophy thus expressed is one of letting the data speak for themselves. Evaluators and other trained analysts are perhaps too quick to apply the esoteric tools of their trade and thus obscure what otherwise would be obvious. Moreover, we are often like builders who leave their scaffolding behind, hinding our findings behind the apparatus used in making them. The use of graphics forces the evaluator to formulate a clear and direct presentation of the findings, free from the complex details of how they were achieved.

An encouraging development in recent years is the increasing availability of computer terminals and software designed especially for producing maps, graphs, and charts. When this technology is fully incorporated into the practice of evalution, the level of evaluation's influence on managerial and political action should begin to rise exponentially. Acquiring the facts is a relatively minor aspect of our work. Packaging and communicating those facts is our principal function.

Comprehensive Modeling

In order for an evaluation to contribute to a comprehensive planning process, it must encompass all major dimensions of the system. When this is attempted on a statewide scale, the range of applicable and available data is staggering. Yet the data come from many different sources, with different definitions, different breakdowns, and different timing. Not only are they hard to assemble but when they are sorted out, fair comparisons are hardly possible. The predicament is one of having too much and too little data at the same time.

Several variables employed in the Georgia study are listed in Figure 1. Most of these variables were examined after breakdown by region or by age group. The first problem, too much data, is evident from the number and variety of variables considered. Few readers will succeed in forming a comprehensive understanding of what the study presents. The second problem, too little data, is evident from the qualifications and caveats necessitated by the facts that each variable influences every other variable and that few of these interactions have been studied. In both connections, the problem is that the variables are used without the integrating structure of a comprehensive model. The mind is capable of handling great complexity, provided that there is a pattern

Figure 1. Some Variables Considered in the Georgia Study

Suicide rate	Evaluated bed capacity
Homicide rate	Licensed bed capacity
Divorce rate	Beds in operation
Unemployment rate	Psychiatric beds per 100,000 population
Estimated mental illness prevalence	Inpatients per 100,000 population
Alcoholic and drug-related mortality	Occupancy rates
Cirrhosis of the liver mortality	Inpatient days
Estimated alcoholism prevalence	Admission rates
Episodes of service	Service stay index
Expenditures	Percent of state within 50 miles of a
Number of clients served	psychiatric hospital
Cost per unit of service	Estimated annual cost per unstaffed bed
Cost per client	Estimated annual cost per staffed bed
Budget recommendations	Psychiatrists per 100,000 population
appropriations	Foreign medical graduates
Expenditures per capita	Psychologists per 100,000 population

to it. Thus, a comprehensive model would enable even more variables to be taken into account without overwhelming the reader.

Development of an adequate model for so complex a system as the total mental health enterprise of a state is a long-term process. The system is man-made, and it will therefore be less susceptible to parsimonious description than the systems of nature. Fortunately, however, the rewards of small progress are sufficient to justify the effort. This will be illustrated and substantiated by ideas elaborated below.

Some Ideas for Next Time

It is important to realize that the evaluation under discussion was not conceived as a one-time effort. Rather, it was done as the first of a continuing series of comprehensive system assessments by the agency. Each assessment will push a little harder and a little farther than its predecessor. Part of the advancement will come from new data and better analyses and from the fact that each new effort stands on the shoulders of previous work. However, the pace and direction of improvement will depend not so much on technical refinements as on the general progress of the larger planning process in which the evaluation effort is embedded. In particular, the fundamental consideration for evaluation is to stay in step with the leadership of this process and not to get too far ahead. Specifically, this means putting the emphasis on issues that the audience is ready to deal with and keeping the presentation simple enough for its members to understand.

In view of these considerations, it may be quite inappropriate to include the ideas for next time elaborated below in a published report. Making these ideas simple for a nontechnical audience would require too much space. Our interest is more in their analytical and pedagogical applications than in their use for a general presentation.

Que Charts: A Managerial Perspective. As illustrated by Figure 1, service systems are burdensomely multidimensional. Evaluation efforts that deal with this multidimensionality by looking at the variables one by one offer only a clerical perspective on what happens. For managerial applications, it is essential to obtain an understanding of interrelationships and linkages among the variables. An approach that is useful in this regard and that serves to illustrate several further points will now be explained in detail.

One important group of variables pertaining to psychiatric hospitals associates admission rate, number of patients served, point-in-time inpatient census, release rate, annual inpatient days, average daily inpatient census, average length of stay, inpatient bed capacity, occupancy rates, and vacancy rates. Observe that these variables are interrelated to the extent that, if any one of them were unknown, its value could be computed from known values of the others. These variables can thus be regarded as embedded in a fully determined algebraic structure.

In addition to the algebraic relationships among these variables, their dynamic and probabilistic relationships should also be considered. A lowered occupancy rate over an extended period might enable the quality of care to be improved, which could lead to an accelerated release rate and a shorter average length of stay. An abnormally high admission rate during a given period could result in a comparable rise in release statistics during a subsequent period. Abrupt cuts in capacity, such as sometimes occur in times of fiscal austerity, could have an influence on admission policies that would result in a gradual slowdown. Similarly, a long-term decline in admissions or length of stay could cause the average daily inpatient census to drop to such a low level that a cut in capacity would be warranted.

Granted, then, that these variables are intricately related, what sort of analysis can bring this complexity into clear view? One approach that seems particularly promising is graphic rather than numerical. The graph will be called a que chart because of its general applicability to what mathematicians call "queing systems." The format is illustrated schematically in Figure 2.

The que chart in Figure 2 shows a Cartesian coordinate system with the horizontal axis representing time and the vertical axis representing number of persons. Three curves are superimposed on this coordinate system. The lower curve, *releases,* represents a cumulative count of all persons leaving the hospital for any reason since time T1, the beginning of the period of analysis. In other words, the height of this curve above the x-axis at some later time T2 is a representation of total releases for the period between T1 and T2. The middle curve, *number served,* represents a cumulative count of all persons receiving service since time T1, including persons for whom service was initiated prior to T1 and was still in progress at time T1. Both this curve and the releases curve use duplicated counts, in the sense that persons experiencing two episodes of service during the period of analysis would be counted twice. The upper curve, distinguished as a dashed line, represents cumulative releases plus program capacity (that is, number served plus vacancies). This statistic is not important by itself, but the curve is useful as a reference line, as described below. In the figure, these curves are smooth, for purposes of simplification. However, it should be recognized that change in this situation is actually a series of discrete events. In a truly accurate graphic representation, each curve would resemble an irregular stairstep.

Remarkably, with only three curves displayed, it is possible to identify all ten variables identified above from features of the resulting

Figure 2. Que Chart

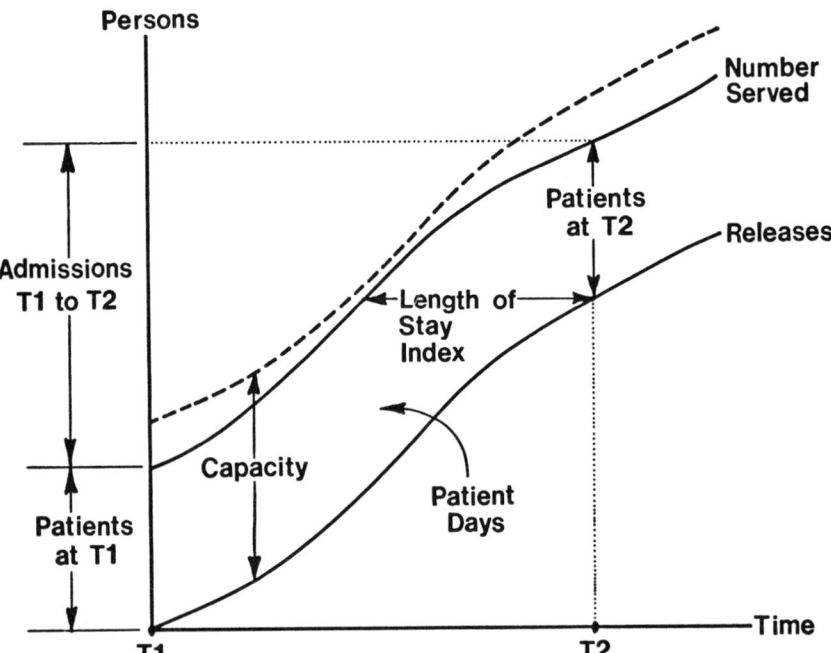

chart. In particular, the following associations may be observed: *Point-in-time inpatient census* is number served to date minus releases to date, a quantity that corresponds graphically to the vertical separation of the number served curve and the release curve at the time in question. *Admission and release dates* in terms of persons per unit time can be interpreted from the slopes of the number served curve and the releases curve. A high rate would correspond to a steep curve and a low rate would be indicated by a curve closer to the horizontal. *Point-in-time vacancy* is capacity minus point-in-time inpatient census, a quantity that corresponds to vertical separation of the upper (releases plus capacity) curve and the number served (releases plus census) curve.

Inpatient days is a bit harder to see. Start by thinking of the area of the chart as being composed of small squares, each of which is one person high and one day wide. Then, the area bounded by the number served curve, the releases curve, and vertical lines through T1 and T2 could be stated in terms of these square person-day units. The resulting quantity would, in fact, be the number of inpatient days during the period between T1 and T2. *Occupancy rates* averaged over a period to yield percent utilization can be interpreted from the relative size of two areas on the chart. In the same way that inpatient days corresponds to the area between the number served curve and the releases curve, bed days corresponds to the area between the releases curve and the upper, dashed line curve. Therefore, the ratio of these areas would be proportional to percent utilization.

Length of stay statistics of two varieties are available from the chart. An especially sensitive indicator, useful for day-to-day management and that we believe to be new in application to human services programs, is labeled on the chart (T2) as *length of stay index.* More generally, it is the fluctuating horizontal separation between the number served curve and the releases curve. Even minor variations in the admission and release rates will be reflected quickly in this statistic. Thus it is a good leading indicator of change in length of stay expectations.

Another indicator, which is related to what is called *service stay index* in the Georgia State Health Plan, is defined as annual inpatient days divided by annual number served. Interpreting T1 and T2 of Figure 2 as the beginning and end of the year, the area of the rectangle bounded by the x-axis, vertical lines through T1 and T2, and the horizontal dotted line would be the annual number served (height) multiplied by 365 (width in days). It follows that the service stay index would correspond to the fraction of this rectangle that represents annual inpatient days (the area between the number served curve and the releases curve) multiplied by 365. Observe that this index would tend to be high for low admission and release rates and low for high admission and release rates.

The power of Figure 2 derives partly from its success at fitting several variables into a single picture, but the full use of the idea is to think of it not as a picture but as a movie. Adding data or forecasts for successive time periods takes the three curves rightward and upward in accordance with a basic rule of the system: the three curves do not cross. With a little practice, the chart can be applied as a simulation model to elaborate various scenarios of change and to gain insight into the relationships among the several variables.

Several points can now be made based on the que chart and the related discussion: First, systems are not necessarily as multivariate as they initially seem. There is often considerable redundancy in the data that is not readily apparent. Second, mathematical modeling, simulation studies, and the like do not necessarily require a computer and a consulting firm. A good set of doodles can often serve the purpose just as well. Third, the clerical perspective of looking at one variable at a time and the managerial perspective of looking at several variables simultaneously yield entirely different perceptions of a situation. Evaluations that offer only a clerical perspective are likely to be discounted by managers for this reason. A major goal of evaluation must be to develop rigorous counterparts of the seat-of-the-pants "models" actually used by managers.

Factor Tables: A Policy Perspective. The que chart described above is exemplary in making possible a simultaneous display of several variables that can be expressed in terms of a common unit of measure. However, for a policy perspective, the main need is to build a framework that can accommodate variables measured in different units. Funding, staffing, and level of service dimensions require different units of measure, and policy questions typically require an analysis of trade-offs among these and other incommensurables.

The dominant concept in management information systems, accounting systems, and evaluation designs is that of breakdowns. Given any number, the first question is "What added up to this?" Hence, we have balance sheets; itemized budget and expenditure reports; breakdowns of staffing and productivity by division, bureau, and unit; breakdowns of sociodemographic indicators by region, county, and census tract; and applications of analysis of variance to every imaginable topic. Breakdowns are fine to have, and the evaluation of the Georgia mental health systems properly includes several. However, there is a serious limitation to breakdowns. Whatever numbers are added up must have a common unit of measure. The breakdown orientation is intrinsically one-dimensional.

Within the boundaries of arithmetic, the only alternative to addition (breakdowns) is multiplication (factors). Applying this observation to a given variable, one might try to devise a factorization to replace the breakdown. For example, the variable "total annual state cost for service X" might be factored as follows:

State cost =
(Gross Cost) × (Proportion State-Funded),
Gross Cost =
(Units of Service) × (Gross Cost per Unit),
Units of Service =
(Episodes of Service) × (Units per Episode),
Episodes of Service =
(Recipients) × (Episodes per Recipient),
Recipients =
(Population of Service Area) × (Recipients per Capita).

Denoting providers (sites) of service X by the identifiers P1, P2, P3, and so on, this factorization can structure a tabular presentation like the one shown in Figure 3.

For another service, such a table might employ a slightly different factorization or start with a different variable, but the general form should be apparent from this example. Note that this factor table format provides a structure that not only accommodates several variables but also

Figure 3. Sample Format for a Factor Table

Providers	(a) Population of Service Area	(b) Recipients per Capita	(ab) Recipients	(c) Episodes per Recipient	(abc) Episodes of Service	(d) Units per Episode	(abcd) Units of Service	(e) Gross Cost per Unit	(abcde) Gross Cost	(f) Proportion State-Funded	(abcdef) State Cost
P1											
P2											
P3											
•											
•											
•											
PN											

Aggregate

several units of measure. This suggests that it may be useful in considering the trade-offs of alternative policies and thereby serve as an antidote to the tunnel vision that afflicts the fiscal- or program-minded manager.

The multiplicative structure of a factor table provides more than a rule for ordering its columns. Like a budget, a factor table is structured so that it has to balance. A change in any cell must be compensated for by a change in one or more other cells. Consider, for example, a reduction in aggregate state cost in the situation outlined by Figure 3. This would be allocated back to the several providers on some basis, and each would then cut back on admissions (column b), service (column c or d), or waste (column e) in order to adjust. While the table provides no estimate of such effects, it does have a structure that impels them to be considered and it provides a worksheet for establishing consistency among the estimates that are made. Much of the administrative and policy planning role can be described in terms of balancing a factor table if the system's main parameters are included.

From the viewpoint of a system evaluator, a useful variant of the factor table is one in which there are two numbers in each cell, one being actual data on performance and the other being the corresponding objective or expectation. Other useful forms of the factor table employ the rows for successive snapshots of a single program over time, for before and after views of experimental and control groups, or for some other designation dictated by an experimental or quasi-experimental design.

In regard to consideration of trade-offs, there is a graphic counterpart of the factor table that may be useful. As an example, suppose gross cost per capita (bcde) is factored as recipients per capita (b) times gross cost per recipient (cde). Suppose further that each of these three variables has its own constituency and that each of the three constituencies specifies a desired level for its favorite variable. Generally, these desired levels will be mutually inconsistent, and they will not be represented by any real program. Artificial data are given in Table 1 to illustrate precisely this circumstance.

A graphic counterpart to Table 1 can be drawn on x–y coordinate axes as follows: Associate recipients per capita with the x-axis. Associate gross cost per recipient with the y-axis. Plot points representing East County, West County, and North County. Plot a vertical dotted line corresponding to the desired number of recipients served per capita by a provider. Plot a horizontal dotted line corresponding to the desired gross cost per recipient. Note that points associated with the desired gross cost per capita must lie along a hyperbolic curve in this coordinate system and represent this curve with a dotted line. The resulting graph is displayed in Figure 4.

Table 1. Some Hypothetical Numbers

		Recipients per Capita	Gross Cost per Recipient	Gross Cost per Capita
	Desired Level	.001	$1,300	$ .25
Providers:	East County	.0007	$1,000	$ .70
	West County	.0008	$1,400	$1.16
	North County	.0009	$1,200	$1.18

Consider the predicament of East County. In terms of recipients per capita, East County is low and would be under pressure to admit more recipients. Responding to this pressure, East County would move over time to the right toward the vertical dotted line representing desired recipients per capita. In terms of gross cost per recipient East County is again low and would be under pressure to move upward toward the horizontal dotted line representing desired gross cost per recipient. In terms of gross cost per capita, however, East County is too high and would be under pressure to move downward and to the left toward the dotted curve representing preferred gross cost per capita. This no-win situation is the reality of most service programs — multiple constituencies to please, conflicting preferences and pressures, inevitable vector sum compromises among the various forces in evidence.

In Figure 4, only three points, representing providers, are shown, but in real applications, there is likely to be a large swarm of points, one for each of the providers or sites among whom comparisons would be made. Monitoring the changing pattern of such a swarm over time would make it possible to analyze which forces are strongest in the policy process. For example, in Figure 4, convergence to the hyperbola of desired cost per capita would indicate that the system was dominated by the constituency for fiscal restraint and geographic equity. Careful consideration of the forces for change at work in a given system should enable the evaluator to identify variables for a factor table that will reveal the relative and composite effects of these forces.

The general idea of a factor table can also be used with columns that correspond to a string of conditional probabilities. For an example of this variation, consider the following generalized program aim: To provide all eligible persons who present themselves for admission to the program with the following sequence of service: diagnostic work-up for each individual to verify need for service; intensive services to each

Figure 4. Sample of a Factor Graph

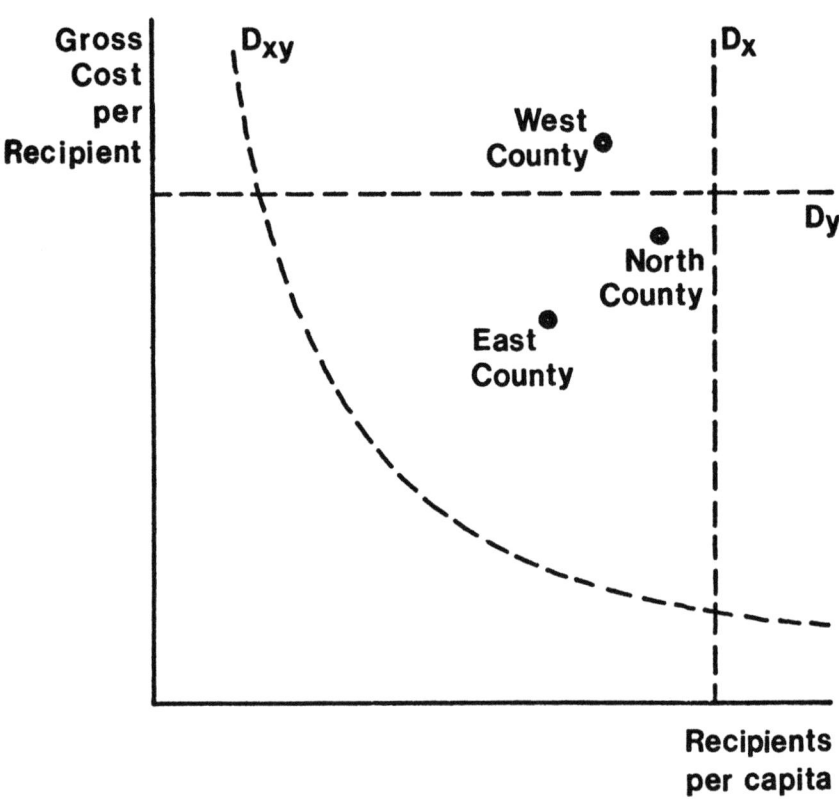

D_x : Desired Recipients per Capita

D_y : Desired Gross Cost per Recipient

D_{xy} : Desired Gross Cost per Capita

individual for three months sufficient to meet the need; and follow-up contact one year later to verify that no further need exists.

The primary variable for a factor table that would represent this program is the probability that no further service is needed, given that a person appears, is eligible, is diagnosed as needing service, receives service, initial need is met, and follow-up contact is made. Using a somewhat more concise notation, we may write this variable as P (no further need/program participation), to be read as "probability of no further need, given program participation." Continuing with this notation and following the rules of probability theory, we may factor as follows:

P (no further need/program participation) =
 P (appearance) × P (eligibility/appearance) × P (need/eligibility)
 × P (service/need) × P (need met/service)
 × P (follow-up/need met) × P (no further need/follow-up)

This factorization would then be applied to build a factor table with a clear and direct relationship to the program's aim and process.

The graphic in Figure 4 and ideas in the associated discussions are derived from material in Keeney and Raiffa (1976). They demonstrate that mathematics is available for handling multivariate preferences and the political characteristics of complex systems. As this mathematics becomes more familiar, the field of evaluation will become less dependent on the methods of the laboratory sciences and better able to relate successfully to the real world of plural perspectives and expectations.

The policy perspective is actually a fusion of several more narrow perspectives, and it consists in an ability to integrate several views into a unified perception. The factor table and factor chart format described here are tools for consolidated reporting and analysis of data representing several perspectives on a system. Hence, these tools are illustrative of what is needed to enable evaluation to influence the thinking and action of policymakers. They speak to policymakers on a policy level, the level of multidimensional balancing and compromise.

Conclusion

The preceding opinions, admonitions, and ideas are drawn from experience in evaluating whole systems, not single programs. Their applicability to the evaluation of single programs is questionable but plausible. The distinction between what is merely a program and what is a system of programs is, after all, quite arbitrary. An evaluation paradigm that works equally well for both extremes of the system-program scale will undoubtedly be developed. Our attention to the system end should be interpreted not as advocacy for an alternative paradigm but rather as work toward an extension of the prevailing program-oriented outlook.

References

Brenner, M. H. "Estimating the Social Costs of National Economic Policy Implications for Mental and Physical Health and Criminal Aggression." In *Achieving the Goals of the Employment Act of 1946 — Thirtieth Anniversary Review.* Vol. 1. Washington, D.C.: Joint Economic Committee, United States Congress, October 1976.

Georgia State Health Planning and Development Agency. "Mental Illness and Substance Abuse." In the *Georgia Preliminary State Health Plan*. Atlanta: Georgia State Health Planning and Development Agency, 1980.

Keeney, R. L., and Raiffa, H. *Decisions with Multiple Objectives: Preference and Value Trade-offs*. New York: Wiley, 1976.

Ronald J. Wooldridge is director of forecasting and modeling, New York State Office of Mental Health, Albany.

Jack A. Bernard is chief of planning for the Georgia State Health Planning and Development Agency.

Index